Praise for

TEACHING TWICE-EXCEPTIONAL LEARNERS IN TODAY'S CLASSROOM

"Emily Kircher-Morris has provided an exemplary resource for educators that clarifies who 2e learners are and how best to meet their instructional and support needs. Practitioners, college students, and researchers will appreciate the practical, research-based information provided in this text. Most impressive are the tools for educators and the student vignettes that appear throughout the book that bring the world of diverse 2e students to life. I highly recommend this text to educators and advocates of twice-exceptional, gifted, and other cognitively diverse students. Well done!"

—Joy Lawson Davis, Ed.D., award-winning author, expert scholar in diversity and equity in gifted and advanced learner programs

"*Teaching Twice-Exceptional Learners in Today's Classroom* is going on my list of recommended reads for all teachers. It's loaded with practical, actionable advice that can be used by educators and parents trying to navigate the often-troubled terrain of educating a twice-exceptional child. The tables, charts, and case studies make it an engaging read, and it covers so many possible scenarios that it will have broad appeal to those in the field. I found myself nodding in agreement many times, and readers will love the respect and feeling of camaraderie that shines through every page."

—Lisa Van Gemert, M.Ed.T., founder, Gifted Guru

"*Teaching Twice-Exceptional Learners in Today's Classrooms* is a comprehensive and user-friendly guide to understanding, supporting, educating, and serving twice-exceptional students not only in the classroom, but also in life. Emily Kircher-Morris has combined her decades of teaching and counseling with her own invaluable life experience to provide a road map for understanding the complexities of twice-exceptional profiles and how they show up in classrooms. This book is filled with strategies for capitalizing on strengths while improving the motivation, organization, and engagement of twice-exceptional learners. We will be recommending this guide to all of our clients."

—Dan Peters, Ph.D., licensed psychologist, co-founder and executive director, Summit Center

"Every teacher of the gifted needs this book! Emily Kircher-Morris has done a fantastic job of combining research and practice to provide doable supports for twice-exceptional learners. Her strength-based approach puts the learner first by getting them involved in the process. She masterfully covers the whole child from understanding the diagnosis to supporting them socially and emotionally. You are sure to find practical tools and strategies mapped out in all the chapters. She includes templates, methods, and techniques to ensure our 2e students find success."

—Richard M. Cash, Ed.D., educator of the gifted, author, and consultant, nRich Educational Consulting, Inc.

"Emily Kircher-Morris draws from both experience and research in putting together this strikingly practical toolkit. Packed with case examples, information, and strategies to support the many types of 2e learners, this book is a great addition to any parent or educator's library."
—**Edward R. Amend, Psy.D.,** clinical psychologist, The Amend Group, Lexington, KY

"*Teaching Twice-Exceptional Leaners in Today's Classroom* is a book that every educator needs, whether they teach special education or general education. It not only offers a structured, insightful look into learners who are so often overlooked, but also practical tools and actionable advice alongside compelling stories of and from twice-exceptional students. These stories, along with Kircher-Morris' professional and personal understanding of the topic, bring the subject to life in a compassionate and relatable way. As a 2e learner myself who was never identified as a child, I was brought to tears by seeing myself reflected in the pages—and knowing that educators now have a resource to understand and support students like me."
—**Amanda Morin,** Associate Director of Thought Leadership & Expertise, Understood, and author of *The Everything Parent's Guide to Special Education*

"Emily Kircher-Morris has crafted an invaluable resource, full of insights, strategies, tools, and resources that will guide every 2e advocate in supporting our twice-exceptional learners. Her poignant student stories remind us to look beneath their 'masks of disability' and 'masks of giftedness' in order to recognize and serve their unique needs—both academic and social-emotional. I just wish this practical guidebook had been available when I was coordinating gifted education, because it goes a long way toward normalizing neurodiversity. And all of us can benefit from her words of wisdom: 'Try. Tweak. Transform.'"
—**Deb Douglas, M.S.,** director, GT Carpe Diem Consulting, and author of *The Power of Self-Advocacy for Gifted Learners* and coeditor of *Empowering Underrepresented Gifted Students*

"*Teaching Twice-Exceptional Learners in Today's Classroom* is a must-have resource for parents and educators. Filled with both information about twice-exceptional students and strategies to address multiple exceptionalities, this resource provides educators with specific ways to support diverse learners immediately. Armed with this resource, educators will be in a much better position to meet the needs of all gifted children, from academic to social-emotional needs and beyond."
—**Christine Fonseca,** licensed educational psychologist, consultant, and author of *Emotional Intensity in Gifted Students*

"As someone who received a formal diagnosis of ADHD at thirty-seven years old, thirty years after being identified as a gifted and talented student in Brooklyn, NY, I am deeply grateful for Emily's efforts to shine a light on how to serve students like me who think a bit differently. By focusing on 'progress, not perfection,' she has created a practical, yet powerful way to bring new partners into this mission and push the rest of us to deepen our understanding of the challenges and benefits of twice-exceptionality and to recognize the boundless untapped potential in students who are told they are defective because their brilliance diverges from the norm."
—**Colin Seale,** Founder and CEO of thinkLaw and author of *Thinking Like a Lawyer: A Framework for Teaching Critical Thinking to All Students*

TEACHING
Twice-Exceptional
LEARNERS
in Today's Classroom

Emily Kircher-Morris, M.A., M.Ed., LPC

For Stephen—
Emily Kircher-Morris

free spirit
PUBLISHING®

Library of Congress Cataloging-in-Publication Data
Names: Kircher-Morris, Emily, author.
Title: Teaching twice-exceptional learners in today's classroom / Emily Kircher-Morris.
Description: Minneapolis : Free Spirit Publishing, 2021. | Includes bibliographical references and index.
Identifiers: LCCN 2020008208 (print) | LCCN 2020008209 (ebook) | ISBN 9781631984853 (paperback)
    | ISBN 9781631984860 (pdf) | ISBN 9781631984877 (epub)
Subjects: LCSH: Gifted children—Education. | Children with mental disabilities—Education.
Classification: LCC LC3993 .K575 2021 (print) | LCC LC3993 (ebook) | DDC 371.95—dc23
LC record available at https://lccn.loc.gov/2020008208
LC ebook record available at https://lccn.loc.gov/2020008209

Free Spirit Publishing does not have control over or assume responsibility for author or third-party websites and their content. At the time of this book's publication, all facts and figures cited within are the most current available. All telephone numbers, addresses, and website URLs are accurate and active; all publications, organizations, websites, and other resources exist as described in this book; and all have been verified as of December 2020. If you find an error or believe that a resource listed here is not as described, please contact Free Spirit Publishing.

Edited by Christine Zuchora-Walske
Cover and interior design by Emily Dyer

Free Spirit Publishing
An imprint of Teacher Created Materials
6325 Sandburg Road, Suite 100
Minneapolis, MN 55427-3674
(612) 338-2068
help4kids@freespirit.com
freespirit.com

DEDICATION

For Dave.

ACKNOWLEDGMENTS

There are many people to thank for their support over the years that has culminated in this book.

The journey to write this book began while I was in elementary school and my mom, Pauline Gouvin, was by my side through it all—advocating for me, encouraging me, and helping me find my homework.

My dad, Allen Kircher, showed me—among many other things—the benefit of keeping a "warehouse full of useless information" in one's brain.

Several teachers understood me—a quirky, impulsive, socially awkward kid—and never shamed me for being myself, especially Tracy Frauen, Linda Brakensiek, Nancy Black, John Guittar, Mike Hartman, and Mary Gismegian.

The Free Spirit Publishing team, including Judy Galbraith, Kyra Ostendorf, Meg Bratsch, Christine Zuchora-Walske, Amanda Shofner, and the rest of the behind-the-scenes crew guided me through this process and patiently answered all of my questions.

Jocelyn Murphy offered her support and assistance with some early stages of this project.

My colleagues at Unlimited Potential Counseling and Education Center have been integral to helping the practice grow and fulfilling our vision of supporting neurodivergent kids and their families, and the board of directors and staff for the Gifted Support Network, who tirelessly advocate for the gifted and twice-exceptional kids in our area.

My amazing clients and their families give me the chance every day to join them on their journey. I'm honored to be a part of their story and have them as part of mine. This book wouldn't exist without them.

My own 2e kids, Grayson, Maggie, and Trevor, who bring more joy to my life than I'd ever thought possible and let me learn through firsthand experience what the parents of my clients are going through.

My husband, Dave Morris, constantly pushes me beyond my comfort zone and provides unending encouragement and support. He is the backbone of our family and my best friend. I love you, Dave.

Contents

PART 2
Interventions for Twice-Exceptional Learners 127

List of Figures

Digital Content

See page 235 for instructions for downloading digital versions of these forms.

List of Reproducible Pages

Foreword

by Jim Delisle, Ph.D.
Distinguished Professor of Education Emeritus, Kent State University

How many times in your life have you said something like this? "If I knew *then* what I know *now*, I would have been a more effective teacher (or counselor, parent, or coach)." We can't travel back in time to erase our mistakes or repair any unintended damage we caused while we were learning the ropes. But we can take comfort in knowing that the twice-exceptional (2e) kids and adults we meet along life's path now will be better served, thanks to the wisdom and guidance offered by Emily Kircher-Morris in her ground-breaking book *Teaching Twice-Exceptional Learners in Today's Classroom*. Indeed, this is a resource that is as useful for veteran educators like me as it is for anyone just starting out in a helping profession like teaching or counseling.

What I found most impressive about this book is the vast set of experiences the author brings into her writing. As Kircher-Morris explains and addresses a cascade of possible 2e conditions—including autism, ADHD, anxiety, depression, dyslexia, and more—she weaves a tapestry of powerful and respectful suggestions for both identifying these exceptionalities and addressing them in a classroom setting. Her frequent use of scenarios involving actual students or clients she has served brings into clear focus what it is like for gifted neurodiverse children and teens. As I read these vignettes, they reminded me of kids I've taught or counseled in my decades of work with gifted students, both neurodiverse and neurotypical. Kircher-Morris has done 2e kids, their parents, and their teachers a great service by so carefully explaining how to help them and by never forgetting that the most effective interventions begin with building a relationship based on mutual trust and respect.

In books like this, it is easy for authors to get so far into the weeds and the jargon that they lose focus on the child. That does not occur in *Teaching Twice-Exceptional Learners in Today's Classroom*. Kircher-Morris writes from a vantage point of practicality and experience. Here are just a few nuggets of wisdom she offers:

- When neurodiverse gifted students achieve at or near grade level, that is not good enough.

- Perfectionism is the denial of any vulnerability.

- Autistic students cannot be bribed out of their neurological wiring.

- If you try to convince students to set goals you think are important without their buy-in, you take away their autonomy.

- A gifted child with a learning disability is a student in the deep end of the pool who doesn't know how to swim.

- It's easier to fight the monster under your bed when you turn on the light.

Some of these ideas are direct quotes from the book, while others are distillations of the author's thoughts, but each of these gems—and there are many more in the book—leave the reader with a fuller understanding of and appreciation for 2e kids and those who care about them. Kircher-Morris provides hundreds of specific suggestions for making the lives of gifted neurodiverse kids more complete and satisfying. You will return to this book so often that its pages will get dog-eared and wrinkled from use, which is the sign of a very worthwhile resource.

Now . . . if only I'd had this book four decades ago.

Introduction

When I was an elementary student in the 1980s, my mother and my teacher saw two different kids. My mother, a special educator, noticed characteristics of giftedness. My teachers saw a disorganized and impulsive child with poor grades. My first-grade teacher noted that my work was always correct, but we had to dump out my desk to find it. By the time I was in third grade, my teachers routinely kept me in from recess because my work was incomplete.

At the end of second grade my mom insisted on testing, and I began participating in the district's gifted education program the next fall. Third grade was the year I learned I was bad at math. To gain entrance to the classroom, we lined up in the hallway and one by one, we quickly answered a multiplication fact flash card. Our teacher would hold up the flash card and signal with her fingers—one, two, three. If you didn't answer before she signaled three, to the end of the line you went. I was always one of the last students in the classroom.

In fifth grade, my teacher pulled me out into the hallway to have a talk. "Do you realize," she asked in her stern voice, "that you are going to fail fifth grade if you don't get your grades up?" She lobbied for me to be removed from the gifted education program because she thought I didn't deserve to participate in it based on my grades.

I'll admit I was stubborn. Every week, that fifth-grade teacher would assign us to write our spelling words five times each. I refused. I already knew how to spell the words. I'd been a finalist in the class spelling bee for several years. Not caring that I already knew how to spell the words, the teacher gave me a zero. Her strategy was unmotivating, to say the least. (Spoiler alert: I did manage to graduate from fifth grade, even without writing my spelling words five times each.)

Through all of this, my mother was my tireless educational advocate. She found a neurologist, who assessed me and diagnosed me with attention deficit disorder (now called inattentive ADHD) at a time when girls rarely received this diagnosis. But by then the damage was done. I had an ingrained sense of helplessness and poor work habits. My teachers never seemed to know what to do with me. I was a twice-exceptional (2e) learner at a time when that term didn't exist. Even gifted-certified teachers had no training on how to teach me.

Since then, I've earned a bachelor's degree in elementary education, a master's degree in curriculum and instruction with gifted certification, and a master's degree in counseling and family therapy. While working on my bachelor's degree, I took a class called Educating the Exceptional Child, which included a single chapter on educating gifted learners. That's just one chapter in four years on meeting the needs of gifted learners—with no mention of 2e learners. Even as I pursued my first master's degree with gifted certification, I still received no training on how to support 2e learners.

I've worked as a classroom teacher, a gifted education facilitator at the elementary and middle school levels, a school counselor, and a mental health counselor in private practice serving high-ability kids and teens. I'm continually amazed at how far we still must go as a community of educators in understanding, advocating for, and teaching 2e learners. But, bit by bit, more educators are finding inventive ways to meet these students' educational needs. Special education and gifted education teachers are collaborating to understand the intersection of giftedness and disability. Classroom teachers are beginning to advocate for accommodations and services for their students who attend both gifted and special education classes. And 2e learners are embracing their unique learning characteristics. We're on the right path, even if the path is still a long one.

Gifted learners in general are statistical outliers; 2e learners are even less common. Their additional layers of neurodiversity further complicate their education. Twice-exceptional learners face challenges for which there is no one-size-fits-all solution. These children deserve to be treated individually and to identify what works for them. When educators, parents, and learners collaborate to find what works, we often discover ways to meet not only academic needs, but also social and emotional needs.

Why I Wrote This Book

The contrasting—and sometimes conflicting or confusing—qualities of 2e students have kept us in the shadows for a long time. We've been misunderstood, disciplined, unchallenged, and left behind. We've been called lazy and unmotivated, knowing in our hearts and minds that we aren't but not understanding why we can't reach this potential everyone keeps telling us we have.

Growing up as a 2e learner led me to the field of education. I became an educator to right the wrongs I experienced as a gifted student with attention deficit hyperactivity disorder (ADHD). Working as an elementary and middle school gifted education teacher, and later as a school counselor, I saw firsthand the struggles 2e students face with inconsistent support. I currently work as a mental health counselor for people who are gifted and 2e, which allows me to support them and advocate for their needs in school. I bring my experience from the office home as I raise my own 2e children. My passion has led me to lift my voice about the needs of 2e kids in other ways too, such as through my podcast, *The Neurodiversity Podcast* (formerly called *Mind Matters*), and this book.

I've written this book to help educators, administrators, and counselors understand learners who are gifted and have a diagnosis that affects their ability to learn. To understand these students, we must look behind the mask of disability that is hiding their giftedness—or the mask of giftedness that is hiding their struggles. We need to recognize how the social and emotional needs of being gifted intersect with the implications of being labeled a troublemaker or an underachiever. Supporting 2e students from a strength-based model allows them to thrive.

My hope is that this book will help bridge the gaps among gifted education, general education, and special education classrooms by providing tools to support 2e learners in each environment where they may find themselves. Students who are gifted might also need special education services or accommodations through a Section 504 plan. Kids with an individualized education program (IEP) may also need the challenge of a gifted program. Tying together these needs and serving the whole child can provide a safety net for 2e kids so they don't fall through the cracks in our education system. A holistic, strength-based approach can help them succeed beyond their elementary and secondary academic careers.

Progress, Not Perfection

Neurodiversity is a broad concept, and gifted kids may experience many manifestations of twice-exceptionality. We're going to cover a lot of ground in this book, and it may seem overwhelming at first. Don't worry! These are ideas, strategies, and knowledge that I've built over almost two decades of work with gifted and 2e learners in both the classroom and counseling office—and I continue to learn new things every day.

My first year teaching, I taught in a third-grade general education classroom. One student in my class was quiet, smart, and quirky, and he loved to talk to anyone and everyone about his passion for motorcycles. One day, the school counselor and I were discussing some of the kids in my class, and his name came up. She looked at me and said, "You know, I think he fits the description of this diagnosis I just learned about at a conference: Asperger's." (For more information on Asperger's syndrome, see chapter 9.) I'd never heard of this diagnosis. This wasn't that long ago. I earned my master's degree in education with gifted certification a few years after that first year of teaching, and the term *twice-exceptional* never came up in that program. I entered the gifted education classroom with no formal training on 2e students.

My experience illustrates three points. First, we are on the frontier of learning about neurodiversity, and we have a long way to go. Second, understanding of twice-exceptionality is just beginning to filter beyond the gifted education classroom to other educational professionals, so a learning curve is to be expected. Third, any and every step toward supporting 2e learners is a step in the right direction. Reading this book and recognizing that gifted learners can also have a disability (and vice versa) is just such a step.

These pointers will help you begin your journey of supporting 2e kids:

- **Use students' strengths to support their struggles.** Leveraging strengths is key to building self-efficacy.

- **Bring students into the process.** Self-awareness and self-advocacy skills will help 2e students far beyond the classroom.

- **Don't be discouraged by gradual progress.** Recognize that a 2e student's struggles didn't appear overnight, and building compensatory skills takes time too.

- **Take a team approach with your colleagues.** This book is meant to bridge the gaps among the general, special, and gifted classrooms, and each of these areas (along with support educators) is vital to meeting the needs of 2e learners.

The goal is progress, not perfection. Supporting 2e kids is a marathon, not a sprint. Gradually using your new knowledge as you become more comfortable with it will help your 2e students.

A NOTE ABOUT LANGUAGE

In this book and in all my work, I'm careful to use language that is appropriate for each diagnosis based on the current terminology preferred by the population I'm describing. For example, the autistic community prefers identity-first language (*autistic student*) instead of person-first language (*student with autism*) because many within the neurodiversity movement recognize that autism is a part of who they are and not a condition they have that needs to be cured. However, I generally use person-first language to describe students with a learning disability (for example, *student with a specific learning disability* instead of *learning disabled student*). Other times, I simply use the legal language as it relates to educational law and advocacy. Language changes as our understanding of neurology and psychology changes. I ask your forgiveness if I use a term that you find unappealing and hope you will trust that at all times, my intent is to provide validation and understanding for 2e learners.

About This Book

This book is made up of two parts. Part 1, "Supporting All Twice-Exceptional Learners," looks at the needs of 2e learners and focuses on the similarities many 2e learners share. Part 2, "Interventions for Twice-Exceptional Learners," discusses 2e learners according to the various labels or diagnoses they may have, describing the specific strengths and struggles that come with each variety of exceptionality.

Chapter 1: Understanding Twice-Exceptional Learners explores our current understanding of 2e learners and how our understanding of these students has evolved over time. It discusses ways to bridge the gap between special education and gifted education programs, as well as how to build an effective interdisciplinary team to support the needs of 2e learners in gifted, general, and special education classrooms. It also provides a resource to help screen for accommodations 2e students may need.

Chapter 2: Designing Strength-Based Instruction for Twice-Exceptional Learners identifies several general characteristics shared by many 2e learners and describes how we can use a 2e learner's strengths to support their areas of difficulty. The Strength-Based Lesson Planning Template in this chapter provides a framework to combine a student's strengths with accommodations for their struggles.

Chapter 3: Social and Emotional Needs of Twice-Exceptional Learners examines the social and emotional needs of 2e learners, including how the learning environment can directly affect their well-being. We'll talk about the impact of perfectionism on 2e learners, including how it can lead to learned helplessness and feelings of shame and vulnerability.

Chapter 4: Motivating Twice-Exceptional Learners takes a deep dive into motivation and understanding how educators can help 2e learners stay motivated in environments that weren't created with their needs in mind. It explores intrinsic and extrinsic motivation through the lens of self-determination theory and discusses ideas to instill a sense of ownership of learning in 2e students.

Chapter 5: Goal-Setting for Twice-Exceptional Learners describes how to harness 2e learners' motivation through goal-setting. It offers specific strategies to help 2e learners set goals that support their areas of struggle. It provides a framework for students to set and reach goals by following a three-step process of self-monitoring, self-assessing, and self-regulating.

Chapter 6: Executive Functioning discusses executive functioning and addresses the ways in which executive functioning struggles affect many 2e learners. It explains how to use metacognition and goal-setting to collaboratively coach students and support their executive functioning struggles.

Part 2, "Interventions for Twice-Exceptional Learners," breaks down the needs of 2e learners into specific diagnoses within three main categories: academic, neurodevelopmental, and emotional and behavioral. Each chapter includes information about how to identify 2e learners who may have these diagnoses, specific social and emotional considerations for the population, and ways to accommodate their learning needs from a strength-based approach.

You may notice there are some diagnoses that aren't covered in this section. For example, this book does not specifically address oppositional defiant disorder (ODD) or Tourette's syndrome. The reasons I have not included these diagnoses (and others) are because the diagnosis is predominantly behavioral and comorbid (co-occurring) with another diagnosis included in the book, because the diagnosis is rarely given to children, or because the diagnosis doesn't necessitate unique educational interventions for 2e learners.

Chapter 7: Academic Diagnoses: Specific Learning Disabilities looks at 2e learners who have academic diagnoses of specific learning disabilities, also called dyslexia, dyscalculia, and dysgraphia. It discusses the barriers to identifying these learners and shares strategies to access special education services. We'll consider the ways 2e students may mask their struggles or their gifts when they have these diagnoses and examine strength-based ideas to accommodate their needs in the classroom.

Chapters 8, 9, and 10 address neurodevelopmental diagnoses, including ADHD (chapter 8), autism spectrum disorder or ASD (chapter 9), and processing difficulties (chapter 10).

Chapter 8: Attention Deficit Hyperactivity Disorder (ADHD) looks at characteristics of 2e learners who have ADHD. It tackles the overlap between characteristics of giftedness and ADHD that can lead to a misdiagnosis or missed diagnosis in 2e learners. It provides strategies for helping 2e students with emotional regulation and rejection sensitive dysphoria, as well as a list of possible accommodations for common struggles faced by these learners.

Chapter 9: Autism Spectrum Disorder (ASD) is dedicated to autistic gifted students. It discusses the difficulty of accessing special education services for autistic gifted learners due to the IDEA definition of educational autism. The chapter defines characteristics of giftedness, autism, and both together to assist with recognizing students. It discusses lesser-known characteristics of ASD, like pathological demand avoidance and alexithymia, along with possible accommodations and modifications.

Chapter 10: Processing Difficulties addresses processing diagnoses, such as central auditory processing disorder (CAPD), visual processing disorder (VPD), and sensory processing disorder (SPD), along with manifestations in 2e learners and ideas for accommodations and modifications.

Chapter 11: Anxiety and Related Disorders looks at anxiety-based diagnoses, including generalized anxiety disorder (GAD), social anxiety disorder or social phobia, separation anxiety, selective mutism, and obsessive-compulsive disorder (OCD). It discusses the fact that anxiety is a common experience in 2e learners simply because they are 2e. It suggests ideas for accommodations and modifications for these learners.

Chapter 12: Depression and Other Mood Disorders is dedicated to gifted learners who struggle with major depressive disorder (MDD), disruptive mood dysregulation disorder (DMDD), and bipolar disorder (BD). We'll look at social and emotional considerations for these learners and talk about existential depression in gifted learners too.

Chapter 13: The Neurodiverse Classroom talks about how we can normalize neurodiversity in our schools and slowly begin both to create systemic change and to empower our 2e students to succeed.

How to Use This Book

Part 1 of this book flows best if you read the chapters in consecutive order, as the strategies therein often rely on information and terminology shared in previous chapters. You can read part 2 in the same way; however, each chapter can also stand alone as a resource for a specific student you are trying to support.

One of this book's major goals is to bridge the divides among gifted, general, and special education classrooms, so please share this resource with your school's special education department, gifted education teachers, school counselors, administrators, and professional learning communities (PLCs). Twice-exceptional learners are often right under our noses and unable to access the services they need. The more people who are on the lookout for 2e students, the more likely they are to be found and given the support they need.

Throughout the book, you'll find easy-to-use informational resources (such as the charts with various possible accommodations and modifications at the end of each chapter in part 2) and reproducible forms for you to use as you serve your 2e students (such as the Accommodations Needs Screener at the end of chapter 1 or the Strength-Based Lesson Planning Template at the end of chapter 2). Mark these pages and use them liberally. All the activities and tools are ones I've used in my clinical practice with 2e learners or during professional development training with teachers who serve 2e students.

You may also notice that many of the strategies shared in this book are helpful not only for 2e learners, but also for other students. While most of the strategies work to integrate higher-level thinking skills and are strength-based, built on common characteristics of gifted learners, you could easily generalize many of the strategies to students who are not officially 2e.

Twice-exceptional students have potential they deserve to realize. I hope you find this book useful as you support all the exceptional and amazing students in your classroom.

Emily Kircher-Morris

Part 1

SUPPORTING ALL
Twice-Exceptional
Learners

Part 1 looks at the big picture of 2e students. In this section we'll explore the legal precedent that advocates for 2e learners can use to help their students qualify for special education services under the Individuals with Disabilities Education Act (IDEA) or accommodations and modifications for a Section 504 plan, how the social and emotional needs of giftedness interact with other areas of exceptionality, and specific strategies in a strength-based model that are useful to support all 2e learners.

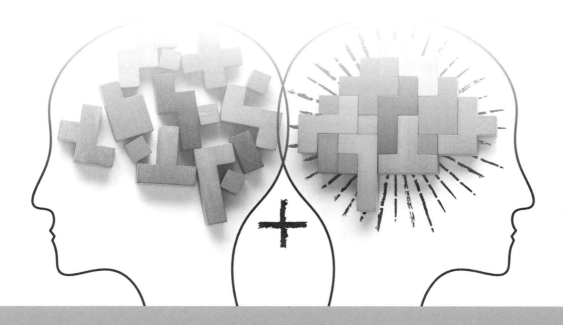

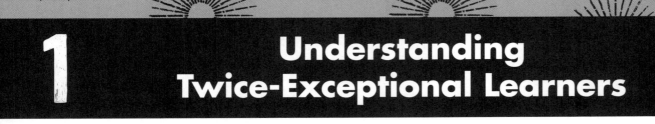

Understanding Twice-Exceptional Learners

1

A twice-exceptional learner is a student who is both cognitively gifted and has a disability as defined by federal or state eligibility criteria. Disabilities include specific learning disabilities, emotional and behavioral disorders, autism spectrum disorder (ASD), ADHD, physical disabilities, and speech-language disorders. Twice-exceptional learners have always been in our classrooms. But only recently have educators really begun to see the struggles 2e learners face. As the field of gifted education has grown, educators have developed a better understanding of these students who are gifted *and* have conditions such as dyslexia, ASD, ADHD, and more. The worlds of gifted education and special education are not mutually exclusive. Where they overlap, we find 2e students.

The term *twice-exceptional* originated as a description for gifted children with specific learning disabilities. Its meaning has expanded to include gifted children with any educational, neurodevelopmental, or mental health diagnoses that may entitle them to services through an IEP or a Section 504 plan. In this book, we will discuss the following diagnoses:

- specific learning disabilities in reading, writing, and math

- ADHD

- ASD

- auditory, visual, and sensory processing disorders

- anxiety disorders and obsessive-compulsive disorder (OCD)

- depression and other mood disorders

Some diagnoses that fall under the 2e umbrella are not discussed in a dedicated chapter or section of this book. The key factor I used to determine which diagnoses to include was the educational impact of the specific diagnosis. I asked myself, "Does this diagnosis require accommodations unique to 2e learners?" Using this yardstick, I decided not to dedicate a chapter or section to oppositional defiant disorder (ODD), for example, because it is a primarily behavioral diagnosis that often co-occurs with another mental health diagnosis, such as ADHD or ASD.

The 1970s were a decade of incredible progress in education. The Rehabilitation Act of 1973 guaranteed accommodations for students with disabilities. In 1974, the Office of the Gifted and Talented was given official status in the US Office of Education. In 1975, the Education for All Handicapped Children Act mandated free and appropriate education for all children

THE EVOLUTION OF 2E LINGO

1980s
gifted/handicapped

Early 1990s
gifted/learning disabled (GLD)

Late 1990s–early 2000s
twice-exceptional, dually diagnosed

2020s
2e, multi-exceptional, neurodivergent

with disabilities. The Individuals with Disabilities Education Act (IDEA) in 1997 and No Child Left Behind (NCLB) in 2004 further cemented the requirement for schools to provide special education opportunities and funding. But beyond the opportunity for grants for gifted education services offered through the Javits grants programs in NCLB, gifted education services have never been federally mandated or funded. This leaves states to determine funding for gifted programming, leading to a wide variety of programs and services offered from state to state.

Because the fields of special education and gifted education evolved separately, 2e learners have a long history of being underidentified and underserved. In the field of gifted education, there's an ongoing debate: should gifted programs serve students identified as gifted based on their ability level or should they serve students who meet a benchmark of academic achievement? Some students have high cognitive ability but not high achievement, some have high achievement but not high cognitive ability, and some have both high cognitive ability and high achievement. (See **figure 1-1**.) The outcome of this debate is important for 2e kids because they have high cognitive ability but often do not achieve high grades.

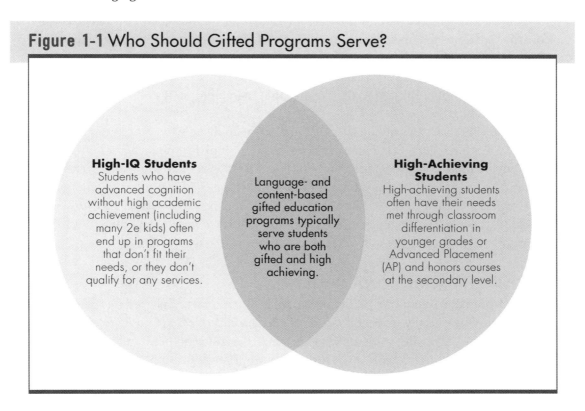

Figure 1-1 Who Should Gifted Programs Serve?

High-IQ Students
Students who have advanced cognition without high academic achievement (including many 2e kids) often end up in programs that don't fit their needs, or they don't qualify for any services.

Language- and content-based gifted education programs typically serve students who are both gifted and high achieving.

High-Achieving Students
High-achieving students often have their needs met through classroom differentiation in younger grades or Advanced Placement (AP) and honors courses at the secondary level.

In the field of special education, teachers are gradually becoming aware of 2e students. These children may not show the typical signs of a learning disability but do, in fact, need the support of specialized services and accommodations. Some students are assessed for learning disabilities or psychological diagnoses, and teachers and parents may be surprised when the students' cognitive ability scores are in the superior ranges.

The 2e community is beginning to find a voice. However, the struggle to provide them ongoing support and services is far from over.

Recognizing 2e Learners

Many 2e learners fly under the radar, especially in the early grades. Academic and social demands are lower for young children, so bright kids with learning difficulties can use their strengths to compensate for their difficulties, thus masking them. As educators, we need to recognize these strengths so we can help students capitalize on them. It is also important for us to be in tune with their struggles so we can be proactive in meeting their needs.

Linda Silverman, Barbara Gilman, Deirdre Lovecky, and Elizabeth Maxwell developed a document called "Checklist for Recognizing Twice-Exceptional Children" (see reproducible on page 28). You can use this tool and share it with families to explore the possibility of twice-exceptionality in students. The diagnoses that may apply to 2e learners aren't always easily recognized even in students who are not gifted and therefore don't have gifted traits masking their struggles. When a bright student in your class is struggling, the checklist can help you determine if there is a reason to pursue additional evaluation. This checklist is simply a tool to start a conversation with other educators or students' parents or guardians. It is not a tool for comparing students. There is no cutoff score that indicates the presence or absence of a diagnosis. However, examining patterns of behaviors and characteristics common in 2e learners through the descriptions on the checklist can help you identify areas for further evaluation. Remember that families might need additional support as they realize that their children may have disabilities along with their giftedness.

Several characteristics on the checklist may seem applicable to many students in many situations. The goal of using the checklist is to look for trends and identify areas that are more of a struggle than others. For example, let's say you have checked "Sometimes/Often" several times for a student who struggles in reading, and you notice that a majority of these checks fall under "Visual Processing Weaknesses" and "Dyslexia or Stealth Dyslexia." This pattern offers a clue about what might be impeding the child's reading success—and what you might want to observe or assess further.

Catching Twice-Exceptionality

Many exceptional students are placed on a single educational path based on their initial referral. Students initially referred for special education services are rarely referred for gifted testing. Likewise, students who are labeled as gifted are seldom screened for learning difficulties. It is important to provide appropriate educational opportunities for students based on their individual learning needs. Gifted education is offered to students because every student deserves to be cognitively challenged at a level appropriate for their ability and to avoid the negative effects (like boredom, perfectionism, and poor work habits) of remaining unchallenged in other class settings. Special education is offered to help provide the supports and instruction needed for students who have struggles that can't be supported solely within the general education classroom. Both are necessary services; some students require both.

SPOTTING GIFTEDNESS IN SPECIAL EDUCATION

To make sure you don't miss gifted students who are already identified for special education, take the following steps:

1. **Train special educators and counselors to spot traits of 2e children.** Students who participate in general education classes may show qualities of giftedness in the classroom. They may also have cognitive assessments on file showing advanced performance in certain cognitive areas despite a full-scale score within the average range.

2. **Use universal screening tools** to catch gifted students who may not be nominated by their teachers. Twice-exceptional learners often fly under the radar.

3. **Find alternative methods to qualify students for gifted services.** Twice-exceptional learners may not have the academic scores often used to qualify students for gifted services. Look for evidence of exceptional creativity or advanced abstract reasoning and problem solving to obtain support services.

SPOTTING SPECIAL NEEDS IN GIFTED EDUCATION

Many characteristics of giftedness overlap with characteristics of special needs. Because of this overlap and because of the stigma surrounding certain educational and medical diagnoses, families and educators may hesitate to address their concerns in the academic setting. They may describe them as signs of asynchronous development or quirkiness. Many in the gifted community are cautious to avoid misdiagnosis by a person unfamiliar with the characteristics associated with high ability.

When a gifted child is showing signs of academic, social, or emotional struggle, the urge to ignore these concerns and label them as traits of giftedness can hurt the 2e child, whose special needs do not get diagnosed. Sorting through the child's behaviors to understand their underlying cause can help distinguish an educational or clinical concern from a developmental issue that will resolve itself with minimal support. A thorough understanding of the underlying cause for the struggle is necessary to determine next steps.

Additionally, the characteristics of students with various diagnoses often overlap. For example, almost all 2e diagnoses include some type of executive functioning struggle. Students can also be multi-exceptional, having multiple diagnoses plus giftedness. In **figure 1-2**, a chart developed by Montgomery County Public Schools in Maryland to help staff understand the commonalities and differences among 2e students, you can see the overlap under the heading "All."

The most effective way to catch twice-exceptionality is for a professional familiar with gifted development to complete a comprehensive evaluation. Training in the characteristics of 2e learners is necessary to identify the learning needs of these students. Appearances can be deceiving with 2e learners. Typical assessment tools may not be adequate to identify their needs. Throughout this book, I will discuss assessment tools for each diagnosis. These discussions will address the subtle things that may be missed by an evaluator unfamiliar with gifted learners. In general, it is important to remember that high-ability learners often compensate for their struggles and that typical scoring standards may not meet the needs of gifted learners. For example, with diagnoses such as ADHD and ASD, an individual with high ability may have scores on a diagnostic assessment that are below the typical cutoff for diagnosis; however, this result may be a "false negative" masking a diagnosis that will become more apparent as the child gets older.

Figure 1-2 2e Commonalities

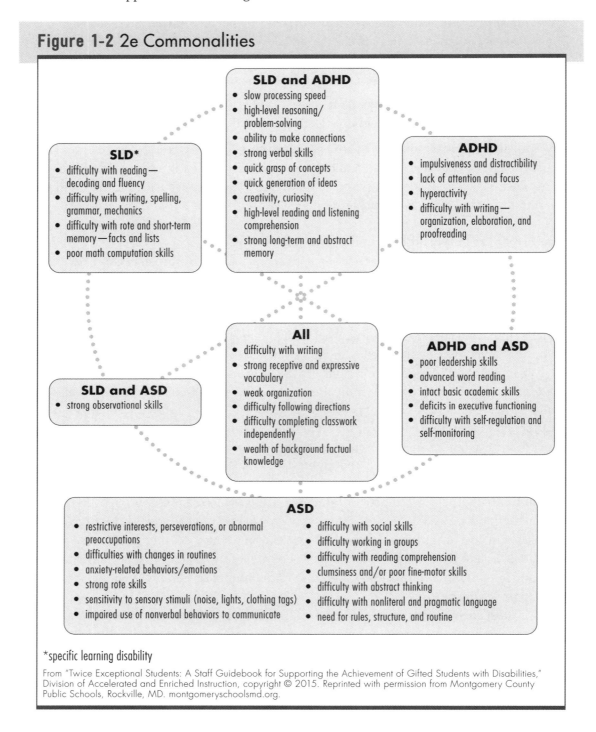

SLD and ADHD
- slow processing speed
- high-level reasoning/problem-solving
- ability to make connections
- strong verbal skills
- quick grasp of concepts
- quick generation of ideas
- creativity, curiosity
- high-level reading and listening comprehension
- strong long-term and abstract memory

SLD*
- difficulty with reading—decoding and fluency
- difficulty with writing, spelling, grammar, mechanics
- difficulty with rote and short-term memory—facts and lists
- poor math computation skills

ADHD
- impulsiveness and distractibility
- lack of attention and focus
- hyperactivity
- difficulty with writing—organization, elaboration, and proofreading

All
- difficulty with writing
- strong receptive and expressive vocabulary
- weak organization
- difficulty following directions
- difficulty completing classwork independently
- wealth of background factual knowledge

SLD and ASD
- strong observational skills

ADHD and ASD
- poor leadership skills
- advanced word reading
- intact basic academic skills
- deficits in executive functioning
- difficulty with self-regulation and self-monitoring

ASD
- restrictive interests, perseverations, or abnormal preoccupations
- difficulties with changes in routines
- anxiety-related behaviors/emotions
- strong rote skills
- sensitivity to sensory stimuli (noise, lights, clothing tags)
- impaired use of nonverbal behaviors to communicate
- difficulty with social skills
- difficulty working in groups
- difficulty with reading comprehension
- clumsiness and/or poor fine-motor skills
- difficulty with abstract thinking
- difficulty with nonliteral and pragmatic language
- need for rules, structure, and routine

*specific learning disability

From "Twice Exceptional Students: A Staff Guidebook for Supporting the Achievement of Gifted Students with Disabilities," Division of Accelerated and Enriched Instruction, copyright © 2015. Reprinted with permission from Montgomery County Public Schools, Rockville, MD. montgomeryschoolsmd.org.

GIFTED BEHAVIOR OR CAUSE FOR CONCERN?

There are a few classic classroom concerns that are associated with giftedness as well. Often, teasing out whether the behavior is a result of a child's high ability or a disability is tricky. Throughout this book, we will discuss a variety of strategies to determine when an assessment or extra support is needed for these behaviors. Here are a few behaviors that can be a sign of giftedness or a cause for concern:

- **Inattention:** Is the child bored because of insufficient challenge, or is the child unable to focus?

- **Impulsivity:** Does the student blurt out answers due to quick processing and copious knowledge, or does the student have an executive functioning deficit in response inhibition?

- **Refusal to write:** Is this perfectionism associated with giftedness, or is it a learning difficulty in written expression?

- **Poor social skills:** Is the child truly unable to interact socially with peers, or does the child have nothing in common with them due to giftedness?

Underserved 2e Learners

Educators across the United States are grappling with the reality of inequities in our schools. Gifted education, in particular, is reckoning with how to identify culturally and linguistically diverse (CLD) students for gifted education programs, after having historically denied these learners access to these programs.

When a student comes from a CLD background, or is an English language learner (ELL), or is economically disadvantaged *and* is 2e, their chance of being identified for gifted services drops dramatically. Shawn A. Robinson authored a paper describing this unique situation and used the phrase *triple identity theory* to describe his experience as a gifted Black student with dyslexia (Robinson 2017). Robinson and Joy Lawson Davis cowrote a chapter on the needs of CLD learners in the book *Twice Exceptional: Teaching Bright and Creative Students with Learning Difficulties* (Davis and Robinson 2018). **They used the term *3e* to describe students whose identities include giftedness, cultural diversity, and a diagnosed disability.**

Who Are 3e Learners?

If 2e learners are twice-exceptional, 3e learners are thrice-exceptional. They have another factor to consider in identification for educational services. The 3e category includes three distinct groups of students at risk of being missed for receiving gifted and/or special education services—CLD learners, ELL students, and economically disadvantaged students (Ritchotte, Lee, and Graefe 2019):

- **Culturally and linguistically diverse (CLD) learners** are students whose households differ in some way from what is considered the majority or mainstream culture of the United States: White, middle-to-upper-income families. For example, these students may have African, Hispanic, Asian, American Indian, or Middle Eastern heritages, to name only a few. Linguistically diverse families may speak another language at home while the student speaks English in academic settings.

- **English language learning (ELL)** students speak primarily a language other than English. They may have had some exposure to English and may speak it in social situations, but they struggle with the more difficult academic language used in classrooms.

- **Economically disadvantaged students** are students who live in poverty. For these students, food and housing stability may be a concern, or they may lack access to appropriate healthcare services. It may be difficult for students living in economically disadvantaged households to compensate for the chronic stress caused by living in poverty.

Barriers to Identifying 3e Students

Bright CLD, ELL, and economically disadvantaged students already face barriers to accessing gifted education services. When you combine these systemic barriers with another disability or diagnosis, the identification procedure becomes even more complex.

Schools that ask teachers to recommend students for gifted services create an obstacle for identifying high-ability students who do not fit the stereotype of a gifted student. Due to common misconceptions about giftedness, many educators overlook 3e students. They may have internalized the (incorrect) image of a gifted student as a highly verbal, high-achieving, compliant student. Students who are 3e do not typically fit this mold, so we need to find other ways to identify and serve these students.

Another barrier to identifying 3e students appears when an adult perceives a student as a discipline or behavior problem instead of a child with an academic, neurodevelopmental, or mental health diagnosis. Think about a Black student who is gifted and autistic. Research shows Black students are less likely than White students to be warned about behavior that's perceived as disrespectful before being disciplined (Wegmann and Smith 2019). This student could be disciplined for a lagging skill that's directly related to their diagnosis—and the teacher's bias. And being cognitively gifted makes it possible that their diagnosis is masked and unrecognized.

CLD and ELL students are less likely to show their cognitive ability on a test that relies heavily on verbal skills. Most IQ tests used for special education and gifted education services are heavily verbal, even though assessment options are available that give a clearer picture for students whose language barriers may suppress their overall cognitive scores. Additionally, educators may not be aware of or willing to use alternative qualification criteria to account for the differences that may appear in cognitive testing.

Strategies for Identifying 3e Students

Here are several steps educators can take to prevent 3e students from falling through the cracks:

- Use universal screening tools to identify gifted learners. When we cast a wider net and give every student the opportunity to show their ability, we are more likely to find all the high-ability students. To account for 3e learners, be sure to compare screening scores with achievement scores and look for signs of discrepancy between classroom achievement and cognitive ability.

- Educate families about characteristics of giftedness and twice-exceptionality. Parents of CLD, ELL, and economically disadvantaged students may lack the cultural capital (experience, knowledge, and connections) to navigate the educational system and advocate for their children. Make sure to provide information in a language appropriate for the family's background.

- Recognize that 3e CLD and ELL students are more likely to show their ability on assessments that do not rely heavily on verbal ability. Choosing appropriate tests is the best way to measure a student's overall ability.

- Connect learning to students' backgrounds and use learning materials representative of their cultural heritage. If students are learning information about a culture that is very different from their own experience, they will be less able to make higher-level connections and analyses commensurate with their ability.

- Examine qualification criteria and look for restrictive identification procedures. The best way to identify gifted learners who don't fit the typical mold is to have several paths to qualify for gifted services that take into account the characteristics of students from diverse backgrounds.

Twice-Exceptional Learners with Physical Disabilities

Gifted students with physical disabilities should not be excluded from the framework of 2e learners. Students who are identified for special education services under the umbrellas of visual impairment (including blindness), deafness, hearing impairment, or orthopedic impairment (such as cerebral palsy) should be considered for gifted education programs and services with the accommodations necessary for them to access the gifted education curriculum.

One of the main difficulties in identifying these students for gifted education services is the fact that they may already be in the special education system. Many students who are placed in special education services are never assessed (or never assessed appropriately) for gifted education services. One study found that of 13,000 students identified for special education services, 330 students had achievement scores above the 90th percentile. Of those 330 high-achieving students, only about 11 percent of them were participating in gifted education services, and the likelihood of those participating in gifted and talented programs being African-American, Hispanic, or female was low (Barnard-Brak et al. 2015). This discrepancy shows the stark disconnect between the special education and gifted education departments in many school districts.

Sometimes, students who begin the special education process are administered a cognitive assessment, and if those scores indicate a child may qualify for gifted education services, the IEP team may provide a referral to the gifted education department. It is important not to rely solely on this process, though. Students with physical disabilities may never receive a cognitive assessment by the IEP team because the basis of their special education services is a medical condition or diagnosis. The IEP team may have used anecdotal information and determined that cognitive skills were not an area of concern and therefore did not need to be assessed.

Universal screening is one way to assess all students for gifted education services. Other standardized or district-wide testing and benchmarks can also provide information about students who should be screened for gifted education services. Additionally, assessment teams may need to be creative and flexible about the best tests that can capture a student's true ability. Your district's school psychologists, psychological examiners, or special education administrators should have access to and knowledge of the tests available within the district and know which will meet individual students' needs, if it appears the tests being used aren't capturing a student's true ability.

NATALIA'S STORY

Natalia had just entered middle school and was getting used to the new routine of changing classes between each period. She had a paraprofessional with her at the beginning of the school year to help her get comfortable with the layout of the school. Natalia was visually impaired and used a cane to help her navigate the halls of the school. Within a few weeks, she was able to leave each class a few minutes early to make her way independently to her next class.

Around the same time, the school got the results of the annual state assessment tests. The gifted education facilitator went through all the results to screen for gifted education candidates. He noticed Natalia's scores were high enough to qualify her for screening for the gifted education program. But when he looked through her file, there was no record of a previous screening for gifted education services. Her latest IEP reevaluation included no cognitive assessments due to the fact that her qualification for special education services was related to a medical diagnosis of visual impairment.

After the gifted education facilitator spoke to the district's special education evaluation team, the school developed a plan to assess Natalia's cognitive abilities. Using a common cognitive assessment, the Wechsler Intelligence Scale for Children (WISC), they assessed Natalia's verbal, visual-spatial, and fluid reasoning skills. Her verbal composite score was above the 95th percentile, but her overall General Ability Index (GAI) was suppressed due to her weak visual-spatial skills. The district chose to enroll Natalia in the gifted education program based on her verbal comprehension composite score and recognizing the impact of her visual impairment. ■

Services and Accommodations for 2e Learners

Services and accommodations for 2e learners take two main forms: IEPs and Section 504 plans. A key factor influencing whether a child is placed on an IEP or a 504 plan is the type of diagnosis they receive. An educational diagnosis is established after the school has conducted its own evaluation and the child has met state and federal criteria for a diagnosis approved under the IDEA. A medical diagnosis is given by a medical doctor or qualified mental health professional and uses diagnostic criteria established in the *Diagnostic and Statistical Manual of Mental Disorders: Fifth Edition* (DSM-5) or the International Classification of Diseases: Tenth Edition (ICD-10).

An IEP is a plan that provides both specialized services and accommodations for a student. An IEP requires an educational diagnosis to qualify, and it includes specific goals and growth targets that are tracked by a special educator. Students may receive their special education services through a resource room, a class within a class (CWC), or a support class built into the child's schedule.

A Section 504 plan is often limited to accommodations and modifications that can be implemented within the classroom. Accommodations provide different strategies for a student to learn the material—for example, listening to an audiobook instead of reading a text, or using flexible seating in a classroom. Modifications change the content or structure of the work in some way—for example, reducing the number of items a student needs to do for a homework assignment. A Section 504 plan is established based on a physical or mental health medical diagnosis and how much the diagnosis affects a student's ability to function in various areas of life. Although services typically provided through special education programs, such as occupational therapy or CWC support, are not the norm for students on a Section 504 plan, they are legally eligible for those services, if their diagnoses would be best supported in this way (US Department of Education Office for Civil Rights 2016). Students who receive support through a Section 504 plan do not receive the same progress monitoring as students tracking growth for a goal stated within an IEP. For a side-by-side comparison of IEPs and Section 504 plans, see **figure 1-3**.

Figure 1-3 IEP Versus 504

	Individualized Education Program	Section 504 Plan
What is it?	An IEP is a plan developed to identify special instruction or related services to meet a child's academic, social, or emotional needs.	A Section 504 plan defines the specific accommodations and modifications a student needs to access the general education curriculum.
How does a student qualify?	The school conducts an assessment to determine the presence of an area of disability as defined by the IDEA. The diagnoses seen in 2e students that fall into this category are specific learning disability, emotional disturbance, educational diagnosis of autism, speech and language impairment, and other health impairment.	Students qualify for a Section 504 plan based on a learning, behavior, or medical condition generally diagnosed outside the school (although the school may conduct assessments to determine the impact of the diagnosis). The disability must substantially impact major life activities for the student in areas such as thinking, learning, concentrating, or performing manual tasks.
What does it provide?	A student with an IEP receives services provided by a certified special educator. Services are defined as a number of minutes a student is in contact with a special educator providing instruction. Student progress is measured annually based on goals set at each IEP meeting.	A Section 504 plan meets a student's needs through accommodations and modifications made in the classroom, like modifying assignments or altering the learning environment. It is possible, but uncommon, for a student to receive special education services, such as occupational therapy or CWC placement.
What agency oversees it?	US Department of Education Office of Special Education and Rehabilitative Services	US Department of Education Office for Civil Rights

Building the Assessment Team

When I worked as a teacher of gifted education programming, I had several students over the years who were identified for IEPs and Section 504 plans. A few times, the case manager or school counselor asked me if I had any observations prior to the meeting. But rarely was I invited to attend the meeting, to be a part of the team determining the educational needs of my students. Sometimes this was due to scheduling issues, because my attendance at the meeting would require a substitute for my classroom. Other times, it appeared the IEP team assumed the meeting didn't really influence gifted services (or that a gifted child's needs would influence the IEP). It was too bad, because I often knew my students better than their classroom teachers did. I taught them for multiple years and had observed them in an environment different from their general education classroom. I attended any meetings I could, but this was generally at my request.

Creating an interdisciplinary team of stakeholders is vital to understanding the multifaceted needs of 2e kids. Each team member brings an important piece of a student's story to the table. Parents and guardians know how the child behaves, reacts, and interacts at home. The classroom teacher knows the student's performance with grade-level curriculum. The special education teacher can help identify what types of supports will be most effective. And the gifted education teacher can help the team recognize the influence of the child's cognitive abilities on their achievement.

Establishing Individualized Education Programs (IEPs)

Families and teachers who want to advocate for an IEP for a 2e child must be battle ready. The biggest hurdle to clear in securing services for a 2e learner is convincing the school to identify the child's need for specialized services or accommodations without limiting support for the child's advanced cognitive development.

A big reason it so difficult to advocate for 2e kids is that advocates and schools tend to focus on different aspects of student achievement. Experts in the field of 2e learners insist that a child's achievement should at least *approach* their ability level. Meanwhile, schools focus on making sure all children are achieving at their grade level. When high-ability children are achieving at or slightly below grade level, they may be achieving far below their true potential. But IDEA does not explicitly support providing services for 2e children unless their achievement grossly lags behind that of their same-age peers.

Twice-exceptional learners often do not get identified for special education or receive IEPs and the services they need for a few reasons. Here are some of those reasons:

- The review of existing evaluation data (REED or RED) meeting held by the school determines there is not enough evidence to go forward with testing. The child is continuing to make progress slowly in areas of weakness or has met the minimum scores needed for the child's grade level on certain benchmark tests. The school uses any progress, even if it is slower than that of same-age peers, to deny assessment.

- The assessment team moves forward with testing, but the student is not far enough behind grade-level expectations to qualify for services. There may be a severe gap between achievement and ability, but the student's scores are within the average or low-average range. The school views the child's achievement scores as a standalone measure, without using the results of a cognitive assessment for context.

- Parents are hesitant to move forward with testing because they don't see the classroom struggles or are worried about the stigma of special education.

- Schools are unsure what services should look like for a 2e child.

Gifted and special educators are uniquely positioned to advocate for looking at the big picture of children's ability, achievement, and social and emotional needs when determining eligibility for services. When you are advocating for 2e students, you may find the following three legal precedents useful to help high-ability children access services:

- Using predetermined "cut scores" to disqualify a cognitively advanced student from special education services is inconsistent with IDEA (Musgrove 2013).

- Schools may not use a single test score to determine eligibility or services. For example, schools may not deny assessment for a child based on a previous test for admission to a gifted program (Musgrove 2015).

- Students qualifying for special education services should include "appropriately ambitious" goals within the IEP (580 U. S. ___ (2017)).

IDENTIFYING 2E LEARNERS AND ESTABLISHING AN IEP

1. **Look beyond the child's cognitive skills; see their struggles too.** Many families and educators explain away areas of concern by attributing them to characteristics of giftedness. Some families may be worried about misdiagnosing their children. However, research does not show that gifted children are being overdiagnosed with neurological or psychological concerns (Kaufman 2018). If anything, they are overlooked. Typical tests for certain diagnoses are normed on the average population and do not consider how symptoms might manifest in high-ability learners. For example, gifted learners with ADHD show fewer symptoms of ADHD than their nongifted peers do because gifted learners are better able to compensate for their struggles.

2. **Advocate for early and proactive intervention.** Early intervention and proactive support are the most effective ways to make progress quickly. The longer we wait to identify 2e children, the more time we lose to help them. Many schools follow a discrepancy model for special education identification: a child's achievement must show a statistically significant lag (often, kids must be at least a grade level behind) before qualifying for services. Advocating for 2e learners requires understanding what disabilities coupled with giftedness can look like and using creative interventions and supports to meet their unique learning needs.

3. **Use the Response to Intervention (RTI) model while recognizing its weaknesses.** RTI is a tool many schools use to monitor the progress of all students in the classroom and provide tiers of intervention based on need. Differentiation can take place within the classroom, in small intervention groups, or outside the classroom for students with the highest levels of need. Some schools also use RTI for providing gifted services. However, RTI isn't great for early identification of 2e learners' needs. For example, a 2e child struggling with reading makes just enough progress to avoid standing out, so the underlying issue of dyslexia doesn't get looked for and addressed.

4. **Complete a Paired Student Data Observation (see below) to quantify behaviors in the classroom.** A typical component of any special education referral is an observation. An objective observation in the classroom by an unbiased staff person can help illuminate classroom behaviors for members of the special education referral team and the child's parents. Many schools use a simple qualitative description of the child's behaviors. The Paired Student Data Observation chart provides both qualitative and quantitative data. It compares the behaviors a child is exhibiting with those of a typical peer in the same environment.

5. **Determine eligibility while keeping cognitive ability in mind.** When the evaluation is complete, it is important to remember that a 2e student's learning profile may not look like those of other students with the same learning difficulties. Resist the myths surrounding the laws of special education and the belief that if a child is at grade level, there's no problem. Here are a few things to keep in mind when you're assessing a bright child for struggles in a specific content area.

   » IDEA does not require a severe discrepancy between the child in question and same-age peers.

   » A gifted learner's achievement should approach their ability.

   » The gap between a child's achievement and ability can be used as a strong indicator of need for an IEP, even if the child's achievement is not significantly below average.

PAIRED STUDENT DATA OBSERVATION

Families and teachers may look at a report card, see As and Bs, and assume things are fine. The struggles of 2e learners aren't always obvious. How can we tease out their struggles when their grades and other work do not show a big problem?

During the process of evaluating a child's needs for a possible IEP, a special education teacher or counselor usually spends time in the classroom observing and recording the child's behavior. The typical observation can be misleading when used for 2e learners if their abilities are masking their difficulties. A Paired Student Data Observation **(figure 1-4)** is one way to objectively quantify what happens during the school day of a student who might be 2e. The observer watches not only the identified student, but also a typical student, recording the frequency of certain behaviors during the same time window. This strategy offers a normative comparison and provides quantitative data to supplement qualitative observations made during this time or provided anecdotally by the teacher. Quantitative data often has power that qualitative data lacks and also helps reduce bias—real or perceived—in the evaluation process. The data can be used to identify and address specific areas of strength and struggle. For a reproducible version of this chart, see page 32.

Once your school has officially identified a 2e student, you may feel like you've reached the finish line. However, writing the IEP and identifying the goals for a 2e learner can be just as tricky. Schools and teachers may not know exactly where to go with goals and techniques because 2e learners don't look like other students with IEPs. The school may even deny services because its educators don't know how to meet the unique needs of the 2e student. It may attempt to place the child on a Section 504 plan instead of providing the minutes needed for specialized instruction or other remediation. But special education and gifted education teachers can get creative with differentiation in their classrooms, just as general education teachers do in their classrooms.

Figure 1-4 Sample Paired Student Data Observation

Student: Tricia A.			Observed by: Mrs. Otto (Counselor)		
Date: 10/5/2020	Observation interval: 1 minute	Start time: 10:25 a.m.	End time: 10:50 a.m.	Activity: writer's workshop	

Behaviors					
Student	On task	Off task	Out of seat	Talking to others	Fidgeting
Student A:	HHT HHT II	HHT HHT III	III	IIII	
Student B: (typical student)	HHT HHT HHT IIII	HHT I		II	

Behaviors					
Student	Rocking in chair	Still but not paying attention	Other: tapping pencil	Other: sitting with head in hands	Other: looking through desk
Student A:	HHT HHT HHT		III	IIII	III
Student B: (typical student)		III			

Notes: When the observation began, Tricia appeared to be searching through her desk for materials. Her writer's notebook was on her desk. She intermittently spoke to a peer. After finding a pencil, she seemed to struggle with getting started. She frequently wrote and erased in her notebook. She exhibited a lot of psychomotor activity throughout the observation, getting out of her seat to sharpen a pencil, get a tissue, and ask the teacher a question. Even the times she was on task did not seem to produce a significant quantity or quality of work. (See attached copy of work from this class activity.)

SIERRA'S STORY

Sierra's parents knew their daughter was struggling even before she started kindergarten. Sierra showed many of the same traits with abstract reasoning and problem-solving as her exceptionally gifted older brother had at her age; however, she was struggling with basic literacy skills. By first grade, her reading was "okay," but her reading fluency was slow and labored. She struggled greatly with understanding what she had read. Her teachers were mostly unconcerned and saw no need for testing, but her parents knew they needed to find out more. An independent cognitive assessment recognized some possible signs of dyslexia, but Sierra's parents were stumped about where to find services. Her parents continued to do their best to support her at home and advocate for her at school.

After her first assessment, Sierra was diagnosed with ADHD, but the medication helped only a little. Sierra's reading struggles grew each year. Sierra's parents asked the school repeatedly and were denied formal testing for a learning disability. The school finally agreed to testing for a specific learning disability during Sierra's fifth-grade year because her grades were suffering. Sierra was administered the WISC, and her overall cognitive ability was in the upper 130s as measured by the GAI. (GAI is a composite score similar to the Full Scale IQ that limits the influence of working memory and processing speed and is often useful when assessing 2e students.) Her overall Reading Fluency Score assessed with an achievement test was 92. At the meeting to determine eligibility for special education services, the school recognized Sierra's struggles, but insisted a Section 504 plan would serve her better than an IEP because the students she would attend special education services with would have much lower ability levels than hers. The school didn't think the services typically provided for a child with a learning disability would work for Sierra because her achievement was "at grade level"—just on the low end of average.

Sierra continued to struggle at the public school, so her parents began exploring other options. They found a local private school specializing in meeting the needs of high-ability learners with learning difficulties. After two years at the new school, Sierra reentered the public school with her skills much closer to her ability level. Her confidence was high. When Sierra transferred back to the public school, the school accepted the IEP established by the private school and provided a daily support class to ease her transition.

The tools used at the private school to boost Sierra's reading skills were the same programs the public school had said wouldn't meet her needs. Without her parents' advocacy (and the ability to afford private schooling), Sierra would have fallen through the cracks. How many Sierras do we miss? ■

Establishing Section 504 Plans

When you are evaluating the necessity of a Section 504 plan, it's important to remember the masking that happens in twice-exceptionality. Students' grades may look fine, but they may be compensating for their struggles with their advanced cognitive ability. Their grades fail to show how much impact their diagnosis has on their daily functioning.

> " Just having the time every day with a teacher who started with the basics and worked through everything with me made a huge difference! I still like listening to audiobooks more than reading, but I'm not scared to go to language arts class anymore.
>
> —Sierra, ninth grader "

Section 504 of the Rehabilitation Act of 1973 is a law that guarantees certain rights to people with disabilities. It requires school districts to provide a free appropriate public education (FAPE) to students who have a physical or mental impairment that substantially limits one or more major life activities (US Department of Education Office for Civil Rights 2018). A Section 504 plan should consider how significantly a student's medical condition limits the student's functioning in a variety of areas. For 2e learners with Section 504 plans, the plans often identify areas of struggle in performing manual tasks, learning, reading, concentrating, thinking, and communicating. However, this is only a small segment of the major life activities identified by Congress.

A Section 504 plan is a tool that helps students, families, and schools proactively scaffold learning success for 2e students. A 504 plan is typically created by an interdisciplinary team that includes the student's parents, general education teacher(s), gifted and special education teachers, and a counselor and/or administrator. Without a formal 504 plan, families must constantly ensure that teachers understand and meet their children's unique learning needs. Many parents and guardians do not have the knowledge or time to do this on a regular basis. When a single document follows a student with special needs, it is much easier for educators to know the student's struggles and plan for accommodations.

EZRA'S STORY

Ezra was a high school student who dealt with significant anxiety daily. He had always earned high grades, so most of his teachers did not see the anxiety just beneath the surface. But his behavior offered clues. Being told to find a group to work with sent Ezra to the bathroom to hide until he came back and was placed in a group by the teacher. Tests sent Ezra into a panic. He tended to hyperfocus on the length of time he took to complete his test compared to other students, and he often stayed extremely anxious for the rest of the school day, hampering his ability to learn and think in the remainder of his classes.

Looking at the qualitative impact on Ezra's daily life was a much more meaningful measure of his disability than looking at his grades alone. After years of advocating, Ezra's mother was finally successful in securing a Section 504 plan to help alleviate Ezra's anxiety. Ezra said that taking a test in a separate setting greatly reduced his test anxiety. With this accommodation, he could manage his anxiety, and the rest of the day was not derailed. ■

WESLEY'S STORY

Wesley became a client of mine when he was in fifth grade. He was identified both as gifted and autistic. His parents attended an initial consultation to discuss their concerns and options for counseling services.

Wesley had received a medical diagnosis of autism in third grade, but his parents had decided not to tell him or the school about it. At first, this seemed to be okay. Wesley did have social struggles, but overall seemed to be doing fine and was viewed as a "quirky" gifted kid. As he got older, though, his struggles increased. His mom thought they should tell both the school and Wesley about the diagnosis. His dad was hesitant. He didn't want Wesley to be treated differently by teachers and feared word would spread to the students, who might then bully him. Like many parents who are unfamiliar with the laws surrounding educational rights, he worried (unnecessarily) that sharing Wesley's diagnosis with the school would prevent him from being allowed to participate in extracurricular activities or being accepted into higher education.

As happens for a lot of autistic gifted kids, Wesley's social struggles became more evident as he got older. By the end of sixth grade, his parents recognized that disclosing his diagnosis was necessary to get him the supports he needed to succeed at school. They began to question their decision to keep the diagnosis quiet, wondering if telling the school earlier might have mitigated Wesley's struggles. ■

SECTION 504 PLAN QUALIFICATION PROCESS

1. **Determine the presence of a medical condition with a diagnosis from a qualified medical professional.** If a child doesn't qualify for special education services, they may benefit from a Section 504 plan. (Note: It is not necessary for a student to go through an IEP evaluation process before qualifying for a 504 plan.) A Section 504 plan is a document specifying the specific accommodations and modifications

needed to help a student with a medical diagnosis succeed. When a child's physical or mental health condition substantially hinders major life activities, a 504 plan can provide the basic changes and supports the child needs to be successful in the classroom. The family generally must provide documentation of the diagnosis to proceed with the Section 504 process.

2. **Determine impacted life activities.** Look at data from the child's school record, including grades, disciplinary records, test scores, and observations to determine the major life activities that are affected by the student's disability. For 2e learners, these may include performing manual tasks, learning, thinking, concentrating, communicating, or reading. How does the child's disability keep them from being able to accomplish these major life tasks?

3. **Exclude mitigating factors from assessment.** Mitigating factors are supports that are in place to help the student. When you are determining the impact of a condition or diagnosis, you must exclude the effect of mitigating factors. For example, if a student's medication helps control their ADHD symptoms, that does not render them ineligible for accommodations or services. The team should consider what the child's level of functioning would be if they were not taking the medication.

4. **Advocate for documented accommodations, even if the school is "already doing them."** Some schools may hesitate to approve a Section 504 plan because the accommodations requested for a 2e student "are available for all students." For example, if all students are permitted to type their assignments instead of handwriting them, a school may feel a Section 504 plan is not necessary for this accommodation. But when a school hesitates to document a child's needs, a few problems can arise. First, even though the teacher and school may usually allow all students to type an assignment, this does not guarantee the 2e student will always be able to type their assignments. A teacher might decide that students must handwrite a certain assignment for a variety of reasons. Documenting the typing accommodation in a Section 504 plan guarantees the right to this accommodation for the student. Additionally, it is important to have documentation of needs being implemented so as students get older, they are eligible to receive these accommodations on standardized tests (for example, through the College Board for Advanced Placement classes).

5. **Empower students to self-advocate through the Section 504 process.** Self-advocacy can be a difficult skill for any student. It can be even harder for a 2e child. A Section 504 plan encourages the student to request accommodations; it provides a comforting safety net.

6. **Need help understanding and implementing a Section 504 plan?** The "Parent and Educator Resource Guide to Section 504 in Public Elementary and Secondary Schools" gives clear and concise information about how to make sure students with a disability have the supports necessary for school success. You can find it online at ed.gov/about/offices/list/ocr/docs/504-resource-guide-201612.pdf.

Supporting Families Through the IEP or 504 Identification Process

1. **Recognize the range of emotions parents and guardians may experience.** I've seen family members feel relief that their children will finally get the help they need, guilt because they didn't notice the struggle earlier, fear that their children will be ostracized or teased if they receive special services, confusion about the entire process, and resistance to having their children labeled. Validate all emotions to help families feel at ease and remind them that teachers are trustworthy people who want only what is best for their students.

2. **Assure families that an IEP or 504 plan is** individualized. Help them see that this process is a tool to help their children in the specific areas they need.

3. **Let parents and guardians know that an IEP or 504 plan is temporary.** When a child no longer needs the supports, the plan is removed. There is no long-term impact on a child's educational opportunities or college application prospects from having these supports or services in place.

4. **In the IEP or 504 meeting, recognize educational jargon and interpret it for family members.** It's intimidating to sit at a table with a group of professionals discussing your child's shortcomings. Many parents and guardians will nod their way through a meeting but leave it with no real understanding of what happened. (If it isn't common practice for you to be invited to these meetings based on your role within the school, talk to your administration or others to advocate for your inclusion. If you are still unable to attend, encourage the parents to take notes and set a time to consult with them after the meeting to go over the plan and answer any questions they may have.)

5. **Reframe the process as empowering instead of negative or critical.** A psychologist friend of mine tells parents who are worried about labeling their child that their child has likely already been labeled—as lazy, unmotivated, or worse. An appropriate diagnostic label can be a positive thing because it helps all involved understand and communicate about what is happening. It shows that a child's difficulty isn't a personal defect; it is a type of neurodivergence. Diagnosis gives kids the power to overcome their difficulties.

6. **Welcome parents and guardians who come to meetings well prepared.** Some teachers feel intimidated by parents who have done their homework and arrive at meetings with binders, notepads, lists of questions, or advocates. Don't worry! Remember that educators and parents are on the same team— the child's.

> " I remember the first meeting I attended for my son. It was incredibly overwhelming. I felt I might be judged by this team of professionals and like I wouldn't know the right questions to ask. They were so great, though, and explained everything as we went through the process. I left knowing my son wasn't going to fall through the cracks.
>
> —**Stacey**, mom of a 2e boy

Types of Accommodations and Modifications for 2e Learners

Whether you are formalizing an IEP, drafting a 504 plan, or developing strategies to support a struggling student, it is important to consider various types of accommodations and modifications. Accommodations typically fall into five categories: behavioral, environmental, evaluative, instructional, and organizational. (See **figure 1-5**.) Throughout this book, I will suggest examples of modifications within these categories for each type of 2e learner.

Figure 1-5: Accommodation Types and Modification Examples

Type of Accommodation	Purpose	Examples
Behavioral	What supports does this child require to manage their emotions and behavior for effective learning to take place?	Twice-exceptional students often do not respond to typical behavior management systems. Possible modifications in this area include creating a collaborative system with the student to monitor behavioral goals, integrating tools for positive reinforcement, and implementing the same behavior system across settings in the school.
Environmental	What can we change about the student's learning environment to help them succeed?	Environmental accommodations change the surroundings of the learner to help improve learning. Preferential seating, alternate locations for testing, and sensory breaks are all examples of ways to modify a student's environment to enhance learning.
Evaluative	How can we modify the ways in which this student shows us what they know during assessments?	Evaluative accommodations help educators fully understand a child's mastery of a topic. Possible modifications include providing a test in segments to avoid anxiety and improve following directions, reading a test aloud to a student, or having someone scribe a test.
Instructional	What are the best ways we can present learning material to this student?	Students learn more efficiently when teachers understand the best way for them to receive information and modify instruction accordingly. One effective instructional modification is shortening assignments by having 2e learners complete the five most difficult problems first and exempting them from the remainder if they show mastery. Other examples are providing a copy of notes for lessons or teaching mnemonic devices.
Organizational	What organizational tools and support does this student need to succeed?	Direct instruction and monitoring of organizational systems can help 2e students learn the skills necessary to remain organized. Frequent communication with families can help students struggling with organization remain accountable.

Brainstorming possible accommodations in each category can be a daunting task. The **Accommodations Needs Screener** (see reproducible on page 33) is an easy tool to help any team of educators and parents or guardians begin to identify a child's areas of need.

Key Points

Twice-exceptional learners are students with advanced cognitive abilities (giftedness) and a neurological, psychological, or physical disability that affects their ability to learn. The area of difficulty is considered a disability by state or federal standards.

- Many 2e learners have abilities that mask their struggles or struggles that hide their gifts.

- Gifted students are less likely than their nongifted peers to be identified for services.

- Twice-exceptional students should be considered for both gifted education placement and special education or accommodations for their struggles. Both areas need support.

- Twice-exceptional students can qualify for services through an IEP or accommodations and modifications through a Section 504 plan.

- Accommodations and modifications within an IEP or 504 plan can be behavioral, environmental, evaluative, instructional, or organizational.

- Accommodations and modifications can made in a multiple areas of a student's daily academic life.

- Stakeholders who understand the nuances of high-ability students with learning struggles need to be part of the team that evaluates and advocates for 2e learners. If a school lacks staff with this expertise, training is essential.

Checklist for Recognizing Twice-Exceptional Children

Linda Silverman, Barbara Gilman, Deirdre Lovecky, and Elizabeth Maxwell

Child's name: _____ Child's gender: _____ Child's birthdate: _____

Your name: _____ ☐ Parent or guardian ☐ Teacher ☐ Counselor

Date: _____

Instructions

The purpose of this checklist is to assist you in recognizing some common characteristics of gifted children with learning disabilities. This is not a diagnostic tool. This checklist has not been validated, and there are no norms. If a child fits many of the characteristics, it would be wise to refer the child for assessment.

Please answer each item as well as you can by checking the appropriate column. Mark "Sometimes/Often" if you have ever observed this behavior.

Item	General Characteristics of the Twice-Exceptional Learner	Sometimes /Often	Not Observed
1	Appears smarter than grades or test scores suggest		
2	Has a sophisticated speaking vocabulary but poorer written expression		
3	Participates well in class discussions but does not follow through with implementation		
4	Has uneven academic skills and inconsistent grades and test scores		
5	Does well when given sufficient time but performs poorly on timed tests and takes much longer to complete assignments and homework than other students		
6	Studies very hard before tests, gets good grades on tests but soon forgets most of the learned information. Needs to restudy it for later tests		
7	Has excellent problem-solving skills but suffers from low self-esteem		
8	Excels in one area or subject but may appear average in others		
9	Performs well with challenging work but struggles with easy material		
10	Is better with reading comprehension than with phonetic decoding of words		
11	Is better at math reasoning than computation		
12	Has wonderful ideas, but has difficulty organizing tasks and activities		
13	Has facility with computers but illegible or slow handwriting		
14	Has a great (sometimes bizarre) sense of humor and may use it to distract the class		
15	Thrives on complexity but has difficulty with rote memorization		
16	Understands concepts easily and gets frustrated with the performance requirements		
17	Fatigues easily due to the energy required to compensate		

Comment:

Item	Visual Processing Weaknesses	Sometimes /Often	Not Observed
18	Struggles with reading		
19	Mixes up plus and minus signs		
20	Has difficulty lining up numbers in calculations		

		Sometimes/ Often	Not Observed
21	Has difficulty copying from the board		
22	Puts face close to the paper when writing or reading		
23	Skips lines and loses place in reading		
24	Uses poor spacing when writing		
25	Tires easily when reading or writing		
26	Makes "careless errors" in written work		

Comment:

Item	Auditory Processing Weaknesses	Sometimes/ Often	Not Observed
27	Does not seem to hear you; may need several repetitions before responding		
28	Mispronounces words or letter sounds		
29	Confuses similar sounding words (e.g., agent and ancient)		
30	Makes grammatical errors in speech		
31	Misunderstands information		
32	Watches other students to find out what to do		
33	Does not pay attention when being read to or during lectures		
34	Has a weak grasp of phonics, reflected in spelling and pronouncing unfamiliar words		
35	Has a loud voice, especially when there is background noise		
36	Responds better to directions when shown examples of what is expected		
37	Is exhausted after prolonged listening, particularly in the afternoon		

Comment:

Item	Sensory Processing Issues	Sometimes/ Often	Not Observed
38	Is clumsy and awkward		
39	Has an odd pencil grip		
40	Does not hold paper in place when writing		
41	Has illegible handwriting and tends to avoid writing		
42	Is poor at athletics		
43	Wears very similar soft clothes every day		
44	Gets upset when brushed against accidentally, as when standing in line		
45	Props self up in chair rather than sitting up straight		
46	Becomes easily overstimulated and may throw tantrums		
47	Has low energy and tires easily		
48	Is uncomfortable with crowds		
49	Has difficulty with transitions		
50	When younger, had difficulty deciding handedness		

Comment:

Item	Attention Deficit/Hyperactivity Disorder Symptoms	Sometimes/ Often	Not Observed
51	Has difficulty awaiting turn		
52	Acts impulsively without awareness of consequences		
53	Intrudes on others		
54	Is in motion as if "driven by a motor"		
55	Has difficulty remaining seated		
56	Fidgets with hands or feet or squirms in seat		
57	Is easily distracted		
58	Has highly variable performance on different days or during different time periods		
59	Spaces out during assignments and homework, often not completing tasks		
60	Is forgetful; may remember only part of an instruction		
61	Concentrates deeply when interested and not at all when not interested		
62	Responds to partial information, thinking understands fully		
63	Complains of boredom, unless work is novel, stimulating, or self-selected		

Comments:

Item	Dyslexia or Stealth Dyslexia	Sometimes/ Often	Not Observed
64	Reads at a lower level than expected for ability; reading may be average but reasoning is superior		
65	Struggles with phonological processing and the learning of sound-symbol relationships		
66	Shows reversals		
67	Has trouble with right and left		
68	Has difficulty learning to read analog clocks		
69	Sequential and rote memory lack permanence		
70	Spelling and math facts may be forgotten after practice		
71	Spells the same word in several different ways		
72	Written output is more difficult than verbal discussion		
73	Struggles to sequence ideas on paper		
74	Is anxious about reading aloud; may leave out words or substitute words with similar meanings or appearance		

Comments:

Item	Autism Spectrum Disorder (includes former "Asperger's Syndrome")	Sometimes/ Often	Not Observed
75	Struggles to read social cues: thoughts/feelings of others, nonverbal responses, body language, motivation of others, and others' response to own behavior		
76	Does not respond appropriately to others' feelings		
77	Shows rigidity: once a decision has been made, it is very difficult to change it		
78	Is inflexible about tasks; will only do them one way		
79	Resists and/or refuses tasks that are not liked, preferred, or self-selected		
80	Shows sensory issues: poor fine-/gross-motor coordination; difficulty with loud sounds, crowds, close proximity to others, touching/jostling, and transitions		
81	Experiences anxiety, particularly regarding social expectations and conventions		
82	Has flat affect		
83	Has difficulty with unfamiliar inferential language, idioms, etc., tending to be more literal, black-and-white		
84	Makes limited eye contact		
85	Unexpected changes often elicit strong emotional distress		
86	Rarely initiates social interaction, and has difficulty responding to overtures by others		

Comments:

Item	Anxiety and Depression	Sometimes/ Often	Not Observed
87	Is very perfectionistic; needs work done just so and obsesses over unimportant details		
88	Is excessively anxious about tests, presentations, projects, and grades, despite usually doing well and obtaining high grades		
89	Is paralyzed and unable to think clearly with items perceived to be too difficult or heavily timed, until able to relax		
90	Worries excessively about things great and small (e.g., school shootings, bullying, whether people like them, getting into trouble, getting things done, dogs, climate change/extinction)		
91	Can't let go of issues and fall asleep		
92	Fears going to school or tries to avoid going to school		
93	Has phobias, such as fear of separation, fear of the dark, fear of burglars breaking in		
94	Obsesses about things (germs, contamination, weight) and can't escape such thoughts		
95	Feels compelled to do things multiple times (e.g., wash hands) or to count or repeat actions		
96	Feels hopeless, worthless, or unhappy, frequently cries		
97	Lacks or has lost motivation		
98	Has very poor self-esteem		
99	Makes statements about wishing to be dead or to have never been born		
100	Makes threats of self-harm or has harmed self		
101	Has a negative or gloomy outlook on life: expresses a lot of negative things about self or others (e.g., calling self a loser, saying no one will ever like them, expressing they hate others or self, feels no one is ever nice to them)		

Comments:

Paired Student Data Observation

Instructions:

1. Choose another student in the classroom to observe in addition to the identified student. This student serves as a "control group" for the data collection period. This student can be chosen at random; often a child who is sitting near the student you are observing can make the Paired Student Data Observation process simpler than watching two students on opposite sides of the classroom. If you are observing a classroom where you don't know the students, you may ask the teacher for a recommendation of a student with typical behavioral and academic abilities to use as the paired student.

2. Identify specific target behaviors to monitor. Some common expected and unexpected behaviors are already included on the chart, such as on-task and off-task behavior. Additional behaviors to monitor can be added.

3. Use a stopwatch to determine the interval each child will be observed and document the child's behavior during that amount of time. For example, at each two-minute interval, a tally mark is made for both students.

4. Continue to document qualitative information about the target students between intervals.

5. Using the tally chart, quantify the behaviors that are observed.

Student:

Date:

Observation interval:

Observed by:

Start time:

End time:

Activity:

Behaviors				
Student	On task	Off task	Out of seat	Talking to others	Fidgeting
Student A:					
Student B: (typical student)					

Behaviors				
Student	Rocking in chair	Still but not paying attention	Other:	Other:	Other:
Student A:					
Student B: (typical student)					

Notes:

Accommodations Needs Screener

Student name:

Behavioral

☐ Struggles to complete work in a timely manner	☐ Talks to or distracts peers	☐ Needs reinforcement for self-regulation strategies
☐ Requires support when working in groups	☐ Engages in attention-seeking behaviors	☐ Engages in task-avoidance behaviors
☐ Does not complete classwork or homework	☐	☐

Environmental

☐ Is easily distracted by other students or stimuli	☐ Rocks/leans in chair	☐ Fidgets with hands
☐ Engages in sensory-seeking behaviors (such as bouncing, running hands along walls, chewing on pencils)	☐ Engages in sensory-avoidant behaviors (resists noisy environments, avoids messy art projects)	☐

Evaluative

☐ Becomes overwhelmed with length of tests	☐ Requires additional time to complete assessments	☐ Tests do not show accurate reflection of learning
☐ Becomes anxious about completing tests	☐ Refuses to complete assessments	☐ Rushes to complete tests
☐	☐	☐

Instructional

☐ Struggles to keep up during lessons	☐ Does not follow written directions on assignments	☐ Disengages in specific style of instruction:
☐ Unable to maintain accurate notes	☐ Misses verbal instructions for activities	☐ Turns in partially complete work
☐	☐	☐

Organizational

☐ Frequently loses items needed	☐ Does not effectively use planner	☐ Completes work but does not turn it in
☐ Desk/locker is unorganized	☐ Unable to estimate time needed for tasks	☐
☐	☐	☐

Designing Strength-Based Instruction for Twice-Exceptional Learners

When gifted students are identified as twice exceptional, the need to address their weaknesses does not negate the need for curricular accommodations and modifications in their areas of strength. Typical opportunities provided for gifted learners should also be made accessible to 2e students. Viewing learners from a holistic perspective is vital to meeting their overall needs. Work with children on a case-by-case basis to define their needs.

Meeting the Gifted Needs of the 2e Learner

Many interventions can help educators meet the cognitive needs of gifted learners. These interventions should not be withheld from gifted students just because they also have special needs. For an overview of enrichment, acceleration, and placement options for 2e students, see **figure 2-1**. For guidance on implementing these tools, check out Susan Winebrenner and Dina Brulles's book *Teaching Gifted Kids in Today's Classroom*.

Figure 2-1 Enrichment, Acceleration, and Placement Options for 2e Learners

Cluster Grouping	
Group several high-ability students together in a general education classroom instead of distributing them among all the classes so the gifted students have academic peers in the classroom and so one teacher can differentiate for them.	
Benefits for 2e Learners	**Possible Obstacles for 2e Learners**
• Cluster grouping allows for strength-based instruction with a group of gifted students in one classroom.	• Schools may have set up a cluster of gifted students in one room and a cluster of special education students in another. • A school may want a 2e student to stay in a CWC to reach required minutes for an IEP. • Some schools do not use cluster grouping.

Most Difficult First	
In subjects following a linear path, such as math or spelling, give students an early opportunity to show mastery of the most difficult items in a lesson.	
Benefits for 2e Learners	**Possible Obstacles for 2e Learners**
• Most Difficult First eliminates the need for students to practice skills they already know. 2e learners struggling with executive function or fine-motor skills may have difficulty completing repetitive work. • This intervention can be dovetailed with 504 modifications for shortened assignments.	• Teachers must coach students on what to do in the classroom once they've shown mastery of a concept. Some type of structured plan or enrichment activity should be provided.

Figure 2-1 continued

- This strategy can be used with all students, regardless of ability, achievement level, or special needs.

Pretesting for a Chapter or Unit
Offer students opportunities to pretest to see if they have already mastered specific content. While the rest of the class participates in the unit instruction, students who've tested out of it complete individualized work outlined in a learning contract with specific goals and outcomes.

Benefits for 2e Learners	Possible Obstacles for 2e Learners
• Opportunities to pretest allow students to avoid redundancy if they have already mastered specific content. • Because 2e learners have needs that can vary greatly between and within content areas, pretesting gives 2e students the chance to show what they know.	• Students must be able to self-regulate to meet the expectations of a learning contract, which can be a struggle for some 2e learners. • Teachers must be prepared to provide differentiation through an individualized learning contract.

Pull-Out Programs
Frequently used in elementary and middle schools, pull-out programs have identified gifted students participating in a resource-room setting for enrichment activities for a certain amount of time per week.

Benefits for 2e Learners	Possible Obstacles for 2e Learners
• Pull-out programs allow many 2e learners to experience school success and increased self-confidence through abstract problem-solving and higher-level thinking activities, which are an area of strength for many 2e learners. • Pull-out programs give 2e learners an opportunity for social and emotional support by spending time with like-minded peers.	• Educators or parents may be concerned with having a 2e learner miss instructional time in the general education classroom. • For a 2e learner with an IEP, minutes needed to meet the legal requirement for special education services may create a scheduling conflict with the times of the gifted pull-out class. • The certified gifted education teacher may have limited experience or training in meeting 2e students' special needs. • Some gifted pull-out programs may have programs that are highly verbal or fast-paced, which may mean a 2e learner requires accommodations to succeed.

Dual Credit and AP Courses
Dual credit courses are high school courses that students can take to earn credit for their high school transcript and college credit at the same time. Advanced Placement (AP) courses are college-level courses that students take during high school; an end-of-course exam can earn them college credit.

Benefits for 2e Learners	Possible Obstacles for 2e Learners
• 2e students are challenged appropriately at their cognitive level. Accommodations and modifications can be made as needed through these classes. • Attending dual credit and AP courses in the structured setting of high school can provide a good introduction to higher-level coursework before transitioning to college.	• Students may not have the prerequisite coursework necessary to enroll in advanced classes if this option was not considered when an IEP or 504 plan was established in earlier school years. • Schools may require a minimum grade point average (GPA) or other criteria to enroll, and 2e students' GPAs may be lowered by their areas of difficulty. • In dual credit and AP courses, some 2e students do not receive accommodations outlined in their 504 plan or IEP.

Subject Acceleration
Students with a single area of strength, such as in math or writing, can attend lessons in that subject with students a grade level above them.

Benefits for 2e Learners	Possible Obstacles for 2e Learners
• Providing appropriate academic challenge in 2e learners' areas of strength allows them to continue to progress while maintaining instruction with their same-age peers for other content areas.	• Logistical challenges arise when a child reaches the end of elementary school or middle school and can't attend subject-accelerated classes within the same school building.

Figure 2-1 continued

	• Scheduling conflicts may occur, often at the elementary level.
	• A 2e student may need accommodations for social and emotional skills that may not be as developed in them as they are in the older students in their accelerated classes.

Early Entrance to Kindergarten
A form of whole-grade acceleration, early entrance to kindergarten allows students to begin kindergarten prior to the official start date for their age.

Benefits for 2e Learners	Possible Obstacles for 2e Learners
• Early entrance to kindergarten is the least disruptive method of whole-grade acceleration because it doesn't require the child to leave established friendships. • The student does not skip any coursework, thus minimizing learning gaps.	• Some state laws require students to be five years old prior to enrolling in kindergarten. • Students may not yet be identified as 2e when entering kindergarten, which could cause struggles later. (It is important to note these struggles would most likely appear even if the child were not accelerated.)

Grade Skipping or Whole-Grade Acceleration
Whole-grade acceleration occurs when a student advances a full grade level prior to completing the grade. This can happen at the end of a school year (for example, finishing second grade and enrolling in fourth grade the next fall) or during the school year (moving from first grade to second grade after the first semester).

Benefits for 2e Learners	Possible Obstacles for 2e Learners
• Appropriate academic challenge for 2e learners can be provided by placing them a grade level above their same-age peers.	• Appropriate tools and supports to make the acceleration decision and shift may not be in place at a school. • Accelerating a 2e learner requires additional analysis and scaffolding to ensure success.

ACCELERATION FOR 2E KIDS?

It is a common myth that accelerating students to participate in classes with older peers is bad for students' social and emotional development. However, research shows this to be false. Two of the most comprehensive resources on acceleration are the report *A Nation Deceived: How Schools Hold Back America's Brightest Students* (Colangelo, Assouline, and Gross 2004) and its follow-up report, *A Nation Empowered: Evidence Trumps the Excuses Holding Back America's Brightest Students* (Assouline, Colangelo, and VanTassel-Baska 2015). These reports show the benefits of acceleration when it's implemented correctly.

The Iowa Acceleration Scale (IAS) is a tool that takes a comprehensive look at the whole child, from achievement scores to whether the child has a sibling in the class above. It is a useful guide for having conversations with teams considering appropriate acceleration for gifted and 2e students.

The Basics of Differentiation for 2e Students

When we look to differentiate curriculum for 2e learners, we should consider their full learning profile to tailor assignments, projects, or units to meet their needs. Differentiation typically refers to modifying instruction to push forward students' strengths. This is called upward differentiation. (See **figure 2-2.**) Take care not to confuse upward differentiation with modifications or accommodations to support students' struggles. (See chapter 1 for more information on modifications and accommodations.)

Teachers can differentiate any of the following three classroom elements:

- **Content:** Content differentiation is changing the *information* that the student learns.

- **Process:** Process differentiation is changing *how the student learns* the material.

- **Product:** Product differentiation is changing *how the student shows* what they've learned.

Figure 2-2 Examples of Upward Differentiation

Learning Objective	Differentiation Strategies
Science: The student will demonstrate understanding of the concepts of mitosis by sorting the steps into the correct order.	**Content:** If the student has already mastered the concepts of mitosis, they could move forward and learn about the process of meiosis and sort the steps into the correct order (depth). Alternatively, the student could research the history of the scientists who first understood and described the process of mitosis and how they learned about it (breadth).
	Process: A student who is already competent in understanding the sequence of steps in mitosis could instead create clues describing the steps using words to indicate the order in which they occur.
	Product: The student could create a board game in which players must answer questions related to cell division and biology to earn cards stating the steps of mitosis. The winner is the player who collects all the mitosis cards and is able to place them in the correct order.
Social studies: The student will use maps to identify regions of the world with specific geographic features.	**Content:** If the student can show understanding of the geographic features within this objective, the teacher could provide more advanced geographic features for the student to learn and locate or ask the student to research how the features form through geologic processes.
	Process: In assessing this knowledge, students with a higher level of understanding could use a map without a word bank; students who need more support could have access to a word bank.
	Product: A student who is already able to identify the geographic regions where specific features are found could create a fictional map, synthesizing information about the geographic features into a new product.
Language arts: After students read a story, the teacher will prompt them to examine metaphors as figurative language and infer the meaning of metaphors from surrounding text.	**Content:** Students with strong verbal abilities can read more advanced text, such as poetry, to infer the meaning of metaphors.
	Process: Instead of being provided the metaphors by the teacher, students could be asked to find the figurative language independently and infer the meanings.
	Product: Students could create contrasting images of the literal and figurative meanings of specific metaphors and explain why they feel each metaphor is appropriate for the meaning intended.

Strength-Based Instruction for 2e Learners

One of the best ways to support the needs of struggling 2e learners is to start by working with their strengths. It may seem counterintuitive to address a 2e learner's needs from a strength-based perspective. You may feel it is necessary to focus on the student's deficits first and postpone developing their strengths. It is easy to fall into the trap that catches many gifted students: the myth that gifted learners don't need special instruction for their strengths because "they'll be just fine on their own." Forgetting the strengths of dually diagnosed learners can lead to stagnation. Focusing on their strengths can improve their engagement and self-efficacy, ultimately leading to further development in the areas where they struggle.

> " The thing I have found more effective than anything else when I am working to differentiate for my 2e kids is involving them in the process! I provide them with some options and ask for their feedback; maybe they have other ideas or can at least give me feedback about what they think they can be successful doing.
>
> —Heather, middle school science teacher "

Many 2e learners see their classmates learn with ease. They don't understand why they have difficulty with things that seem simple for others. Strength-based instruction gives 2e students the confidence they need to overcome their challenges. When you guide 2e students to success, you can prevent learned helplessness. Proactive strength-based instruction stops negative thinking from becoming habitual.

Many 2e learners have both innate abilities and learned strategies that help them overcome their difficulties; however, these vary greatly from student to student. Understanding the interplay between a student's compensatory strategies and innate strengths is a good starting point for this type of instruction. Once you've identified a student's strengths, you can help the student leverage those skills to promote success. Asking students to explore ways to integrate their strengths into daily classroom instruction can help them build independence and personalized learning strategies to use in the future. The rest of this section describes six common strengths of 2e students and how to use them in strength-based instruction:

- openness to experience
- holistic or global thinking
- visual-spatial thinking skills
- logical thinking
- creative and divergent thinking
- comfort with technology

Openness to Experience

High-ability learners are generally very curious about new information, whether they seek broad information on a wide range of topics or they prefer to delve deeply into a single topic. Many gifted learners have above-average creativity. In this context, the term *creativity* means artistic and imaginative creativity as well as originality and problem-solving. Additionally, cognitively gifted students tend to learn at a rapid pace and need fewer repetitions to retain new concepts and information.

SIGNS OF OPENNESS TO EXPERIENCE

- active seeking of information and desire to comprehend new concepts
- ability to intuitively understand abstract concepts and patterns

- initiation and enjoyment of philosophical conversation

- quick understanding of new concepts

- active imagination and appreciation of fantasy

USING OPENNESS TO EXPERIENCE FOR STRENGTH-BASED INSTRUCTION

- Adjust pacing to the speed at which the student can grasp the concept. For 2e students who learn new skills easily but struggle with other aspects of the curriculum, practicing work they've already mastered can cause resistance and demotivation. To keep these students challenged, compact curriculum and find alternative ways to assess for content already mastered.

- Provide opportunities for self-directed learning. Gifted students have a passion for learning novel concepts. Give 2e students the chance to learn about a related topic and share their learning with the class. Provide a clear outline of expectations and time lines to help the student stay on track.

- Give 2e students a variety of options for showing what they've learned. These students thrive when they are learning, but their area of difficulty may hinder them from exhibiting the true level of their knowledge.

Holistic or Global Thinking

Twice-exceptional learners who are holistic or global thinkers are students who see the big picture easily but get bogged down in the details. Many of these students learn intuitively, drawing from prior knowledge and linking seemingly unconnected pieces of information. Sorting through global understandings and expressing them in detail can be overwhelming for 2e students. These students may get frustrated when they're asked to follow a list of instructions without explanation of why or how to do so.

When 2e learners struggle to understand the logic behind certain tasks or assignments, they may refuse to participate. Provide top-down instruction by starting with the big picture, to help 2e learners understand how the smaller pieces fit into it. You can also capitalize on 2e learners' cognitive strengths by giving them opportunities to create their own path to achieving the learning objective.

TARIQ'S STORY

Tariq was gifted and autistic. He had been looking forward to eighth grade because it was the first year Spanish was offered as a course, and Tariq was fascinated by world cultures. When he enrolled in the class and was asked to pair words with pictures and use vocabulary flash cards, he lost interest and began to struggle on quizzes and tests. He didn't see the connection between these basic activities and learning how to speak the language. His teacher integrated immersive opportunities for Tariq to read more complex Spanish and listen to Spanish speakers so Tariq could use his prior knowledge to begin dissecting the language and building skills. Through this holistic learning opportunity, Tariq capitalized on his intuitive ability to make real-world connections with the material. ■

SIGNS OF HOLISTIC OR GLOBAL THINKING

- is able to solve a complex math equation but unable to explain the steps used to find the solution

- embarks on a big project with enthusiasm and quickly loses interest because the logistics are overwhelming

- frequently uses figurative language, making unique or complex connections

- appears disorganized; struggles with organizational systems that use too many steps

- struggles to work in groups because other group members don't understand their vision

- needs to understand the purpose of completing an assignment or project before engaging in the task

- has difficulty with time management because it is hard to separate tasks from the whole

USING HOLISTIC OR GLOBAL THINKING FOR STRENGTH-BASED INSTRUCTION

- Teach holistic or global thinkers to work backward from their ideas. Validate their ideas, then give them structure (in the form of graphic organizers) to help them break down and see the steps needed to achieve their goals.

- When you introduce a new concept, provide an overview of the topic to be covered and each of its parts. For example, start a history unit with a time line of events and predict the effect of some of the first events on the time line. Or teach a math unit by starting with the end algorithm students are expected to learn and diagramming each of the steps they will be learning in the process. This way, global learners can understand the end goal of a unit or lesson before following the steps to achieve it.

- Find ways for students to make concrete-to-abstract or abstract-to-concrete connections from the content to other areas. When you teach students about a concept, look for concrete examples of it. For example, if you are teaching students about cause and effect in reading, ask them to brainstorm specific examples of cause and effect they've seen in their lives. If you are teaching about specific animal adaptations in biology class, ask students to identify other types of adaptation that take place outside the animal world.

- Encourage 2e students to be leaders by explaining what leaders do: they provide a vision and ideas, but also have to collaborate with and listen to others in order to reach the finish line.

- Provide a variety of tools to help students organize their thoughts. Graphic organizers, word maps, time lines, and outlines are very useful for helping holistic or global thinkers stay on track, but these students often won't gravitate toward these tools independently. Let students choose which tools they feel are the most useful for them. Offer frequent guidance on how to use the tools effectively.

■ Give latitude to students who tend to jump from topic to topic or complete steps out of order, especially on longer-term projects. This method of putting the pieces together to complete the larger task may not make sense to you, but to the global thinker, it is like putting together the pieces of a puzzle one section at a time and then bringing the sections together at the end.

REYNA'S STORY

Reyna had anxiety and obsessive-compulsive disorder. Her worries manifested in a lack of focus at school and deteriorating rapport with her teachers. Reyna's existential awareness was beyond her years. An eighth-grade student, her concern for people less fortunate than her was intense, and she struggled to make sense of life's randomness. To cope with her distress, she would often come up with elaborate plans for how she wanted to help people throughout the world. Once, she wanted to initiate a drive at school to collect money for food; another time, she developed the ambitious plan to create and sell greeting cards made by kids with disabilities to raise funds to support mental health. When she shared her thoughts and concerns with her parents and middle school teachers, the adults often responded with pragmatism and failed to validate her ideas. When a social studies teacher read an essay Reyna had written about her desire to help families in need, the teacher allowed Reyna to begin an independent project that fueled her passion and integrated the civics concepts they were currently learning. Reyna was able not only to create a project that was meaningful for her, but also to delve more deeply into the content of the course and alleviate many of the symptoms of her anxiety by pursuing her passion of helping those in need. ■

Visual-Spatial Thinking Skills

Many 2e students have strong visual-spatial skills compared to their verbal abilities. Our classrooms typically rely on language-based tools to convey information, whether it is reading in a book, listening to a speaker, or writing in narrative form. These are all linguistic methods. Visual-spatial teaching relies on visual literacy, which is the exchange of information through visual imagery.

What we aren't talking about in this section is "learning styles" (often referred to as visual, auditory, and kinesthetic learning styles). When educators talk about learning styles, they are labeling children as having specific learning strategies that always work best for them. The concept of learning styles is considered a neuromyth (Macdonald et al. 2017). All students learn better when material is presented in multiple formats. For our purposes, visual-spatial learners are students who have a significant discrepancy in their abilities. For example, in a full cognitive assessment, a student may have an extremely high visual-spatial reasoning score and weaker ability in verbal comprehension. There is a pervasive assumption that students with a specific learning disability in reading decoding have heightened visual-spatial skills; however, research does not support this assumption (Crogman, Gilger, and Hoeft 2018).

SIGNS OF VISUAL-SPATIAL THINKING SKILLS

- has difficulty putting thoughts into words, whether orally or in writing
- struggles to interpret language that is solely spoken, written, or gestured
- struggles with phonics-based reading skills
- prefers geometry to algebraic concepts
- solves math problems in their head; is resistant to writing down the steps used to arrive at a solution
- thinks mostly in pictures (as opposed to words)
- doodles and draws often

USING VISUAL-SPATIAL THINKING SKILLS FOR STRENGTH-BASED INSTRUCTION

- Allow students to show learning through visual means: diagrams, artwork, and models.
- Use multisensory methods of instruction, such as charts, graphs, and manipulatives.
- Integrate visual and performing arts opportunities, both active and passive.
- Teach students to integrate visual components into their work, such as doodling to improve memory retention and visual note-taking.
- Use mind maps and graphic organizers to help students organize their thoughts prior to engaging in writing activities. (See **figure 2-3**.)
- Find infographics to complement content (or create your own, or have your students create them for you).

TRUMAN'S STORY

Truman's struggles with written language were directly tied to his slow processing speed and lagging fine-motor skills associated with his ASD diagnosis. The fourth-grade curriculum had increased expectations for writing, and he was quickly falling behind in his classwork. He felt extreme frustration when he tried to write down his thoughts, and he struggled to speak when he became emotionally dysregulated. During these emotional times, well-meaning teachers who pressured him to communicate, either orally or in writing, often accelerated the dysregulation. This led to a fight-flight-freeze response from Truman.

Cognitive testing from Truman's special education evaluation identified visual-spatial reasoning as an area of significant strength. His teachers were able to help Truman both regulate his emotions and show his learning by using visual-spatial strategies to support him. Providing a visual schedule allowed Truman the chance to read and process information at his own speed, which was especially useful for days when his schedule varied from the norm. He created a system of index cards with words and pictures on them that he could use to communicate when he was experiencing dysregulation. When teachers began finding ways to present material visually, whether through videos, diagrams, or other means, Truman was able to keep pace with his classmates. ■

Figure 2-3 Mind Mapping

Susan Daniels's book *Visual Learning and Teaching* is an excellent guide to integrating visual-spatial learning into K–8 classrooms. Mind mapping is one way to use students' visual-spatial abilities to organize their thoughts and share information. This mind map shows the ideas and things that are important to a middle school student named Jessica.

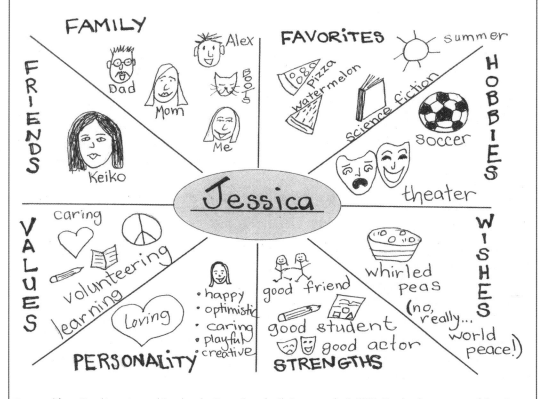

Logical Thinking

Many 2e learners have exemplary logical thinking skills. Finding direct connections and following them to the next step is natural and comforting for these learners. These are the students who often question the reason why a certain task needs to be done or why a math problem has to be solved a certain way—and their teachers had better be prepared with an answer! Strength in logical thinking can be related to analogical reasoning; these students understand the relationships between concepts and not only can infer the comparisons in analogies but also can create their own analogies and comparisons.

SIGNS OF LOGICAL THINKING

- makes unexpected connections between seemingly unrelated or abstract concepts
- recognizes and calls out illogical reasoning by peers or teachers
- easily categorizes and classifies concepts
- looks for direct evidence and details as supporting information

- enjoys playing with hypothetical situations ("If this happens, what would happen next?")

- finds humor in wordplay and double meanings

- can extrapolate patterns beyond what is expected or anticipated

USING LOGICAL THINKING FOR STRENGTH-BASED INSTRUCTION

- Provide structure and opportunities for concrete, logical steps in projects and assignments. Make sure the objectives of lessons and projects are clear, so students can see the way the skills build on one another.

- Work with students on metacognitive strategies and explicitly teach about how logic plays into higher-level thinking skills, such as analysis, evaluation, and synthesis.

- Teach logic (from a philosophical perspective) to help students reason. Engage in authentic discussions to process concepts such as motivation, duty, and responsibility.

JAYLYN'S STORY

I observed Jaylyn, a second grader, in her classroom to help develop a plan for teacher support. She was active and anxious, and she often called out in class. The day of the observation, the students were seated on the floor, and the teacher was leading them through an activity to learn about cause and effect.

The teacher said, "So, the third little pig built a house out of bricks. What was the effect of this?"

Beginning to speak while she raised her hand, Jaylyn answered, "The wolf couldn't blow it down! But, when you think about it, building the brick house was an effect, too, right? The cause for that was the third pig saw the other two pigs building unsafe houses—" The teacher interrupted Jaylyn and directed the conversation back to her planned lesson. Jaylyn stopped talking and withdrew into her mind, blissfully unaware the teacher had shut her down. I imagine her wheels were turning about all the various causes and effects in the simple story.

The teacher's reaction had been one of mild frustration. She hadn't noticed the complex logical thinking Jaylyn was exhibiting, working backward in the story and making inferences from information that wasn't explicitly stated. Instead of validating and elaborating on Jaylyn's comment, she ignored it and proceeded with the lesson for the rest of the class. ■

Creative and Divergent Thinking

Students whose strengths are in creative and divergent thinking often find themselves isolated in school. They may not qualify for gifted services because many cognitive assessments don't accurately capture the ability of divergent thinkers, or if they do qualify, they struggle to succeed in highly academic and analytical gifted programs that are a mismatch for their abilities.

Many 2e learners show creativity and divergent thinking skills. The connection between creativity and ADHD is well documented (Fugate 2018). These students not only are artistic and musical, but also thrive in the areas of fantasy and imagination. The gifted classroom may lend itself to meeting the needs of these learners, giving them opportunities to develop many of their own projects and plans, but modifying the general education curriculum can prove a bit trickier.

PROGRAMMING MISMATCH

To identify as many gifted learners as possible, a district I worked in had a tiered identification approach. Students who passed the initial screening were given an achievement test; if they passed the achievement test, they went on for an individual IQ test. If they did not pass the achievement test, they were given a nationally normed creativity inventory and could qualify to go on for the individual IQ test based on those results. Our team noticed a pattern: students who qualified solely on the creativity inventory struggled in our program. Their giftedness didn't always fit with the structure of the highly academic gifted program.

SIGNS OF CREATIVE AND DIVERGENT THINKING

- engages easily in new activities

- elaborates on basic ideas in unexpected ways

- shows great flexibility when brainstorming or formulating ideas and plans for projects

- creates original and unique products or ideas

- excels in visual or performing arts and/or creative writing

USING CREATIVE AND DIVERGENT THINKING FOR STRENGTH-BASED INSTRUCTION

- Encourage a climate that invites questioning and exploration of concepts through open-ended prompts, questions with many "right" answers, and self-directed projects.

- Validate thought processes by allowing students to explore concepts formulated from their divergent thinking; ask them to research and report back to the class if they are looking for answers you don't know.

- Give a variety of options for exhibiting learning: puppet shows, movie trailers, narrative fiction, sculptures, and so on. Let students propose their own ways to show their learning.

- Use inquiry-based instruction models to allow students to explore concepts independently. Use essential questions to keep them on track but allow students some independence in the process.

LOGAN'S STORY

Most teachers saw Logan's behavior as problematic, even when she was in elementary school. As a sixth-grade student with a diagnosis of ADHD, she still struggled with behavioral inhibition. She often drew the class's attention away from the topic at hand. Her questioning could be brought back on topic, but her divergent thinking was frustrating for teachers, who felt she was being disrespectful or defiant. Teachers often shut her down and shamed her for her questions. As a result, Logan often refused to complete her schoolwork in those classes.

As Logan's grades dropped, her parents had her start working with a math tutor. In the one-on-one setting, her tutor was able to dive into Logan's divergent thinking to lead her back to understanding the concepts and skills necessary for the lesson at hand. Her performance in the class improved when she had the opportunity to question and understand the bigger connections about algebraic concepts like radicals and transcendental numbers. ■

Comfort with Technology

Many 2e students—indeed, many kids in general—are extremely experienced with and comfortable using technology, whether they use it to connect socially with friends or have taught themselves how to hack the parental controls on their smartphones, tablets, computers, or televisions. Capitalizing on their technological know-how is a great way to remove barriers and help them engage. Twice-exceptional students who struggle to maintain attention or use fine-motor skills for lots of writing will also thank you.

SIGNS OF COMFORT WITH TECHNOLOGY
- produces work through technology that's greatly superior to their "analog" work, showing greater depth and complexity
- is excited about opportunities to use technology, even when the same task done without technology would not be exciting
- has wide experience with and understanding of technological usage and principles, such as computer coding languages
- frequently gets in trouble for using technology at inappropriate times during class

USING COMFORT WITH TECHNOLOGY FOR STRENGTH-BASED INSTRUCTION
- Use technology to provide accommodations whenever possible, such as audio recording, text-to-speech software, typing, or taking photos of notes.
- Set clear boundaries about permissible technology activities before use.
- Use technology as a tool to help students who struggle socially with group work or collaboration. Students may feel more comfortable communicating through technology or collaborating on a shared document instead of negotiating the work face-to-face.
- Give students with technological strengths the role of tech support in cooperative learning groups.

JOSEF'S STORY

Josef was an eighth grader with clinical depression and anxiety. In my gifted education class, he rarely completed or turned in his work and appeared to struggle greatly with maintaining motivation on any longer-term projects. For a research project, students could choose the type of product they preferred to create to present to the class. When Josef chose to do a digital slide presentation, I worried that he just wanted to play on the computer during time that should be used for research—or that he was choosing it because it would be easy for him.

When it was time to exhibit student projects, Josef requested that we turn off the lights for his presentation. We watched his presentation, which was complete with auto-timing, narration, music, and effective animations to show connections between concepts. This may not sound amazing *now*, but this was in the early 2000s, when the technology was fairly new, and Josef used skills he had not been taught at school. He had taught himself, through trial and error, how to maximize the capabilities of the slide software. It was the proudest I'd seen him the entire year. ■

Addressing Areas of Difficulty

Strength-based instruction is an excellent place to begin planning for meeting 2e learners' needs. However, I also recognize that teachers can't simply ignore students' areas of struggle. Throughout this book, we'll discuss ways to support struggles specific to each diagnosis a student may have.

Strength-based instruction for 2e students isn't just growing students' strengths. It's also integrating these strengths with appropriate remediation for students' weaknesses. (See **figure 2-4**.) Take the time to develop a plan collaboratively with stakeholders across all disciplines to guarantee you meet the varied needs of the 2e learner. Multidisciplinary teams should include general education teachers, special education teachers, counselors, administrators, and parents or guardians. Additionally, the team should invite the gifted education specialist to participate and advocate for the child's cognitive needs. I'm surprised and disappointed every time I attend a meeting to discuss the needs of a 2e student and a representative from the gifted education department hasn't been invited.

Figure 2-4 Remedial and Supportive Service Options for 2e Learners

Cotaught Class or Class Within a Class (CWC)
Cotaught classes allow students with similar needs to be clustered within a single class. In addition to placement within one class, the class also has a special education coteacher. The coteacher is responsible for supporting the needs of the identified students, providing small-group or individualized instruction, and modifying assignments or tests as needed for each learner. Cotaught classes are created by the special education department or school administrators when a small group of students need access to similar services without needing remedial instruction in a separate classroom.

Benefits for 2e Learners	Possible Obstacles for 2e Learners
• 2e learners can be placed in appropriately challenging classes with a designated teacher to support their needs. Students don't have to be removed from the classroom to receive the support.	• A special education teacher designated to support the 2e student's needs may not be trained to modify instruction for 2e learners. • Cotaught classes or CWCs may not be offered for higher-level courses, such as honors or AP courses.

Figure 2-4 continued

Resource Room	
Students attend their classes with the rest of their peers and go to a designated special education classroom for support at assigned times or on an as-needed basis.	
Benefits for 2e Learners	**Possible Obstacles for 2e Learners**
• Students can attend their classes with similar-ability peers and use the resource room for support when needed. If certain assignments don't require additional support, they can remain in their class.	• Teachers in the resource room may not have as much experience with upper-level curriculum or access to resources necessary to support the curriculum at the correct level. • Students may refuse to go to the resource room if they are concerned about peers judging them for needing additional support.

Self-Contained Classes	
Self-contained classes are generally focused on a single skill area (such as reading, math, or social skills). The minutes students spend in these classes can vary widely, depending on need. Students may attend as a replacement for the time spent in their general education classroom for that subject. Study skills, social and emotional needs, and remediation may take the place of an elective class at the middle or high school level.	
Benefits for 2e Learners	**Possible Obstacles for 2e Learners**
• Additional minutes with a focus on direct instruction can support the lagging skills of 2e learners and help them catch up.	• At the middle and high school levels, students often have to give up an elective to attend a self-contained class. For 2e students, electives may be the areas where they excel, such as band or art. • Because of 2e learners' cognitive strengths, placement in a self-contained class may mean working at a too-slow pace; they may need additional modifications to account for their abilities.

Response to Intervention (RTI)	
Schools using RTI assess all students with universal screenings and provide supports as needed, regardless of the presence or absence of a medical or educational diagnosis. Students receive targeted interventions to improve lagging skills, and progress is monitored continuously to ensure growth.	
Benefits for 2e Learners	**Possible Obstacles for 2e Learners**
• Groupings for interventions are generally fluid, meaning 2e learners can move in and out of them based on their needs. • Interventions are often in the same classroom or held grade-wide at the same time, so many students are moving from class to class, removing the stigma of receiving interventions.	• Twice-exceptional students who are progressing slowly may be masking their struggles and may not get identified for services. • The RTI model may prolong the identification process for students who need more direct support and intervention. • Schools that provide enrichment for gifted students as an intervention during RTI time may prevent 2e students from receiving enrichment by placing them in remedial intervention groups instead.

Consultative Services	
Consultative services involve a related service provider, such as an occupational therapist, school psychologist, or speech-language pathologist, who provides training and consultation to teachers to meet students' needs or who meets with the student occasionally to work toward a measurable IEP goal.	
Benefits for 2e Learners	**Possible Obstacles for 2e Learners**
• A school with a professional who can provide training and tools for teachers to meet the needs of 2e learners could use this model effectively without needing to provide specialized instruction outside the classroom. • Although the number of minutes a student receives direct services is defined, there can be flexibility in when and how those minutes are met.	• Some schools may not have personnel trained to provide consultative services that meet a 2e student's needs.

Figure 2-4 continued

Section 504 Plans Based on medical instead of educational diagnoses, students receive accommodations and modifications to support their educational needs.	
Benefits for 2e Learners	**Possible Obstacles for 2e Learners**
• A Section 504 plan typically does not remove a student from regular classes because it has no required minutes of instruction.	• Teachers in advanced classes may be unaware of a student's accommodations or modifications, especially if they are used on an as-needed basis. Students and their families may need to advocate strongly for the plan to be followed. • Some schools or teachers are hesitant to allow 2e students to participate in honors, AP, or gifted courses with accommodations, believing the appropriate placement for them is in a lower-level class. (This discrimination based on disability is illegal.)

Strength-Based Lesson Planning

Differentiating lessons for any student takes time. When you are planning a strength-based approach for a 2e learner, reflect on how you can integrate the student's strengths while accommodating their struggles.

The Strength-Based Lesson Planning Template walks you through this reflection and helps you consider the varied needs of 2e learners. (See **figure 2-5** for two sample completed templates. See page 52 for a blank reproducible version of the template.) You can use the Strength-Based Lesson Planning Template by following these steps:

1. Identify the lesson objective and/or essential question. What should students know when they have completed this lesson, unit, or project?

2. In what format will the lesson be taught to the entire class?

3. What strengths do you notice in the 2e learner? (Don't limit yourself to the following examples if the student has other unique strengths that can be useful.)

   ■ openness to experience

   ■ holistic or global thinking

   ■ visual-spatial thinking skills

   ■ logical thinking

   ■ creative and divergent thinking

   ■ comfort with technology

4. In what areas does the student struggle? Does the student have a specific educational or medical diagnosis that should be considered?

5. How can you challenge the student with upward differentiation?

6. What strategies can support the student's struggles? (Refer to chapter 1 for information on the types of accommodations and modifications available.)

Figure 2-5 Sample Strength-Based Lesson Planning Templates

Student Name Molly P.	
Lesson Objective/Essential Question	• The learner will use the writing traits of voice and word choice to create a fictional diary entry for a character from a student-chosen novel. • "How can I write from the point of view of a fictional character?"
Format of Lesson	Writing workshop with independent writing and one-on-one student-teacher conferences
Student Strengths	Integrating Strengths for Upward Differentiation
• Artistic ability • Creative, divergent thinker • Above-average reading and comprehension • Comfortable with technology • High verbal ability	[X] Content ☐ Process [X] Product • Help Molly find developmentally appropriate books that are both challenging and in her areas of interest. • Brainstorm with Molly different ways to complete objective with greater depth/complexity—create a blog for character? Write/illustrate graphic novel page?
Student Struggles	Accommodations and Modifications to Support Difficulties
• Difficulty writing more than a few sentences by hand • Trouble staying on task	[X] Behavioral ☐ Environmental [X] Evaluative ☐ Instructional ☐ Organizational • Set up frequent check-ins with Molly to help her stay on track with work completion. • Ask Molly to elaborate on her written work orally to determine mastery of voice and word choice.

Student Name Trevor P.	
Lesson Objective/Essential Question	• The learner will implement economic principles of supply and demand when creating a budget for a fictional company. • "What financial information do I need to create a budget for a company?"
Format of Lesson	Continuing lesson of economic simulation unit; independent work
Student Strengths	Integrating Strengths for Upward Differentiation
• Strong visual-spatial thinker • Good at spotting patterns and connections; big-picture thinker	☐ Content [X] Process ☐ Product Modify process to challenge Trevor to include data in graphs and charts to support his reasoning.
Student Struggles	Accommodations and Modifications to Support Difficulties
• Diagnosis of specific learning disability in math fluency and concepts • Hesitant to take risks; does not believe he can accomplish tasks independently	☐ Behavioral ☐ Environmental [X] Evaluative [X] Instructional ☐ Organizational • Provide calculator for calculations. • Do not count off for mathematical mistakes if application of economic principles is correct.

Key Points

- Teachers can support the strengths of 2e students through a wide range of placement options; being 2e should not prevent them from participating in programs for high-ability learners.

- Teachers can use upward differentiation to challenge 2e students' strengths. Content, process, and product are all areas in which material can be brought to a higher level.

- Many 2e students have learning and personality characteristics that serve as strengths in the academic setting. Some common ones are openness to experience; holistic or global thinking; strong visual-spatial, logical, and creative or divergent thinking skills; and comfort with technology.

- When possible, 2e students' areas of struggle should be addressed within the context of the students' areas of strength. A variety of models for remedial or support services for 2e learners can be used to support their struggles.

Strength-Based Lesson Planning Template

Student Name	
Lesson Objective/Essential Question	
Format of Lesson	

Student Strengths	Integrating Strengths for Upward Differentiation
	☐ Content ☐ Process ☐ Product

Student Struggles	Accommodations and Modifications to Support Difficulties
	☐ Behavioral ☐ Environmental ☐ Evaluative ☐ Instructional ☐ Organizational

Social and Emotional Needs of Twice-Exceptional Learners

The social and emotional needs of gifted children differ from those of other students. Add in one or more additional exceptionalities, and those needs become complicated. In the following story, Timothy experienced social and emotional struggles common among twice-exceptional learners: His self-confidence was low because his grades didn't reflect his ability, his friendships suffered because he started acting out in class to deflect from his difficulties, and he felt simultaneously bored with his schoolwork and anxious about his performance. He floundered for years as his needs went unrecognized.

TIMOTHY'S STORY

Timothy wasn't identified as an exceptional learner until fifth grade. His grades were poor, his parents suspected an attention-related diagnosis, and his teachers were worried about his reading skills. The school decided to move forward with an assessment for a specific learning disability. When the report came back, it said Timothy had dyslexia *and* was cognitively gifted. His parents were shocked and his teachers confused. Timothy wasn't surprised at all.

"I felt misunderstood," he explained during a counseling session when he was in sixth grade. "My teachers were impatient because I understood all the concepts before we even started the unit but bombed the tests. I was always getting in trouble for doodling or being off-task too. The other kids made fun of me and never wanted to be in a group with me because I worked so slowly. My parents thought I wasn't trying. Eventually, I did kind of stop trying."

Timothy experienced the dichotomy of twice-exceptionality before he even knew he was 2e. He saw other students succeeding and was frustrated that he wasn't doing as well, even though he knew he grasped the concepts quicker than they did. ■

The Self-Concept of 2e Learners

Self-concept is how you define yourself—the image or idea you have about the kind of person you are. Your self-concept is based on your beliefs and how you interpret the reactions you get from others. Self-concept can be a general view or a view within a certain domain, such as academic, social, or emotional self-concept. Children's self-concept is directly related to the support they do or don't receive from the individuals and environment around them.

Research shows that gifted students have a better general self-concept and a higher academic self-concept than their nongifted peers have. Twice-exceptional learners, on the other hand, have a self-concept lower than that of students who are identified as only gifted or as only having a learning difficulty (Rinn 2018).

The biggest factor causing low self-concept in 2e learners is the mismatch between the student and the school environment. Twice-exceptional kids are often stuck without the skills they need, in classrooms with teachers who don't speak their language. Imagine being transplanted to a country where you don't speak the language and you have no idea how to navigate your surroundings—and you have no Google Translate! You might try to ask for help, but how do you even begin to do so? People might try to speak to you, but they give up after realizing you don't understand them. How long would it take for you to feel frustrated? How long would it take for you to feel isolated? You have the *ability* (potential) to do what is needed to survive, but you don't have the skills (practical tools). Without the support of the people and environment around you to build the needed skills, you would be left to struggle.

Academic Self-Concept

The first step in supporting a 2e student's social and emotional self-concept is to meet their academic needs. The primary focus of schools for learners is to meet their academic needs; however, this is exactly the area where 2e students begin to fall through the cracks of our educational system. Twice-exceptional learners often don't show signs of struggle the same way other students do and don't receive the interventions that would be most helpful for them.

Their academic self-concept can suffer for a variety of reasons. Perhaps their grades don't reflect their understanding of the material. Twice-exceptional students may be capable of more difficult work than they are given. If adults perceive their struggles as a lack of effort, this misunderstanding can damage a student's academic self-concept. Finally, 2e learners who aren't considered or don't qualify for gifted services struggle because their advanced cognitive skills aren't being engaged.

In order to meet the academic needs of 2e learners, we need to first identify them as early as possible. Universal screening for gifted programs is a good start, but the next steps schools should take is to compare those universal screening scores to achievement scores. Are the scores similar or discrepant? A bright student whose achievement is much lower than their ability is showing warning signs of being a 2e learner.

Once a student is identified as 2e, schools can take a strength-based approach to presenting the curriculum to them. (See chapter 2 for guidance on creating strength-based lesson plans.) A student's academic self-concept is built on a foundation of feeling successful, so digging into a student's weaknesses over and over, day after day, will wear down their resilience and academic self-concept.

Finally, ensuring that 2e students are eligible for and able to participate in appropriate gifted education classrooms helps support their academic self-concept. Even if they struggle in the general education classroom, success in a setting that fosters their abstract reasoning and creative thinking skills is a huge confidence-booster.

Social Self-Concept

Twice-exceptional students may struggle with social relationships—not only at school, but also at home. Some gifted individuals struggle with peer relationships in general.

This is usually not because of lagging social skills, but more often because they have few shared interests with their same-age peers. Many gifted students' social lives begin to thrive in high school, where they can take advanced courses with like-minded peers and get involved in clubs related to their areas of passion. In high school, gifted students are no longer required to stay in a classroom with students grouped together simply because they are the same age. Twice-exceptional students often have a different experience. They struggle to fit in with same-age students in their regular classroom, but they may not truly fit in with students in their gifted or advanced classes either.

The parent-child dynamic in a family also greatly influences a child's social self-concept. Twice-exceptional children and teens who struggle with executive functioning, emotional regulation, or academic performance may have parents or guardians who can't understand why their bright children aren't doing better. Well-intentioned parents may take an authoritarian stance to attempt control behavior concerns. They may also frequently remind children about their poor academics. These actions can undermine positive relationships, damaging children's social self-concept.

You can help 2e students develop strong social relationships through group opportunities based on the students' interests. Robotics clubs, Pokémon leagues, chess clubs, or interest-based book clubs can give 2e students a chance to develop friendships outside the academic setting (which they might find intimidating or stressful). Groups such as these can be open to students from a range of grade levels, allowing for varied levels of ability and maturity.

Explicit social skills instruction can also be helpful for 2e students who struggle with these skills. It is easy for adults to get frustrated with a student who acts impulsively, seems fearful of nonthreatening social interactions, or struggles to collaborate with peers. It is tempting to think problematic social behaviors are intentional or manipulative due to the asynchrony of 2e students' cognitive abilities and social skills. Students reprimanded for lagging social skills are more likely to have a poor social self-concept. When we approach these situations with the belief that students do well when they can, we can help them build social skills without shaming them. Explicit instruction can take the form of modeling or redirection in the moment ("I can see you and your friend feel the other isn't listening. One way to show you are listening is to restate the other person's comments in your own words. You can restate what you heard by starting your sentence with 'So, what I hear you saying is . . .'") or more directive, guided lessons in small groups facilitated by a counselor or teacher.

Emotional Self-Concept

Often the academic and social perceptions of 2e learners feed their emotional self-concept. Struggling academically and being placed in inappropriate academic settings can harm a child's emotional self-concept. If a 2e student is experiencing negative events daily, this chronic stress can lead to loneliness, helplessness, frustration, or worry.

Because twice-exceptionality is typically identified at older ages than giftedness alone or disability alone, many emotional reactions of 2e learners may become habitual. Missing the opportunity for early intervention may mean that 2e learners miss out on learning healthy emotional reactions to frustration. Having structure and support to overcome obstacles is a major factor in children's development of perseverance and resilience. We can't help kids overcome obstacles we don't know exist.

Students who constantly experience emotional dysregulation often suffer long-term impacts. These students may develop learned helplessness and avoidance behaviors and may experience burnout. These emotions are symptoms of students in chronic survival mode. They are hard to unlearn.

Providing opportunities for 2e students to feel successful is a major component of helping them build a strong emotional self-concept. This can happen through strength-based curricular opportunities or facilitated social opportunities with like-minded peers. Increasing the frequency of situations where they can succeed will enhance their emotional self-concept.

One of the basic tenets of the therapeutic counseling relationship is understanding that people, even children, are experts in their own lives. This means the emotions they experience and share are valid, even if we don't understand or relate to them. Adults can bring this mindset into interactions with young people. Creating a place where it is okay to share emotions about a situation is important. Rather than trying to convince a student their emotions are wrong, we can validate and normalize their experiences and emotions.

Twice-exceptional students who struggle with emotional regulation also benefit from the normalization of their experiences. Although an emotional reaction may be out of proportion to a triggering event, we can connect with our students and validate their initial emotions about the experience while helping them develop skills to regulate those emotions. (See **figure 3-1**.) Sharing thoughts is often easier than sharing emotions for 2e learners, because many of them struggle with emotional awareness. If they can't label their feelings, start with their thoughts.

Figure 3-1 Validating Student Emotions

Instead of Saying This	Try Saying This
You're overreacting.	I can tell you feel angry/upset/sad. Can you tell me what you're thinking?
Why aren't you working? Stay focused.	I'm guessing you stopped working because you feel frustrated. Am I close?
I can't help you unless you tell me what is wrong.	I'm ready to listen when you're ready to tell me what happened. Signal me when you're ready.
You look like you need to calm down.	Your body language is showing me that you are uncomfortable. What's up? Is there something I can do to help?
There's no reason to be worried about this little thing. Just be brave!	I can see you are so nervous about this. Let's brainstorm solutions that can help you feel safe.
Cheer up! Think about all the good things that are happening.	I understand feeling disappointed, and it is okay to feel that way. What could help you feel better?

Disclosing Diagnosis to Students

The decision to disclose a 2e diagnosis to a student is usually made by a parent or guardian. However, families often consult teachers in making this decision. And because teachers work with students daily, teachers need to be able to talk frankly with students about their diagnoses.

Some parents aren't hesitant to tell their children about gifted identification. Many gifted students already know they learn differently from their peers. Helping them understand why supports their social and emotional needs. Discussion about their learning characteristics and why they participate in advanced classes or a gifted program helps students become better self-advocates.

Telling students they've been diagnosed with a learning disability, mental health concern, or neurodevelopmental disorder can be more difficult. Some parents don't want their children to feel or be seen as different. They may worry that knowledge of the diagnosis will become an excuse for poor behavior or effort. Sometimes, parents are skeptical of a diagnosis. But just as cognitively gifted learners know they're different, 2e learners are already quite aware that they learn differently from their peers. Confirming what they already suspect is validating.

Knowledge is power. Helping 2e learners understand their learning characteristics will help them develop self-acceptance and self-compassion. Clear and concise discussions about their strengths and weaknesses are empowering. They bring students into the process of determining what works for them in the educational setting and what doesn't.

If you know a student's parents have already disclosed their twice-exceptionality to them, it may be appropriate to initiate a one-on-one conversation with them to help them build awareness of their neurodivergence. When you talk to a student about their twice-exceptionality, let the student lead the conversation. This can help them feel some control over the situation. Any discussion of struggles can naturally bring up feelings of discomfort. Allow a student to stop a conversation and resume it later, if needed, to help them process the information at their own pace. (If an official diagnosis hasn't been made or a student's parents have yet to tell the student about the diagnosis, this conversation could simply focus on a student's strengths and struggles without labeling a diagnosis.)

Twice-exceptionality comes with both strengths and struggles. Emphasizing how twice-exceptionality is a student's unique learning profile can help the student understand that their characteristics are simply different from others', not inferior to them. Remind students that even their weaknesses have a bright side. For example, people with ADHD are often divergent thinkers, autistic individuals draw on the strength of logical thinking and problem-solving, and people with dyslexia often have excellent creative and artistic abilities.

Here are some questions you might ask to begin a conversation with a student about their twice-exceptionality:

- What do you know about (student's diagnosis)?
- Which strengths and struggles of this diagnosis do you see in yourself?
- How do you think these strengths and struggles influence your schoolwork?
- How do you think your strengths and struggles affect your relationships with friends, family, classmates, and teachers?
- How do you think your diagnosis and giftedness influence each other?
- What are the best ways for me to help you?
- What questions do you have about being 2e?

Ultimately, talking to 2e students about their learning characteristics is something a trusted adult will need to do, gently and matter-of-factly. Gifted kids are intuitive, and they are going to want to know why they need more or different help than their peers need. The long-term negative impact of not telling children about their diagnosis is greater than the short-term discomfort of an awkward conversation and a shift in daily interactions to support the learner's needs. Twice-exceptional learners need to know themselves so they can make informed decisions about their futures.

Helping Parents Talk to 2e Kids About Diagnosis

Helping parents and guardians understand their child's diagnosis is key to supporting the child as a team. Parents need information about their child's diagnosis, strategies to support their child at home, and a sense of hope that things will be okay. Parents' reactions to finding out their child is either gifted or has another exceptionality can vary. They may feel relieved their child will now get help. They may feel fearful that somehow their child is going to struggle through their whole life. Taking a neurodiversity-affirming approach to supporting parents of 2e kids is key to helping them understand their child's needs. A neurodiversity-affirming approach includes recognizing and accepting a person's neurodivergence without trying to change them to conform to societal expectations; neurodivergent people deserve accommodations and don't need to be cured or fixed.

If a parent is uncertain about whether they should disclose a diagnosis to their child, educators can assure parents that giving the child a name for the thing that they already know is there can be liberating. It turns "I'm dumb" or "I always mess everything up" to "I learn differently from other kids" and "I can cope with my diagnosis." Another fear parents face is that their child will use the diagnosis as an excuse when they do poorly. Some students may try to deflect their struggles with a quick "Not my fault, I have (fill in the blank)." But given the tools and strategies to succeed, students stop externalizing the behavior and take ownership of self-advocacy and implementing the strategies they need to succeed.

Cultural Awareness with Families of 2e Learners

Being culturally responsive when discussing the needs of 2e students with families from CLD backgrounds is important. Whether a language barrier makes it difficult to communicate with a family effectively or a family's cultural heritage conceptualizes mental health issues differently than the majority culture in the United States, it is important to be aware of these possible differences at the starting point. Here are some considerations for talking with families about a mental health or neurodevelopmental diagnosis:

- European Americans tend to view most mental health diagnoses from a perspective aligned with that of the medical community. Members of Latinx and African American communities may interpret concerns related to mental health symptoms as outcomes of spiritual or moral character.

- Families may view mental health issues as socially damaging or matters to be dealt with privately within the family. They may not want to expose concerns to educational or medical professionals.

- Access to medical care or psychological evaluations may be limited for families who are economically disadvantaged. Specialists who can provide the type of evaluation many 2e students need to receive an accurate diagnosis are available to middle-to-upper-income families but are often unavailable to families who cannot pay for these services.

- Language barriers can impede healthcare and diagnosis. A parent of a CLD or ELL student may have difficulty explaining their concerns to a doctor without the help of a bilingual medical professional or interpreter.

- Being a member of a marginalized group can have lasting impact on a parent's trust in the educational system. Parents from CLD backgrounds may be cautious about negative feedback from schools, concerned that implicit bias is influencing the educators' views. Building rapport and gathering subjective information from the parents can help minimize this barrier.

KARISSA'S STORY

The process of 2e identification was a long one for Karissa. Her parents struggled to accept that the characteristics they were seeing in their daughter were more than just typical developmental concerns. The picky eating and clothing sensitivity, the difficulty making and keeping friends, and the epic meltdowns had finally led to an autism diagnosis.

After learning the diagnosis, Karissa's parents couldn't decide whether to share it with her. Karissa was an academically successful fifth grader. Her parents thought that if she didn't know about her diagnosis, maybe she would learn coping skills to overcome her weaknesses. Maybe they could tell her about the diagnosis when she was older, if it became necessary.

As time went on, Karissa began to show an extremely negative emotional and social self-concept. Her parents saw negative self-talk increase, and Karissa began to resist going to school. Through conversations with parents of other autistic 2e kids, Karissa's parents realized that they needed to tell Karissa about her diagnosis.

Over the course of several counseling sessions, I talked with Karissa and her parents about the implications of being gifted and autistic. Karissa asked questions and listened carefully to information about the diagnosis. She agreed that many of the characteristics sounded like her.

Over time, Karissa began to understand her struggles. Viewing her difficulties through the lens of being 2e normalized them. She saw that while she was unlike many kids, her experiences were common among kids like her. She began to self-advocate at school and home. She found that using coping skills was easier when she understood that she needed them because of the way her brain worked, not because she was bad or dumb.

"I always thought there was something wrong with me," Karissa said in session. "Now I just know that this is the way that I'm wired, and I need different tools than other kids." Talking to Karissa about her diagnosis empowered her, and she embraced her role in the neurodiverse world. ■

Perfectionism

Perfectionism doesn't always look like the stereotypical overachiever who studies for multiple hours a night and obsesses over getting 100 percent on every assignment.

BOOKS FOR DEALING WITH PERFECTIONISM

For parents, guardians, and educators:
- *Letting Go of Perfect: Overcoming Perfectionism in Kids* by Jill L. Adelson and Hope E. Wilson
- *Perfectionism: A Practical Guide to Managing "Never Good Enough"* by Lisa Van Gemert

For students:
- *What to Do When Good Enough Isn't Good Enough: The Real Deal on Perfectionism* by Thomas S. Greenspon
- *What to Do When Mistakes Make You Quake: A Kid's Guide to Accepting Imperfection* by Claire A. B. Freeland and Jacqueline B. Toner

Sometimes perfectionism is a frustrated student tearing up or crumpling a paper before yelling at a teacher that an assignment is stupid. Sometimes it is a student who finishes their work but never turns it in and has a poor report card because the grade book is filled with zeros.

For 2e students, perfectionism can be especially insidious. Living up to the expectations of giftedness is harder when a student has a disability. Twice-exceptional kids facing perfectionism might understand a concept but be unable to explain their thoughts in writing, leading to frustration and embarrassment. If 2e learners cannot regulate their emotions when their work doesn't measure up to their own expectations, they may experience a fight, flight, or freeze reaction instead of verbalizing their emotions and asking for help.

Perfectionism can be a risk factor for concerns in the future. It can predict a variety of future problems, including anxiety, depression, eating disorders, and even suicide (Ruggeri 2018). Proactively recognizing and helping students with perfectionistic tendencies is important for their long-term well-being.

Where to Look for Perfectionism

When I talk to parents about the possibility that their children's behaviors are associated with perfectionism, I get a lot of confused stares. "You mean my kid, with the trash-heap backpack and a mountain of dirty clothes on the bedroom floor, is a perfectionist?" Yep—could be. Perfectionism is rarely shown in all domains. Its appearance depends on the individual's personality and abilities. Following are a few situations in which perfectionism often shows up:

- **An area of relative strength:** A student who is an excellent musician may become a perfectionist about practicing and maintaining first chair in the band. The student may practice obsessively after school and get frustrated when a piece of music takes a long time to learn. However, this student may not think twice about turning in an essay rife with spelling errors and grammatical mistakes, because they believe they are hopelessly bad at writing.

- **A highly competitive environment:** Competition—explicit or implicit—can really fan the flames of perfectionism. Many students view any type of assignment that is graded as a competitive event, even if the scores are kept private. (And let's be honest: kids are terrible at keeping their grades to themselves.)

- **A focus on outcome instead of process:** When students only see success or failure in an endeavor, they are more likely to feel perfection is necessary. Students who recognize the importance of learning through the process of the activity instead of the resulting final product are less likely to experience perfectionism.

- **An assignment without a right or wrong answer:** Many perfectionistic students find comfort in completing assignments with ideal results. If they can find the answer in a book or they have been taught how to solve a problem, they feel comfortable and confident. When they must complete open-ended assignments, like essays that require inference or personal opinion, students who struggle with perfectionism may freeze. Many 2e learners who are black-and-white thinkers have trouble with this type of assignment.

SHAYLEE'S STORY

A middle school student, Shaylee had never gotten anything but an A on a report card. As the content of her coursework progressively got more challenging, the number of hours Shaylee spent on her work increased. Eventually, Shaylee was staying up past 11:00 every night to keep up with her homework. Shaylee was a 2e student with anxiety and depression. Her anxiety drove her perfectionism to an exponential degree. Her parents set boundaries on how much time Shaylee could spend on her homework. They hoped to limit the hours she spent going over her work to ensure accuracy. They also coached her on using her time efficiently.

Shaylee began to avoid turning in work that wasn't perfect in her eyes. She would keep assignments that she felt she could improve, believing the reduction in grade associated with turning in the work late was better than the grade she'd receive for imperfect work. Shaylee's fear of not being perceived as a top student prevented her from asking for help when she didn't understand the work or needed extra time.

As time passed, Shaylee realized she couldn't keep up with her work this way. Instead of trying to scale back or prioritize her tasks, she went to the opposite extreme. She avoided doing any work at all. At home, Shaylee binged on television shows. Because of her anxiety, her parents feared pushing her. They didn't want to trigger a panic attack or depressive episode.

Shaylee started seeing me for counseling to help with her anxiety. During counseling, Shaylee described her feelings of helplessness. She'd grown comfortable and dependent on being the student who always had the right answer. "I never had a lot of friends," she explained, "but knowing that the teachers liked me and thought I was a good student helped me get through the days." Over time, we worked to understand her fear of making mistakes. We gradually built skills to desensitize her to turning in work with errors or even work that was incomplete. Shaylee's anxiety and perfectionism peaks at the beginning of each school year, but Shaylee and her gifted education teacher work with the other teachers to build trusting relationships so she feels comfortable asking for help. Shaylee's perfectionistic fear still sometimes returns, but overall, she has made great progress toward seeking a healthy level of success instead of requiring a debilitating level of perfection. ■

Helping 2e Learners Overcome Perfectionism

Students' beliefs about themselves and how they learn influence their ability to overcome the barrier of perfectionism. These strategies can be helpful:

- Emphasize process instead of product. The journey the student takes is more important than the destination. Even an incomplete project has value to the learning process.

- Encourage students to reflect on what they've learned when they make a mistake. Remind them that mistakes are opportunities to learn. Understanding the benefits of a growth mindset can be a helpful cognitive strategy to reduce perfectionistic behaviors. (For more on growth mindset, see chapter 4.)

- Help students recognize the feelings, thoughts, and behaviors they have when they are striving for excellence versus when they are experiencing perfectionism. Does their self-talk change? Does their body feel different? Once they are aware of these signals, they can use various coping skills (like reframing their thoughts or asking for help) to overcome perfectionism.

- Guide students to recognize that everyone has a unique profile of abilities. Their individuality is what makes them who they are, and self-acceptance of all parts of themselves—even the things that may be hard for them—is valuable.

- Coach students to reduce feelings of discomfort surrounding vulnerability. For more information and guidance about vulnerability in 2e students, read on.

Shame and Vulnerability in 2e Learners

Perfectionism is the denial of any vulnerability. People who have perfectionist tendencies fear that any errors they make will be seen and judged negatively by others. This perceived judgment triggers shame, which in turn causes distress.

Author Brené Brown writes about the difference between guilt and shame in her book *The Gifts of Imperfection* (2010). She describes guilt as the feeling that we've *done* something bad or wrong. Shame, however, is the feeling that we *are* bad or wrong for the thing we've done. Guilt externalizes a mistake and lets us act to fix it. Shame internalizes mistakes.

Twice-exceptional learners whose difficulties are unrecognized or misunderstood may have a hard time separating themselves from their mistakes. When they struggle in school, they tell themselves or hear from others that they are the cause of their own problems. For example, ADHD students are called lazy, autistic kids are labeled as stubborn, and dyslexic learners feel that they're dumb. Perfectionism becomes a way to hide this shame. Students may think, "If I don't ever make any mistakes, people won't realize I'm stupid," or, "If I stop trying, I can't make any mistakes."

The relatively late diagnosis of twice-exceptionality for many 2e learners compounds the problem of shame. When these students are young, they can compensate for their struggles, and academic success comes more easily. They understand their strengths, and their intelligence may become part of their identity. When these students grow older and content becomes more difficult or social and executive function expectations grow beyond their compensatory capabilities, the resulting confusion can lead to shame and fear of being discovered as a fraud.

As educators, we need to teach 2e students not to deny vulnerability but rather to become comfortable with intentional vulnerability. Feeling vulnerable is scary for a 2e learner. Bright learners may simply be unfamiliar with vulnerability, or they may have had negative experiences with vulnerability in the past. We need to coach 2e learners on how to express their vulnerability and build relationships so these students feel safe to do so.

STRATEGIES TO COACH VULNERABILITY

- **Model your own vulnerability through self-disclosure.** We all make mistakes, and we all have insecurities. Share about a time you felt vulnerable at school or had to ask for help when you were afraid of what someone would think of you. Ask for forgiveness from your students when you mess up, whether it is a grading error on a paper or overreacting to a situation you misinterpreted. In addition to modeling vulnerability, explicitly state what you are doing and why it is important.

- **Provide a script for students.** Help them find the right words when they are feeling vulnerable and need help. Use the reproducibles **Asking for Help (Grades 4 and Up)** (page 68) or **Asking for Help (Grades K to 3)** (page 71) to facilitate a problem-solving session with your 2e learners (individually or in a group setting) about the ways that work best for them to ask for help.

- **Have conversations requiring vulnerability in private.** Acknowledging a mistake or the need for help is difficult enough. Having a conversation about it in front of a room full of peers is paralyzing.

- **Give students time to process their emotions and circle back, if necessary.** This may be most needed when you're working with students to help them accept responsibility for mistakes involving other students. (For example, a student hurt another student's feelings.) Requiring children to apologize before they are genuinely ready do so can undermine children's willingness to apologize in the future and increase feelings of shame.

- **Offer options.** The heightened emotions of many 2e students can make it hard for them to express their vulnerability. If students can't talk about what they need, give them the option to write about it instead. If coming up with their own words to write is too difficult, give them options with checkboxes or hand signals to indicate their thoughts. Communicating this way with students may take additional time, but if they are in shutdown mode, it can expedite their recovery and build trust that you won't push them too far in the future.

WHEN STUDENTS DECLINE ACCOMMODATIONS

Many 2e students do not feel comfortable accepting accommodations from their teachers. As students get older, they become more aware of the fact that they are getting additional help or support their peers are not getting. They may worry about other students' perceptions of this help. Or they may feel that accommodations give them an unfair advantage.

Establishing a bunch of accommodations that a student will refuse to use is a waste of time. To avoid such resistance, try bringing 2e kids into the process of developing their own accommodation plans. Let students express their level of comfort with accommodations and tell you how they think they could best be helped. Frank conversations about the student's comfort level with certain accommodations offer an opportunity to discuss the benefits of the accommodations and help students understand and accept their unique learning profile. Students should know their accommodations so that if teachers aren't using them, students can self-advocate with the teacher, a case manager or counselor, or their parent or guardian.

Fear of Failure and Fear of Success

Tied in with perfectionism, shame, and vulnerability are the fear of failure and the fear of success. Fear of failure is easy to understand. Fear of success is a little harder to understand—but for 2e learners, the fear of success can also be debilitating. With their complex strengths and weaknesses, 2e learners may fear success because they are unsure of their ability to keep succeeding. For a comparison of these two fears, see **figure 3-2**.

Figure 3-2 Fear of Failure Versus Fear of Success

	Fear of Failure	Fear of Success
Feels Like	• Constant worry that errors are being judged by others and one's worth as a person is contingent on success	• Being propelled forward against one's own will; pressure to continually reach the next level of skill without consideration of one's wishes or desires
Looks Like	• Excessive effort to avoid challenging tasks and perceived mistakes or failure	• Hesitation to take on new skills or tasks; indecision about future; masking of skills in academic or social situations
Sounds Like	• "What if I look dumb?" • "I haven't been taught how to do this. I'd better not risk messing it up." • "Other people do this better than me."	• "What if I love med school but hate being a doctor?" • "People will like me more if I'm not the best." • "If I get better at playing piano, people will expect me to keep getting better. Eventually, I'm going to let them down."

Learned Helplessness

Learned helplessness is a struggle I see often in 2e students. A combination of perfectionism, reliance on unnecessary supports, or a poor academic self-concept can lead students to refuse to attempt tasks that feel difficult. They may wait for a teacher to approach them to help, intentionally do poorly on assignments, or check multiple times with the teacher on the same assignment to see if their work is on the right track.

It is easy for well-meaning adults to fall into the trap of offering too much assistance to struggling students. Their effort to build up students' academic self-concept can backfire, leaving students afraid to attempt any task without adult reassurance. The reverse is also possible: an adult may push a student too hard, assuming the resistance to a task is laziness or unwillingness to try.

A major component of learned helplessness in 2e learners is their high ability. From a young age, learning may come easily to them. They understand many topics rapidly. As a result, many gifted learners end up thinking that effort is not necessarily a good thing. When they inevitably face a difficult task, they may avoid the task to preserve their identity as "the smart kid." Simple replies such as "I can't do this" or "This is too hard" become common refrains.

With encouragement and support, these students can begin to put effort into their schoolwork. If this effort brings success in grades or visible progress, all is well. However, if it backfires—doesn't bring success—students faced with a challenging task may avoid the effort next time. They may ask, "What if I try and I don't succeed?" Rather than redouble their efforts, 2e learners may fall into a trap of learned helplessness.

ROHAN'S STORY

Rohan was working on a research project in his fourth-grade gifted classroom. Diagnosed with ADHD, ASD, and sensory processing disorder (SPD)—and probably struggling with a written language learning disability, although it had never been assessed—he found it overwhelming to muster the focus and time commitment required to sit, find facts, and handwrite them on note cards. The teacher in his gifted education classroom was not very accommodating and expected him to keep up with the rest of the class. He'd spent hours over several days working on this task with minimal progress. He was very behind in his research, so his teacher sent it home with him so he could try to catch up.

His dad asked me for advice. "I want to just scribe for him," he said, "but I also don't want him to become dependent on other people writing for him. I'm worried his teacher will be upset that he hasn't written the note cards himself." I told Rohan's dad not to worry about the teacher and help his son get the note cards written.

He did, and I talked to Rohan's teacher about the accommodation. Once the tedious task of writing the note cards was complete, Rohan created an exemplary final research project. It was on a topic he was passionate about and excited to share. His ability to verbalize his thoughts came through when the obstacle of sitting, focusing, and copying information was removed. ■

Accommodating or Enabling?

Does providing accommodations teach kids bad habits? Do accommodations enable students to avoid the hard stuff? Do accommodations leave kids with gaps in the academic and emotional regulation skills they'll need for success later in their academic careers? These questions are understandable and valid.

Try to remember that 2e kids learn and think differently from their peers. What would be the easy way out for a neurotypical kid may be the accommodation a 2e student needs to build skills and autonomy. Accommodations are like giving a step stool to a child who's too short to reach the highest shelf. Will the child need the ladder forever? It depends on how tall they grow before they reach adulthood. Maybe they'll have a few growth spurts and will abandon the step stool. Maybe they'll always need a bit of a lift to reach that high shelf. Our goal is to help students be successful and find the structure that allows them to be autonomous.

The key to preventing accommodations from enabling poor habits is twofold. First, students should be told what the accommodations are and why they are being provided. Second, the responsibility for using accommodations should gradually be transferred to

Figure 3-3 Development of Learned Helplessness

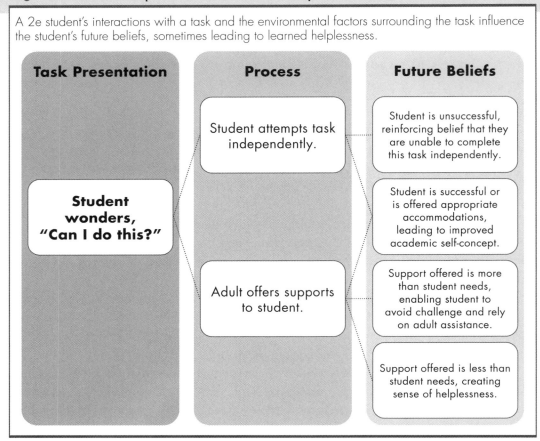

A 2e student's interactions with a task and the environmental factors surrounding the task influence the student's future beliefs, sometimes leading to learned helplessness.

Task Presentation

Student wonders, "Can I do this?"

Process

Student attempts task independently.

Adult offers supports to student.

Future Beliefs

Student is unsuccessful, reinforcing belief that they are unable to complete this task independently.

Student is successful or is offered appropriate accommodations, leading to improved academic self-concept.

Support offered is more than student needs, enabling student to avoid challenge and rely on adult assistance.

Support offered is less than student needs, creating sense of helplessness.

the student. Awareness about accommodations empowers the student and reduces the likelihood of dependence on others to manage their difficulties. If adults are running around behind the scenes providing a ton of accommodations for students without their awareness, those accommodations can easily become enabling.

Many 2e learners already have negative beliefs about their abilities. They may automatically assume they are going to fail. It is often better to provide 2e students with more support than necessary and gradually remove it than to wait for them to fail before offering accommodations.

Here are some questions to help you determine if assistance is appropriate or if it might encourage practices that lead to learned helplessness:

- What is the primary objective of the activity? Will the accommodation interfere with the achievement of this objective? *Example: The primary objective of a science review packet is to review the concepts learned. Allowing a student to use (coherent) abbreviations in their answers instead of writing out every word fully and using complete sentences does not impede the student from achieving the objective of the assignment.*

- Is the accommodation something that is easily accommodated in the future? Or is it delaying a skill that will eventually become necessary? *Example: Scribing on exams for a student who will soon take the ACT or SAT and will be required to write independently on that test may lead to some level of learned helplessness. Scaffolding to build student autonomy and success toward the goal of writing independently will serve this student in the future.*

■ Is the accommodation long-term or short-term? If it is long-term, is it sustainable? *Example: Helping a student with attention difficulties complete a task within a limited amount of time so they do not fall behind is a short-term accommodation. Allowing a student with dysgraphia to type their work is a long-term accommodation, but it could be sustainable.*

Key Points

■ Twice-exceptional students may have low academic, social, and emotional self-concepts, although their comfort in each area may vary.

■ Twice-exceptional students may be perfectionistic, especially if schoolwork has typically been easy for them.

■ Helping students learn to become vulnerable and feel comfortable asking for help is valuable for 2e kids. Self-advocacy skills are critical for their continued success.

■ Mindfully making accommodations is not enabling a student to be helpless. Appropriate accommodations prevent learned helplessness.

Asking for Help (Grades 4 and Up)

Do you ever get the feeling that you should be able to do everything on your own? Maybe schoolwork is usually easy for you, but once in a while, an assignment or project is harder than you expected. You might feel as if you're speeding along and then—oof!—you hit a brick wall.

When this happens—let's say on a written assignment—do you ever react in one of these ways? Check any reaction that sounds familiar:

☐ I stare at my paper for a very long time, hoping I'll be able to come up with something to write.

☐ I begin writing. I erase my writing. I start writing again. Then I erase again.

☐ I try to get something written on the paper, even if I know my work is probably wrong, because I just want to get it done and not think about it.

☐ I walk to my teacher's desk, show my blank paper, and say, "I don't get it."

☐ I read and reread the instructions to see if anything clicks. If it doesn't, I raise my hand. When my teacher comes to me, I explain which part of the assignment is too hard or confusing so my teacher can help me understand.

Asking for help is not always easy. When you ask for help, you're admitting that you aren't perfect. But guess what: you aren't supposed to be perfect. No one is perfect. Your teacher and your parents are there to help you learn. That's what school is for, right? It would be a waste of time if you already knew how to do everything you were supposed to learn in school, wouldn't it?

How do you feel about asking for help?

No problem!   *A little awkward*   *Ugh! The worst!*

⟵————————————————————————⟶

1 2 3 4 5 6 7 8 9 10

Here are some reasons kids might have trouble asking for help. Check any that you've experienced.

☐ I feel embarrassed that I need help.

☐ I'm worried I'll get in trouble for not understanding.

☐ Asking for help makes me feel like I'm not smart.

☐ I don't want other students to judge me.

☐ I feel like I should be able to do it on my own.

☐ It isn't fair for me to get more help than other kids get.

☐ I think asking for help is like cheating.

☐ I haven't had to ask for help before; why should I ask now?

☐ I feel better if I can just do it on my own.

Part of asking for help is feeling safe about asking for it. Feeling safe means you trust the person you're asking. You need to believe that the person will be able to help you and will do so without making you feel guilty or dumb. Who are the people in your life you can trust in this way?

Once you realize you need help and you've figured out who you can trust, you can use the following script chart to build a request for help. Choose one part of your request from each column. If the words in this chart don't quite fit your situation, just remember the four steps—introduction, problem, need, and question—and come up with your own words.

Step 1: *Introduction*	Step 2: *Your Problem*	Step 3: *Your Need*	Step 4: *Question*
I need help.	I'm overwhelmed.	I think I need to review the instructions.	Is that okay?
I don't understand something.	I don't know how to do this problem/task.	I think I need a reminder or hint.	Can you help me with that?
I'm confused.	I can't tell what these directions mean.	I think I need a break.	Is now a good time?

Read the following scenarios and use the script chart to come up with a request the student in each scenario could use to ask for help.

- Ian is working on a math assignment. He doesn't know how to apply the skill to the word problems. He starts to get frustrated, but then takes a deep breath and decides to ask for help.

- Daniella is mad at herself because of the science test score she just got back. She is so disappointed, she feels like she is about to cry.

- Joanna is trying to do her social studies assignment, but she is really confused about what to do next.

What if you need help, but it is too hard for you to ask out loud? You could ask for help in a different way. Which of these ideas do you think might work for you? Check any that you'd like to try. Do you have other ideas?

☐ Agree with your teacher on a secret hand signal to request help.

☐ Write your request for help on a note or on a whiteboard.

☐ Have a check-in system with your teacher. For example, your teacher asks if you need help, and you reply on a scale of zero to five, with the size of the number showing how much help you need. (You could also hold up your fingers to show how much help you need.)

☐ When you're assigned a task or subject that is often tricky for you, meet with your teacher for a short conference, regardless of whether you think you'll need help.

☐ Other ideas:

Are there any other obstacles that might prevent you from asking for help when you need it? What are they? Brainstorm possible solutions with your teacher and take notes in the space below.

Asking for Help (Grades K to 3)

Teachers: Read these stories aloud and facilitate a class discussion using the questions for each scenario.

Omar

Omar's favorite subject was math. He was proud that he had memorized all his multiplication tables before everyone else in his grade. Every time Omar got back a math paper, it showed that he'd solved every problem right.

Omar got sick and had to miss a few days of school. When he returned, his teacher gave him some of the math work to make up from when he was gone. He looked at the assignment and got a confused look on his face. He hadn't seen problems like this before. Omar sat and stared at his paper for a long time, getting angry at himself because he couldn't figure out how to solve the problems on the paper. Pretty soon, he had tears in his eyes. One of his friends asked him if anything was wrong, but Omar was embarrassed to say he didn't know how to do the math work and told his friend everything was fine.

Questions:

1. What is the problem in this story? (Possible answers: Omar couldn't figure out his math homework; Omar was upset that the math assignment was too hard.)

2. Why did Omar feel so upset about the math assignment? (Possible answers: He felt like he should be able to solve the problems himself; he felt like he wasn't smart in math anymore.)

3. What solutions could Omar use in this situation? (Possible answers: Omar could ask his friend or a teacher for help; Omar could take the work home and get help from his parents.)

Neveah

Neveah listened as her teacher gave instructions for their writing assignment. They were supposed to write about the most exciting thing they had done over the summer. Neveah tried to think back over her summer. They had done some things that were fun, like go to the pool and visit their grandmother, but she couldn't think of a single thing that was "exciting." Neveah watched the rest of the class start writing their paragraphs. She picked up her pencil and tried to write—but the words wouldn't come! She was so afraid that whatever she wrote would be wrong and she didn't know what the right answer was if there was nothing "exciting" she'd done over the summer. When her teacher came around to check, Neveah covered her paper because she didn't have anything written yet and she was worried she'd get in trouble. She began to stress out because she knew if she didn't finish, she'd get a bad grade.

Questions:

1. Why is Neveah having a hard time with this assignment? (Possible answers: She can't think of anything exciting she did over the summer; she's afraid she's going to get a bad grade.)

2. What could Neveah do to solve this problem? (Possible answers: Ask for ideas from her teacher; ask if she can make up something to write about.)

After reading and discussing these scenarios, brainstorm with students the reasons why someone might not want to ask for help. Next, create a list with students of emotions that someone might feel if they needed to ask for help (possible responses: embarrassed, worried, stressed, nervous, confused, comfortable, calm).

Finally, create with your students a chart showing a variety of strategies to ask for help (similar to the following sample). Keep it as an anchor chart in your classroom. Let students be creative and find ways that help them feel safe to ask questions.

I Can Ask for Help		
When should I ask for help?	**Who should I ask to help me?**	**What should I say?**
• when I feel stuck • when I don't understand the directions • when I think I'm doing my work wrong	• my teacher • a classmate • my parents	• "Can you help me with this?" • "I'm confused by the directions." • "Will you tell me if I'm on the right track?"

Motivating Twice-Exceptional Learners

Motivation is the drive to move toward a goal. It is the combination of the desire to reach a goal and the willingness to take action to achieve it.

In the field of education, we talk about motivated and unmotivated students. The term *motivated students* calls up visions of students who participate in class, raise their hands, and do the extra credit. We generally think of unmotivated students as the kids who sit sullenly in the back of the classroom with their heads on their desks and turn in their work late (if at all).

Of course, these are oversimplified stereotypes. Motivation is individual and contextual; it depends on the person, the domain, and the task. I've never met someone who's completely unmotivated in all areas of life.

The struggle twice-exceptional learners face in school is complex. Because of their advanced cognitive skills, they may be highly motivated by the content being taught—but their learning difficulties may prevent them from engaging with the work as teachers expect. Perceived failures, unchallenging work, and unrecognized or unsupported learning needs can lead a child to check out of academics over time. In an article on the role of motivation in learning and work, researchers D. Betsy McCoach and Jessica Flake assert, "Ability without motivation is like wind without a windmill. The energy produced by the wind must be harnessed to produce electricity. So too must ability be coupled with motivation to produce achievement" (McCoach and Flake 2018, 201).

AMARI'S STORY

Amari arrived in my counseling office as a quirky sixth grader. He talked pretty much nonstop. With no hesitation, he'd tell me his strong opinion about almost any topic. I loved his quick wit, and his unfiltered thoughts helped me understand exactly what made him tick.

When I first met him, he was not yet identified as a 2e learner. His parents were running circles around the school, trying to advocate for his needs. He was identified as gifted in math and attended an accelerated math class—which he was failing.

As I worked with Amari, his parents, teachers, and I struggled to find a way to motivate him and keep him moving along. We made progress in fits and starts. Eventually, Amari was diagnosed with ADHD, ASD, and a learning disability in written language expression. He'd been compensating for these struggles for years; his high ability had masked them. His lack of motivation resulted from years of frustration at developing basic skills, weak executive functioning skills causing day-to-day struggles, and adults exasperated by a greatly talented child not reaching his potential. ■

What Is Motivation?

Motivation is:

- the inner energy that directs and regulates behavior

- choosing some goals and not others

- starting work toward a goal

- persevering in the work toward the goal

- the cause of progress toward a goal

- influenced by personal characteristics and social and environmental factors

- a determining factor in high- and low-achieving students

- enthusiasm, engagement, passion, and flow

Renzulli's Three-Ring Model of Giftedness

Educational psychologist Joseph Renzulli created a three-ring concept of giftedness. He says giftedness manifests when a student shows high levels of three different characteristics: above-average ability, creativity, and task commitment (motivation). When the three characteristics intersect, we find gifted behavior. (See **figure 4-1**.) Imagine a student in your class who exhibits above-average ability and creative ideas but lacks task commitment. This student would probably be an underachiever, not living up to their potential. Renzulli describes task commitment, or motivation, as a high level of interest in a certain area, a capacity for perseverance and hard work, high standards for one's work, and a willingness to accept criticism (Renzulli 2005).

Figure 4-1 Renzulli's Three-Ring Model of Giftedness

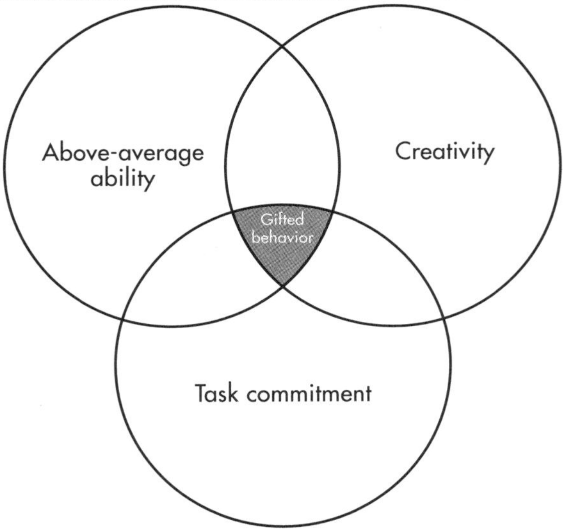

Adapted from "Graphic Representation of the Three-Ring Definition of Giftedness" by Joseph S. Renzulli in *Conceptions of Giftedness*, edited by Robert J. Sternberg and Janet E. Davidson, © Cambridge University Press 1986, 2005. Reproduced with permission of Cambridge University Press through PLSclear.

The Impact of Stress on Motivation

Stress strongly influences motivation. A little stress can be good. A little stress is the push that helps us seek a promotion or get the house cleaned before the relatives come over. For students, manageable stress helps them study a little extra for an upcoming test or check their work for mistakes. The distinction between positive stress (eustress) and negative stress (distress) is important. Positive stress is the excitement of a new opportunity—a little kick of adrenaline to get us moving toward a goal. Negative stress is fear and anxiety when the stress hormone cortisol kicks in.

Neuroscientists are constantly learning about the negative impact too much stress has on a person's overall health and wellbeing. They've found that increased levels of chronic stress harm our cardiovascular health, metabolic functioning, and neurological and psychological performance (Sousa 2016). Too much stress reduces our ability to make decisions and use cognitive flexibility and increases avoidance behaviors (Morgado and Cerqueira 2018).

Chronic stress can take many forms. As schools learn to be trauma-informed, we're recognizing that students from economically disadvantaged families face chronic stress when they live on a day-to-day basis with food insecurity. Families who move frequently due to housing insecurity face the stress of being in survival mode as they repeatedly acclimate to new situations and environments. Students in these families can't rely on the stability of a consistent home environment. Students facing systemic bias due to being from culturally and linguistically diverse (CLD) backgrounds may also experience the toll of trauma due to chronic stress.

Twice-exceptional students often experience chronic stress when they must learn in environments that don't match their needs. These environments cause an immense amount of daily stress. Let's look at this idea through the lens of "flow." When we experience a balance of challenge that is appropriate for our skill, we achieve a state of flow. We feel highly motivated and engaged. If challenge is high, but ability is not, the result is anxiety. If challenge is low, but ability is high, boredom is the likely outcome. Finding this balance is always difficult for gifted students, who may enter the classroom already knowing much of the content that will be taught. Between 20 and 49 percent of students show achievement over one year ahead of the grade level curriculum in English language arts; in math, 14 to 37 percent of students are ahead by a year (Peters et al. 2017). It's even trickier to find the right challenge level for 2e learners. A certain level of content may be an appropriate challenge for their ability, but they may not have the skills needed to show their ability. Because flow is elusive for them, they are constantly either bored or anxious.

As educators, we must work to adjust the learning experience for 2e students to match their learning needs. We must also help them build coping skills to manage the stress in their lives. You'll find information on coping skills later in this book. For information on self-advocacy, see chapter 5; for information on mindfulness, see chapter 11.

Theories of Motivation

Because of the complex nature of 2e learners' academic, social, and emotional needs, we need to understand how motivation influences their effort and success in the academic environment. We'll discuss three main theories of motivation in this chapter: goal orientation theory (also known as growth mindset theory), attribution theory, and self-determination theory. The three theories shed light from different angles on what motivates (or demotivates) learners. After exploring these ideas, we'll talk about how to harness the force behind each to help 2e students find success.

Figure 4-2 Theories of Motivation

Theory of Motivation	Asks
Goal orientation theory (mindset)	"Is it worth trying to do well?" "If I try to do well, will I succeed?"
Attribution theory	"Why am I doing well or poorly?" "If I succeed or fail, is it something I can control?"
Self-determination theory	"Why do I want to do well?" "Who is in control of my motivation and effort?"

Goal Orientation Theory or Mindset

Goal orientation theory says that two types of goals motivate us to learn new skills: performance goals, which focus on outcomes of learning, and mastery goals, which focus on building skills. A student with performance goals generally has a fixed mindset. A student with mastery goals generally has a growth mindset (see **figure 4-3**). If you are an educator, you've probably heard about growth mindset and fixed mindset. Educators have been using these terms widely since Carol Dweck published her book *Mindset: The New Psychology of Success* in 2006.

Figure 4-3 Performance Versus Mastery Goals

	Performance Goals (Fixed Mindset)	Mastery Goals (Growth Mindset)
Example	"The main thing I want when I do my schoolwork is to show how good I am at it."	"It's much more important for me to learn things in my classes than it is to get the best grades."
Belief	Ability is a fixed trait that cannot be changed.	Ability is a fluid trait that can be developed.
Response to failure	Helplessness: "I'll spend less time on this subject from now on."	Resilience: "I'll work harder in this class from now on."

Goal orientation theory suggests that students who have a growth mindset will be more likely to challenge themselves and persevere through difficult content because they believe their achievement can be changed based on the amount of effort they put forth. Students with a fixed mindset are more likely to quit when things get difficult because they believe their achievement is immutable and if they are unable to accomplish a task or reach a solution, it is most likely because they have reached the top of their ability and further attempts will not prove successful.

Twice-exceptional learners may be prone to developing a fixed mindset because their past experience may have included perceived failures. When comparing their performance to other students, 2e learners may see what their gifted peers are able to produce while their twice-exceptionality prevents them from accomplishing the same. Students might also have a fixed mindset in some areas and a growth mindset in others. For example, a student may show a strong growth mindset in math but a fixed mindset in writing and physical education.

Students who develop a fixed mindset have two styles: approach or avoidance. A student with approach style strives to achieve, possibly leading to perfectionism. A student with avoidance style focuses on avoiding failure or showing weakness. Avoidance style often looks like learned helplessness. (See chapter 3 for more on learned helplessness.)

Learned helplessness in 2e students can come from a variety of causes. Being given unchallenging schoolwork may lead learners to feel that this level of work is all they can manage. Placement in remedial classes without appropriate challenge to meet their gifted needs also reinforces a fixed mindset. Likewise, being placed in gifted or advanced courses without appropriate supports can limit a 2e learner's self-efficacy.

Fostering a growth mindset in 2e learners is one way to help them make progress. Shifting the focus from grades to the process of learning can combat learned helplessness, perfectionism, and apathy.

> **" Why should I give 100 percent effort when I know that 75 percent effort will get me an A?**
> **—Ezra, ninth grader "**

With all the attention mindset has received over the last decade, it is easy to believe that changing a fixed mindset to a growth mindset is the solution to all motivational struggles in learners and that students who develop a growth mindset will see significant gains in academics. Recent research that includes more longitudinal data about implementing growth mindset shows the gains in achievement are not as great as once hoped. The results of this meta-analysis show growth mindset does, however, appear to be most beneficial for students from economically disadvantaged families (Sisk et al. 2018). From a counseling perspective, it seems the benefits in emotional regulation for students who develop the internal self-talk skills associated with a growth mindset may be worthwhile, even without any immediate academic benefit. While helping students focus on the learning process is important, this strategy can't stand alone. Teachers must also understand attribution theory and self-determination theory to give 2e students their best opportunity to become self-directed learners.

ELISHA'S STORY

Eighth grader Elisha was gifted and had a diagnosis of OCD and depression. When it came to academics, she had a rigid fixed mindset. She had always gotten straight A's and expected nothing less from herself. She eventually became fixated on her performance, choosing not to turn in work if she was afraid it wouldn't live up to her standards. Her teachers told her she could turn in incomplete work, and they would grade it based on what was finished. Elisha refused. At home, she avoided homework and panicked when a deadline approached.

We talked through this at length. Elisha had internalized the educational system's method of measuring students and was unable to separate learning as a process from the grading of the product. She had great difficulty understanding that the process was more important than the product. Her ingrained beliefs made it challenging to move Elisha from a performance goal (fixed) mindset to a mastery goal (growth) mindset. ∎

Attribution Theory

A major factor influencing motivation is the degree to which people feel able to control their success or failure. Attribution theory examines whether students believe that they can influence their success or that their performance depends on factors outside their control. Internal attribution is when someone credits an outcome to factors such as ability, effort, or personality. External attribution is when someone ascribes success or failure to luck or the influence of other people (such as a teacher's favor or disfavor).

Learners develop these beliefs through their experiences. Twice-exceptional learners, who often experience intermittent successes and failures, may find it easy to believe they have no control over their outcomes and that they must be due to external factors. Results that are predictable and consistent are easier to attribute to internal factors. For example, gifted students with strong study habits may believe diligent preparation is the cause of their good grades. Twice-exceptional learners may study just as much but earn a high grade one week and a low grade the next depending on the content covered, the test style, or their emotional regulation skills.

Figure 4-4 Internal Versus External Attribution

	Internal Attribution	External Attribution
Factors	Internal and controllable	External and uncontrollable
Success	Due to hard work, understanding task	Due to luck, teacher's favor
Failure	Due to insufficient effort or using a wrong strategy	Due to lack of ability or bad luck

AMARI'S STORY

When we learned about Amari at the beginning of this chapter, he had recently been diagnosed as 2e with ADHD, ASD, and a written language learning disability. After Amari was diagnosed as a 2e learner, his school gave him an IEP to support his learning needs. However, even with these supports in place and a case manager helping Amari complete his schoolwork and build his skills, his grades continued to flounder.

In sixth grade, math was Amari's least favorite subject. He was barely passing, even though he had great natural strength in math. He had a lot of incomplete work and completed work that he didn't turn in. His test scores were the only thing keeping him afloat. During our sessions, Amari would rant about his frustration with his math teacher, who he felt was unfair to him. "She doesn't like me! I can't turn in my late work to her because she'll just refuse to grade it," he lamented. He refused to believe there was any possibility of doing well in the class because he felt the teacher disliked him. He felt he had no control of the situation and showed zero motivation to change it.

In seventh grade, Amari excelled in math. The teacher gave him choices about how to complete his work and how to turn it in. He felt in control of the situation. This led to a cycle of growing self-efficacy, and the internal locus of control stoked his motivation. He was named Math Student of the Year. ■

Self-Determination Theory

Self-determination theory is similar to attribution theory but focuses on intrinsic and extrinsic motivation. In self-determination theory, varying degrees of intrinsic and extrinsic motivation exist along a continuum. The theory recognizes that while true intrinsic motivation is ideal, it isn't always realistic. For example, there aren't many people who will practice math facts just for the love of flash cards. A realistic view of motivation is necessary to help 2e learners engage and find success in school.

Self-determination theory identifies six levels of motivation. The top three levels are self-determined types of motivation. This means the person is motivated based on their own desires, and they can self-regulate their effort based on their valuation of an activity. The bottom three levels are external types of motivation.

- **Level 6: intrinsic motivation.** The activity itself is the motivator and the reward. Someone who loves to read is intrinsically motivated because the reading itself is the reward.

- **Level 5: integrated regulation.** An external reward and a person's sense of self are intertwined. For example, a student who enjoys writing for the school newspaper and wins an award for their work is experiencing integrated regulation.

- **Level 4: identified regulation.** Someone recognizes external rewards for an activity, and they decide these rewards are important enough to work for. Students who do homework because the effort will help them earn good grades and get accepted to college or earn a scholarship, which they value, are experiencing identified regulation.

- **Level 3: introjected regulation.** Someone is motivated to complete a task because it is expected, even though they may not have any desire to do so on their own or may not see the value in doing it. For example, a parent or teacher assigns a task, and the student complies because it is expected.

- **Level 2: external regulation.** A student engages in an activity strictly because they are trying to earn a reward or avoid a punishment. This type of regulation is the least effective in helping a child build a sense of self-efficacy. It often leads to inconsistent behavior.

- **Level 1: amotivation.** A student completely lacks motivation and cannot be spurred to act by rewards or punishments. This student probably exhibits extreme avoidance behaviors.

To facilitate intrinsic motivation in our students, we have to work within the existing academic system. Helping students understand their motivation and effort will serve them well throughout their lives. Remember that motivation fluctuates from topic to topic, day to day. When you are working with a 2e student, examine the multiple factors that may influence their level of engagement and motivation so you can use the best strategies to help them in the moment. Motivation needn't *always* be intrinsic. I mean, how many of us do our taxes for the sheer joy of it? We are probably motivated by some combination of a sense of duty and the prospect of reward (a tax refund) or punishment (a costly penalty). Without those extrinsic motivators, we probably wouldn't make the effort. (Well, at least most people I know wouldn't!)

Many 2e learners have trouble equating the steps needed for a task to the big picture. A student with ADHD who doesn't turn in work might cognitively know that a zero in the grade book will bring down their grade, but that doesn't mean they really grasp the long-term impact it has on their future opportunities. An autistic student might complete their work as expected because they are experiencing introjected regulation; in their black-and-white world, schoolwork is a thing they are supposed to do because teachers and parents expect it. However, they don't really understand or embrace the value of an assignment.

FOSTERING INTRINSIC MOTIVATION

Our goal as teachers isn't necessarily to push kids to be intrinsically motivated all the time. Teaching 2e students about intrinsic and extrinsic motivation can have great benefits in student self-awareness. If a student recognizes they aren't feeling interested in a project, they can examine the reasons why. When we teach students the questions to ask themselves, we empower them to take control of their motivation.

Figure 4-5 Extrinsic to Intrinsic Motivation Continuum

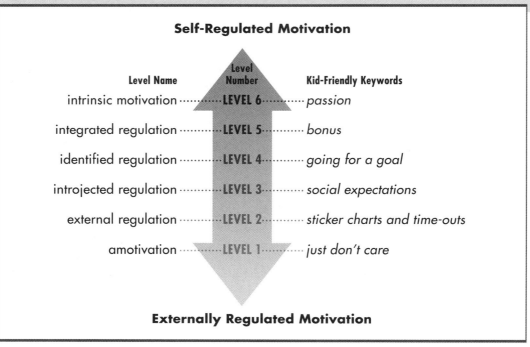

The following types of lessons are more likely to develop intrinsic motivation in students (McCoach and Flake 2018):

- optimally challenging
- interesting and enjoyable
- moderately novel
- intellectually stimulating

- taught inductively
- lacking a content ceiling
- involving higher-level cognition
- allowing multiple solutions
- involving ambiguity and unanswered questions

EMILY'S STORY

Fifth grade was a rough year for me. The compensatory skills I'd picked up earlier in elementary school were no longer effective. I struggled to complete and turn in work and my desk was often pushed against the wall so I couldn't talk to other students. I spent time each day out in the hallway, usually because the class was grading the work I hadn't turned in yet.

I was, however, a motivated learner. For example, each fifth grader chose a state to research and completed a project on it. I spent days researching and organizing and writing, and this was before we had the internet! I remember my colored pencil drawing of Michigan on the cover of my report, carefully placed in a plastic sleeve, and my pride when I turned in that project. That was one of few bright spots that year.

My teacher had an elaborate behavior management system. She described it as a positive system. I'd describe it otherwise. We started each week with our name written on five index cards. (That's the positive part—we started each week with all five cards, and "all we had to do" was keep them.) Each time I didn't turn in work when it was due or I was off task, my teacher let me know, and I had to walk across the classroom and place one of my cards in a basket. Any cards left still in a student's possession the end of the week were collected for a drawing. The winner got a soda or candy bar from the teacher's lounge. *And,* if you kept all five of your cards, the teacher would send a positive note home—you know, one of those cutesy little teacher notes with a saying like *I did a bear-y good job this week* and a picture of a teddy bear. Of course, I rarely earned a note home. Even the shame of walking across the room to turn in a card, the pride of being able to show my mom that I'd kept all five of my cards all week, or the temptation of winning a full-sugar, full-caffeine soda from the teacher's lounge couldn't motivate me to get my act together.

My problem wasn't motivation. It was an executive functioning deficit. No amount of lost recess time or cards getting turned into the basket was going to teach me the skills I needed to be successful. ■

THREE COMPONENTS OF SELF-REGULATED MOTIVATION

Self-determination theory says that three components are necessary for someone to feel intrinsically motivated: autonomy, competence, and relatedness. If someone is unmotivated, looking at these three areas may reveal the cause. This is especially important for 2e learners. They may have low motivation caused by external factors but attributed to internal shortcomings, such as laziness or defiance. The fact that they are both gifted and have a learning difficulty means that people may miss the latter, depending on their compensatory skills. When we take the time to examine external factors first, we allow students' true motivation to shine.

Autonomy

Autonomy is having feelings of volition and control over one's environment. You have probably had the experience of being told to do something and feeling resentful of the person who told you to do it. If they had only *asked*, you probably would have been happy to comply.

Students feel the same way. When you tell them to do something a certain way, they may be able to complete the work as directed. But how does this command influence their motivation? Lack of autonomy can lead students to feel helpless to have any sway over their environment or actions.

Students with unique learning needs often are those who would benefit most from autonomy but are offered it the least. Because schools tend to focus on areas of weakness and remediate the concepts a child struggles to learn, the path for this learning often follows a regimented and linear process. When given some independence to choose their own ways of doing things and to use their strengths to build on skills they have already developed, students not only feel successful but recognize they can achieve success without being told what to do every step of the way.

When teaching discrete topics, like math skills, history, or science, we can give students autonomy by allowing them to pick how they would like to show mastery. When the learning objective is more abstract, such as comparing and contrasting, we can give students the latitude to choose their own subject. Structural or environmental choices (for example, letting kids choose where to sit or what medium they'd like to use for showing their work) can also help facilitate a feeling of autonomy.

Teachers may undermine student autonomy when they are unintentionally manipulative. For example, practices that cause shame or guilt will lead students to feel anxious and reliant on teacher approval instead of fostering independent learning and confidence. Removing privileges or direct punishment of students will also reduce student autonomy. If the goal is to help students feel intrinsically motivated, they need independence to make mistakes and control their own work.

To foster student autonomy, you can use the following strategies:

- When you're reviewing a topic for assessment, have students engage in self-assessment and identify their own strengths and weaknesses. Assign a certain number of items to complete for review, but let the students choose which items to complete based on their self-assessment.

- Let students create their own time line for a project and identify how they would like to chunk the material into manageable pieces. As a bonus, this strategy builds executive functioning skills.

- Give kids options for assignments based on engaging them in a variety of higher-level thinking skills. As a classroom teacher I used a point system, with more points available for more difficult items, to discourage students from always choosing the easy options. I usually structured this system based on Bloom's Revised Taxonomy, although the Depth of Knowledge (DOK) framework would also work.

- Individualize feedback on student behavior. Create an environment that supports students in problem-solving when behaviors are keeping them from learning. Handle concerning behaviors discreetly and emphasize that you know the student can improve and you are there to help them.

AIDEN'S STORY

Aiden was a seventh grader who was gifted and had ADHD. He struggled with motivation. Classroom teachers throughout his academic career thought he was lazy and apathetic. They saw a child who refused to participate in group projects or do more than the bare minimum on assignments. Aiden's gifted teacher, however, saw a different student—one who regularly went above the basic requirements and produced intricate and well-thought-out projects.

Aiden and his gifted teacher noticed the discrepancy and started to investigate. They asked themselves, "What differs in these environments that encourages Aiden to produce exemplary work in one and mediocre work in the other?" Aiden realized that in his gifted classroom, he loved having the latitude to determine how to show what he was learning. The regular classroom, with work that Aiden felt was too easy and group work with kids who tried to take over, demoralized Aiden. The lack of autonomy dissolved his motivation.

With this awareness, Aiden and his teacher could advocate with his classroom teachers. With a mix of appropriate pretesting to guarantee his existing knowledge and skills, and a contract stating how he would show his learning, Aiden began to shine. In addition to producing work that was appropriate for his cognitive ability, he also began to complete the more mundane work. His overall feeling of autonomy improved his baseline motivation, and he was now more willing to comply with the "necessary" work. ■

Competence

Competence is feeling capable of interacting with one's environment. When was the last time you did something that was really difficult? How long did you stick with it? If you opted to quit, your feelings of competence were probably low. If you did stick with the task, what helped you persevere? I imagine that you felt some competence—you believed that if you kept trying, you would eventually accomplish your goal.

Twice-exceptional learners are more vulnerable to feeling incompetent than their neurotypical peers are because of their complex mix of abilities and struggles. Because they have high cognitive ability, they and others often expect them to learn concepts or demonstrate skills easily. However, their second exceptionality stands in the way. Executive functioning deficits may hinder their progress. They may struggle with reading fluency and their comprehension lags. They may be risk averse due to anxiety. Whatever the reason, competence eludes them, and they need more help.

Teachers can foster competence by making sure students are always working at an appropriate level. Work that is too challenging will cause students to feel helpless; work that is not challenging enough will cause students to feel bored. Individualizing work is key to keeping students engaged. When students feel competent in a subject, they will also feel motivated to pursue the subject further.

Teachers may undermine student competence when their expectations are constantly changing. When expectations are unpredictable or disorganized, a student may feel lost. Criticism without the support to correct also undermines student competence.

MALIK'S STORY

Malik entered sixth grade with a positive attitude, ready for a fresh start. Elementary school had ended with some difficulty for Malik, who had been identified as both gifted and having clinical depression. His depression was episodic, and when it was peaking, he had a hard time with peer relationships, concentration, irritability, and motivation.

Malik's strongest subject was math. He was looking forward to his first opportunity to take an advanced math course. His teacher, however, believed that because this was the first math class that would eventually lead to AP courses, she needed to weed out students who couldn't meet high expectations.

Within two weeks, Malik was struggling. He said the teacher criticized his work for inconsistencies, even when he understood the concepts. He felt like she jumped all over the place in her teaching to find gaps in what they'd previously learned. He felt dumb and was ready to quit and enroll in the general education math course. The rapid pacing, lack of positive feedback, and chaotic classroom had led to Malik's loss of competence and motivation.

Malik's counselor listened to his concerns. When she reviewed his test scores and previous math class performance, she knew the advanced class was where he needed to be. Considering Malik's tendency to struggle with negative thinking, she invited Malik and his math teacher to a conference. The math teacher was able to show Malik that he was progressing appropriately through the class and informed him about the format of the class and what to expect in the future. This began to restore Malik's feeling of competence and motivation, and he was able to complete the class successfully. ■

Relatedness

Relatedness is feeling reciprocal connection with others (caring for them and feeling cared for by them). Do the student and the teacher have a relationship? Does the student feel cared for by the teacher? Does the student also care for the teacher?

Students most easily relate and connect with teachers who show interest in them, both as people and as students. There are many ways to foster this connection. To build relationships, teachers can allow students to have a voice in classroom procedures and avoid procedures that are punitive. Showing interest in student's personal lives and passions and integrating them into both daily conversations and classroom assignments is another way for a student to feel they are seen by their teacher. Taking the time to talk and work through problems is another way to develop a sense of relatedness between teachers and students.

There may be teachers, especially at the middle and high school levels, who have so many students that it is difficult to develop the one-on-one relationship discussed in the previous paragraph. There is a second way relatedness can manifest in the classroom. Students can feel this sense of connection with the *content* that is being learned. A student who is motivated to learn about a particular topic will make a connection to it, fulfilling this ingredient for motivation.

Must a student like a teacher in order to learn from them? Not necessarily. But I think the bigger question is this: if students don't relate to a teacher, will they *want* to learn from that teacher? Will they feel motivated to do what that teacher asks?

CLD learners have another obstacle to consider when it comes to developing a sense of connection with their teachers. In the United States, there is a big gap between the racial diversity of the students in our schools and the educators who serve them. The National Center for Educational Statistics found that 51 percent of all students in elementary and secondary school in the United States in 2015 were non-White (National Center for Education Statistics 2017a). Meanwhile, only 20 percent of teachers come from culturally or ethnically diverse backgrounds (National Center for Education Statistics 2017b). Taking the intersectionality of race and twice-exceptionality into consideration helps create the foundation for developing a solid relationship.

CLD students who've experienced racism or microaggressions may be cautious about trusting the adults in power, especially if those adults are part of the majority culture. Some teachers may unintentionally create barriers through statements and expectations that are based on middle-and-upper-income White cultural norms. For example, many students from CLD backgrounds have to code-switch between their home and school environment. Code-switching occurs when a certain dialect or syntax is used in one environment but it isn't considered acceptable in another environment. For example, it may be acceptable for Black students to use the slang word *finna* (meaning "fixing to" or "going to") in casual settings; however, there is an expectation to use formal English in the academic setting. If educators discipline students who struggle to code-switch, they may be missing an opportunity to connect with a student on a personal level and undermining the potential for a student to trust them in the future. Cultural awareness and training helps teachers establish a classroom structure that feels safe and trustworthy for all students.

Twice-exceptional learners are vulnerable to experiencing disconnection at school. Many teachers don't understand 2e students or know how to work with them. Without a baseline understanding of these students' educational and psychological needs, teachers may inadvertently place unrealistic expectations on them. When students perceive a teacher as cold, distant, indifferent, or critical, they are less likely to cultivate a relationship with the teacher. This disconnect can hinder student motivation.

Self-Actualization and Motivation

Abraham Maslow was a psychologist who created a developmental model to understand the path humans take toward reaching their potential (self-actualization). One of his main contributions to the field of psychology is called Maslow's hierarchy of needs. Maslow described the needs all humans have and how certain needs are built upon others. The base level of Maslow's hierarchy (which is pictured as a pyramid) describes physiological needs as the foundational needs all humans must meet first—sleep, food, and shelter, to name a few. The level above physiological needs describes needs associated with helping a person feel safe, such as economic security and safety from physical harm. Above this level is love and belonging, and above that is esteem. Esteem is the level we associate with academic learning—feeling confident, being able to take cognitive risks, and feeling respected by others. The top of the pyramid is self-actualization, with skills related to morality and creativity.

Maslow is often cited when educators talk about social and emotional needs. It is extremely important when providing a trauma-informed educational setting to be cognizant of the needs at the bottom of the pyramid. Does the child feel safe at home and at school? Are their physiological needs met or do they experience food or housing insecurity? Awareness of and support for these needs is a vital component of providing a trauma-informed school environment. To connect this with our discussion about 2e learners, though, let's look at the pinnacle for a moment: self-actualization.

Self-actualization is the desire to become the most that one can. It is easy to see the link between self-actualization and motivation. When we are motivated, we are working to become the best we can be. I think there is a common misconception that self-actualization is some type of place we reach, like the monk meditating on the top of the mountain. A more realistic view of self-actualization is that it's the *process of seeking* that pinnacle—the constant effort to align our life with our desires and values.

When we give students the opportunity to drive their own lives and learning, we enable them to become self-actualized. The three components of intrinsic motivation in self-determination theory—autonomy, competence, and relatedness—are also components of self-actualization. (See **figure 4-6**.)

Figure 4-6 Maslow's Hierarchy of Needs and Self-Determination Theory

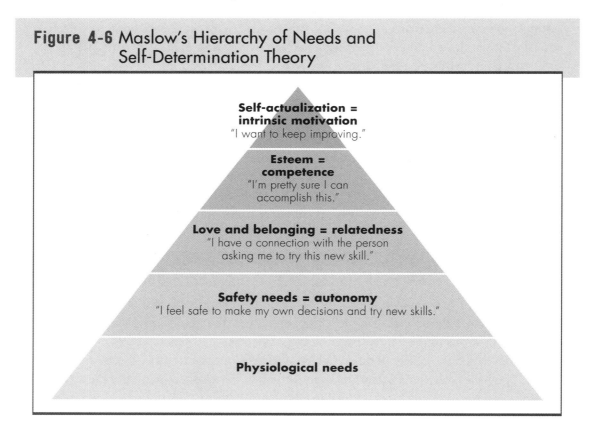

Self-actualization = intrinsic motivation
"I want to keep improving."

Esteem = competence
"I'm pretty sure I can accomplish this."

Love and belonging = relatedness
"I have a connection with the person asking me to try this new skill."

Safety needs = autonomy
"I feel safe to make my own decisions and try new skills."

Physiological needs

LISA'S STORY

I started working with Lisa when she was in middle school. She was strong-willed and struggled with emotional regulation. After we'd worked together for some time, Lisa was diagnosed with ADHD and generalized anxiety disorder.

When Lisa entered high school, she began refusing to go to school. The combination of feeling overwhelmed by work she hadn't completed and the feeling that nobody understood her paralyzed her in the mornings. She complained of frequent stomachaches and headaches, manifestations of her underlying anxiety.

Lisa experienced many peaks and valleys throughout her high school years. She would get back on track and have several weeks of excellent attendance, homework completion, and test scores. Then something would set her back. Often it was being called out by a teacher in front of her peers for forgetting something or talking over the teacher. This triggered her anxiety and undermined her relationship with the teacher. Although her 504 plan said that any disciplinary conversations should be conducted in private, her teachers rarely remembered this accommodation. She didn't look like a student with unique learning needs because her ability masked her struggles. Once Lisa's relationship with a teacher was damaged, it was practically impossible to recover, and Lisa's willingness to invest time or energy in completing work for the class evaporated.

Lisa's school counselor noticed this pattern and worked on Lisa's schedule to put her in classes with teachers who either had already built rapport with Lisa or were known for having strong relationships with students. To help improve relationships on Lisa's end, she and I worked on her own skills to self-advocate and express vulnerability instead of shutting down. ■

Praise, Rewards, and Punishments

The academic system in North America has rewards baked into it. Grades are a reward for good work. Then we have class rewards (fill a jar with marbles for a class prize), individual rewards (earn a sticker for every 100 percent on a spelling test or clip up for good behavior), and schoolwide awards (Math Student of the Year). Verbal praise is another kind of reward. ("Great job on your science test!" or "I really like the way Jenae is sitting quietly at her desk.")

All these rewards are well-meaning, and let's be honest: we're not going to get rid of them. But it is important to be aware of the impact of praise and rewards and use them constructively. Inappropriate praise can hamper a child's motivation, especially when it focuses on a child's inherent ability instead of their effort. Rewards are often unnecessary to motivate people of any age and can even diminish motivation in the long run.

Quite often, the default when working with an identified 2e learner is to emphasize the progress they are making. We should consider the value of offering this kind of praise or reward. Many times, praise and rewards come from a position of power. How does praise offered from a teacher impact a child's feelings of autonomy, competence, and relatedness? Consider the two scenarios in Cassidy's story.

CASSIDY'S STORY

Cassidy was a gifted fourth grader with dysgraphia. She struggled with fine-motor skills and putting her thoughts into words, and therefore had trouble initiating writing assignments. During writer's workshop, she got frustrated and completed a few sentences while many students in her class completed their entire first draft.

Scenario 1: Her teacher, recognizing Cassidy's frustration, stopped at her desk to offer feedback: "Nice job, Cassidy. You're making progress." Cassidy appreciated the kindness, but the comment did not help her. Cassidy did not feel independent or competent because she saw the other students around her making much more progress while she kept getting stuck. Her teacher's kind words actually reduced Cassidy's feeling of connection. Cassidy wondered why her teacher didn't recognize how hard this was for her or seem to think she needed any help.

Scenario 2: Her teacher, recognizing Cassidy's struggle, asked Cassidy to come to her desk for a conference. The teacher asked Cassidy some clarifying questions before offering any feedback: "What do you like about the piece you are writing so far? What are you having trouble with? How can I help?" The teacher offered several options for assistance. This brief interaction allowed Cassidy to provide her own self-praise by allowing her to reflect on what she was doing well, fostering a sense of competence. Her teacher gave her autonomy to determine what would help her the most. Cassidy felt connected to the teacher, who was taking time to help Cassidy reflect on her work. ◼

The difference between these two scenarios is subtle. Neither is a "bad" interaction between a teacher and student. The second scenario, though, empowers the student to become more motivated and less dependent on the teacher. It puts Cassidy in charge of her own learning, instead of relying on her teacher. If we rely on rewards to lure students to the finish line, the student doesn't learn how to get there independently, or know where to go once they arrive. And we are stuck in a loop of providing rewards and praise, without motivating the student to pursue success without us.

We are teachers for a reason. We want to help our students, and seeing students struggle triggers an innate urgency to fix the problem. (If you are a parent or guardian, you can probably relate to this sentiment within a family context too.) Giving verbal praise or tangible rewards may help in the short term, but it doesn't teach the skills necessary for students to self-regulate and self-motivate.

Here's the thing: rewards and punishments don't work—at least not for long. Compliance earned by bribery or punishment may help in the short term, but they foster a sense of dependence (external regulation).

Here's the other thing: many behavior systems—colored cards, clip charts, emojis, ClassDojo, and so on—focus on rewards and punishments. One thing I learned during my years in the classroom is that the only kids who comply with these systems are the ones who don't need them. The kids who are going to follow directions when you ask them to clip down probably would have complied with a brief conversation and redirection.

For 2e kids, these systems are often the most strictly enforced and the least effective. For a kid who struggles to self-regulate, it's better to focus on microgoals and

HOW TO SPICE UP YOUR PRAISE

Effective praise is a useful way to provide feedback to students, but make sure you aren't undermining your own efforts by giving ineffective praise. The acronym **SPICE** can help you remember how to deliver effective praise.

S — sincere: Authentic praise comes from a place of genuine appreciation and recognition of a job well done. Twice-exceptional students who already have poor self-concepts are skeptical of praise and will recognize when it is undeserved. Insincere praise can undermine trust in your relationship with the student and have the opposite of the effect you'd hoped for.

P — personal: Focusing the content of your praise on the obstacles a specific student has overcome is meaningful because it relates directly to the growth that student has made. Praise that compares a student's achievement to others can feed into a fixed mindset and a belief that if they aren't always succeeding at levels higher than those around them, they are failures.

I — fostering independence: Offering praise as a student is learning a new skill can be encouraging. Students generally need less praise as they become more proficient at a skill. Praise for a skill the child is already adept at completing feels fake and can cause the student to rely heavily on praise, even on tasks they should be able to accomplish independently.

C — consistent: Twice-exceptional learners may have difficulty interpreting communication, so praise that is direct and tied to a specific action and is given in a timely manner (as soon as possible after the task is completed) can help reinforce your specific expectations. If you offer praise nonverbally (such as with a nod or a thumbs-up), it can be helpful to precede using this communication with a brief conversation about what the communication means.

E — emphasizing effort: For a student who is struggling, the attempt of a new task may be the biggest obstacle they face. Twice-exceptional students may not have control over the outcome of a test or assignment because of their disability. They *do,* however, have volition over the amount of effort they use. (Note: there are times when 2e students can't control their effort, such as when they are emotionally dysregulated.) When you emphasize effort, you empower kids to keep trying.

---

metacognition to build awareness than to take away their recess. (For more on microgoals and metacognition, see chapter 5.) Lean on the 2e student's cognitive strengths. Bringing them into the problem-solving process builds independence and confidence.

Remember that rewards and punishments are two sides of the same coin. Not earning a reward often feels like a punishment. Giving one student a reward often means withholding this reward from another student or students. If we give a reward for a behavior once, kids may feel slighted if the reward isn't offered the next time.

We also have to remember that 2e learners' struggles are part of who they are. A child with ADHD is going to struggle with executive functioning—and no sticker chart will make that go away. No autistic student is going to be bribed out of their neurological wiring. We shouldn't ask students to change who they are; instead, we need to help them figure out learning strategies that work for them.

What's My Motivation?

You can use the reproducible forms on pages 92–98 to facilitate a discussion about the types of motivation each student feels and to help them evaluate their motivations in various situations. When students understand the varying levels of motivation, they can self-evaluate when they feel disengaged. This self-evaluation leads to a greater level of self-awareness, which in turn helps students persevere.

Here's how to use the reproducible forms with your students:

- **Types of Motivation (Grades 5 and Up) (page 92):** Introduce the types of motivation. Discuss the differences. Each type of motivation is linked with a kid-friendly word or phrase to help students remember the driving force behind it. Using these words instead of the official names will help students understand them.

- **Types of Motivation (Grades 1 to 4) (page 93):** Modified for younger students, this chart includes only four levels of motivation with an example of each. Using the kid-friendly terminology will help students remember the different types of motivation. An image to help students with the concept is also provided for each type.

- **Motivation Scenarios (Grades 5 and Up) (page 94):** Cut the scenarios into separate cards. Use the scenarios to facilitate a discussion, with students drawing a card and identifying which level of motivation the scenario describes. Answers are not included because there may be more than one way to arrive at an answer. Allow students to defend their responses.

- **Motivation Scenarios (Grades 1 to 4) (page 95):** Read the scenarios with students. Students circle the level of motivation they believe fits the situation. Discuss with students how they reached their responses. A copy of scenarios and descriptions of the level of motivation appropriate for each precedes the reproducible.

- **Motivation Evaluation (Grades 5 and Up) (page 97):** Have students evaluate their own motives and interests to identify situations in which they feel varying levels of motivation.

- **Motivation Evaluation (Grades 1 to 4) (page 98):** Have students evaluate their own motives and interests to identify situations in which they feel varying levels of emotion. Students may write sentences or draw, depending on their ability.

Key Points

- Twice-exceptional kids often are labeled as unmotivated because adults around them don't understand their unique needs. Explicit teaching about motivation can help students better understand themselves and find ways to harness their interests or goals into actionable steps.

- Goal orientation theory is the basis for growth and fixed mindsets. Twice-exceptional students benefit from working toward performance goals focused on progress instead of mastery goals that may be based on grade-level expectations.

- Attribution theory of motivation examines how a student accounts for their successes and failures and whether they see them as influenced by things inside or outside their control.

- Self-determination theory of motivation breaks intrinsic and extrinsic motivation into levels, recognizing that most situations are not completely intrinsic or extrinsic. In self-determination theory, the three key components of intrinsic motivation are autonomy, competence, and relatedness.

Types of Motivation (Grades 5 and Up)

Feeling motivated means that you want to do something. The reasons for wanting to do something can change from person to person. Sometimes people are motivated because of their own thoughts and wants. Other times, they are motivated by forces outside themselves.

Level 6: PASSION	**Intrinsic motivation** is when you want to do something because you love to do it. Doing the activity is its own reward.
Level 5: BONUS!	**Integrated regulation** is when you want to do something you enjoy and there is a bonus of some external positive outcome.
Level 4: GOING FOR A GOAL	**Identified regulation** is when you may not especially enjoy an activity, but you do understand and value the benefits that come from doing it.
Level 3: SOCIAL EXPECTATIONS	**Introjected regulation** is when you know you have to do something because it is expected, even though it isn't something important to you.
Level 2: PRIZES AND PUNISHMENTS	**External regulation** is when you do something either because you are going to get a reward (like a prize or recognition) or because you want to avoid a punishment (like a detention).
Level 1: JUST DON'T CARE	**Amotivation** is a total lack of motivation. Even if there were a reward or punishment, you wouldn't be motivated to do it.

Types of Motivation (Grades 1 to 4)

MOTIVATION is the feeling you get inside when you WANT to do something. Sometimes we are motivated to do things; sometimes we do them even though we don't really want to. Here are some of the different ways people can feel motivated.

Level 4: **LOVE** "I'm doing this because I love it!"		Pablo loves building with Lego blocks and spends hours doing it for fun.
Level 3: **GOAL** "I don't really like doing this, but I decided to keep doing it because it will help me reach a goal."		Greta doesn't like to clean her room, but she wants to paint her room a new color, and she knows keeping it clean will help her convince her parents to let her redecorate.
Level 2: **HAVE-TOs** "I don't want to do this, but my teacher or parents tell me I have to do it."		Pranav has trouble getting ready on time in the morning. His mom told him if he gets ready on time, she'll give him a sticker, and when he has ten stickers, he can have a playdate. He isn't really motivated to get ready faster, but he does want to have a playdate!
Level 1: **DON'T CARE** "There is no way I want to do that."		When Rubi's mom signed her up to play on a soccer team, Rubi told her mom she did not want to play soccer. Even though her mom tried to give her a reward for trying a new sport, there was no way to convince Rubi to give the sport a try.

Motivation Scenarios (Grades 5 and Up)

Charles loves Legos. They are the main thing he requests for gifts and he spends many hours at home assembling and creating Lego structures.	Clarissa is an okay student and does pretty well on tests, even though grades aren't important to her. Her parents know she is smart and expect her to get A's and B's on her report card, so she works to keep her grades at that level.	Orlando earns video game time based on his behavior at school. If he has a positive report from his teacher, he gets extra time that evening to play his favorite video game.
Briella really likes to cook, but she doesn't like cleaning up. Her parents tell her if she doesn't clean up after herself, she can't cook anymore. Cooking is important enough to her that she makes sure to clean up after herself.	Malachi thinks the homework he is assigned for his math class is boring and pointless. His parents, however, expect him to get all his work turned in on time, so he makes sure to do it.	Ben likes learning about biology, but he struggles on his tests. Through trial and error, he has learned that rewriting his notes into outline form is one of the best ways for him to review what he has learned for the tests. It takes a lot of time and is pretty boring, but it is worth it because it helps him do well in the class.
Weight training isn't exactly Dania's idea of fun, but she loves swimming and has been swimming competitively since she was seven years old. Dania goes to weight training twice a week because she knows it will help her as a swimmer.	It might sound weird, but Haley really likes to help clean the house. Vacuuming is fun for her, and organizing things feels like a problem-solving game. Haley would clean the house even if she weren't asked, but the allowance she gets is nice.	Jayde spends hours creating keychains and bracelets. She finds the activity relaxing. She sells the items to her family and friends, using some of the money for savings and the rest for more supplies.
Ever since Brayden learned how to play Minecraft, it has been his favorite game. He chooses to play it more than any other video game and plays it every day.	It doesn't bother Tariq when his room is a mess, but his parents tell him he has to keep his room clean. He takes time each night to pick up his clothes and organize his desk.	Claudia's favorite subject is history. She reads about historical events and watches tons of videos on historical people. She has found this information useful at school and always gets A's in her history class.
Elizabeth paints or draws every single day. She loves to look back on the artwork she has created and see how much progress she has made over the years.	Samir was really burnt out on playing baseball. After playing for several years, he just didn't enjoy it anymore. His parents and teammates tried to convince him to play another season, but he still didn't feel like playing.	Jesse was not a morning person. Even though his parents tried everything to get him to wake up on his own so he wouldn't be late, he just wasn't worried about it.

Motivation Scenarios (Grades 1 to 4)

Read each scenario. Circle the level of motivation you think fits for each.

Orlando earns video game time based on his behavior at school. If he has a positive report from his teacher, he gets extra time that evening to play his favorite video game.	Level 4: LOVE  Level 3: GOAL Level 2: HAVE-TO Level 1: DON'T CARE
Briella really likes to cook, but she doesn't like cleaning up. Her parents tell her if she doesn't clean up after herself, she can't cook anymore. Cooking is important enough to her that she makes sure to clean up after herself.	Level 4: LOVE  Level 3: GOAL Level 2: HAVE-TO Level 1: DON'T CARE
Ever since Brayden learned how to play Minecraft, it has been his favorite game. He chooses to play it more than any other video game and plays it every day.	Level 4: LOVE  Level 3: GOAL Level 2: HAVE TO Level 1: DON'T CARE
Jesse was not a morning person. Even though his parents tried everything, like giving prizes or grounding him, to get him to wake up on his own so he wouldn't be late, he just wasn't worried about it.	Level 4: LOVE  Level 3: GOAL Level 2: HAVE-TO Level 1: DON'T CARE

TEACHER KEY:

Note: Scenarios may have multiple possible responses; responses provided are examples only. Allow students to justify their responses.

....

Orlando

Orlando earns video game time based on his behavior at school. If he has a positive report from his teacher, he gets extra time that evening to play his favorite video game.

Level 2: have-tos—Orlando isn't in control of whether or not he earns his reward.

....

Briella

Briella really likes to cook, but she doesn't like cleaning up. Her parents tell her if she doesn't clean up after herself, she can't cook anymore. Cooking is important enough to her that she makes sure to clean up after herself.

Level 3: goal—Briella is determining her own effort to pursue something she enjoys.

....

Brayden

Ever since Brayden learned how to play Minecraft, it has been his favorite game. He chooses to play it more than any other video game and plays it every day.

Level 4: love—The activity is its own reward, and Brayden is self-motivated to do it.

....

Jesse

Jesse was not a morning person. Even though his parents tried everything, like giving prizes or grounding him, to get him to wake up on his own so he wouldn't be late, he just wasn't worried about it.

Level 1: don't care—Jesse's parents have tried to reward or punish him, but they can't seem to motivate him to improve.

Motivation Evaluation (Grades 5 and Up)

Student name:

Intrinsic motivation (PASSION)

Intrinsic motivation is when you want to do something because you love to do it. Doing the activity is its own reward.	Example: Abigail was motivated to research and learn about horses because it was a topic she really loved.	When do you show intrinsic motivation?

Integrated regulation (BONUS!)

Integrated regulation is when you want to do something you enjoy and there is a bonus of some external positive outcome.	Example: Terra really loved to write and felt an internal drive to write often. Her writing earned very good grades in language arts too.	When do you show integrated regulation?

Identified regulation (GOING FOR A GOAL)

Identified regulation is when you may not especially enjoy an activity, but you do understand and value the benefits that come from doing it.	Example: James collected Pokémon cards and was always trying to collect more. He volunteered to do extra chores at home to earn money to purchase more.	When do you show identified regulation?

Introjected regulation (SOCIAL EXPECTATIONS)

Introjected regulation is when you know you have to do something because it is expected, even though it isn't something important to you.	Example: Payton knew that his parents expected him to do his homework and his teachers expected him to turn it in every day, so he did it, even though he thought it was kind of a waste of time.	When do you show introjected regulation?

External regulation (PRIZES AND PUNISHMENTS)

External regulation is when you do something either because you are going to get a reward or because you want to avoid a punishment.	Example: Xavier worked quietly on his assignment because he didn't want his name written on the board. Also, he knew if he finished early, he'd get a piece of candy.	When do you show external regulation?

Amotivation (JUST DON'T CARE)

Amotivation is a total lack of motivation. Even if there were a reward or punishment, you wouldn't be motivated to do it.	Example: Madison didn't like cleaning her room and avoided it altogether, even though she knew she might get in trouble for not doing it. It didn't bother her that her room was messy.	When do you show amotivation?

Motivation Evaluation (Grades 1 to 4)

Name: _____

Write a sentence or draw a picture that shows an activity that goes into each category for you.

Level 4: LOVE "I'm doing this because I love it!" 	What is something you do because you love it?
Level 3: GOAL "I don't really like doing this, but I decided to keep doing it because it will help me reach a goal." 	What is something you do because it helps you get closer to reaching a goal?
Level 2: HAVE-TOs "I don't want to do this, but my teacher or parents tell me I have to do it." 	What is something you do because someone will give you a prize for it or because someone tells you to do it?
Level 1: DON'T CARE "There is no way I want to do that." 	What is something you choose not to do, even though others might want you to do it?

Many twice-exceptional learners have a habit of goal vaulting. Gifted kids often learn easily, so just before they reach a goal they've set, they raise the bar for themselves. When they get close to that higher goal, they raise the bar again. The long-term effect of goal vaulting is that students feel like they're always striving but never achieving—meanwhile ignoring all the work they've done and all the progress they've made. It leads to a sense of stagnation and lack of accomplishment (Webb et al. 2007). That's why goal-setting is a vital part of working with 2e students. Effective goal-setting helps students crystallize their progress and recognize the work it took to get there. Whether you are working with them to monitor their progress toward an academic goal, to build self-regulation, or to develop goals to include in an IEP, set collaborative and appropriate targets and benchmarks.

ANDREW'S STORY

Andrew had musical abilities well beyond his years. He'd begun playing piano in early elementary school and trombone in middle school. Now in high school, Andrew was the only freshman with a solo in marching band, and he was first chair in the concert band. He also played in an elite traveling jazz band. Despite these accomplishments, he consistently felt frustrated when he came across a new skill or piece of music that posed some difficulty. He would slip into negative thinking, helplessness, and depression.

First, I worked with Andrew to reflect backward from his current level of success. This helped him see the goals he'd already vaulted past and reminded him of all the work he'd already done. Next, we broke down his future goals into microgoals and set up a plan to measure his progress. The first microgoal we established focused on cognitive flexibility to manage his uncomfortable emotions. Each day Andrew practiced his music, he rated each of three factors: How new is the piece of music to him? How well did he feel the practice went? How comfortable or uncomfortable were his emotions after he finished practicing? When Andrew and I examined this data for patterns, it helped him realize in a concrete way that the more he practiced and the more familiar he become with a piece of music, the less frustration he felt. This was much more effective than simply giving Andrew strategies to reframe his thinking or calm his emotions; it allowed him to assess the situation independently and gain some objectivity to overcome his frustration and feelings of inadequacy. ■

Motivation and goal-setting are inherently linked. Motivation is the drive to move toward a goal; goal-setting is clarifying the goal and establishing concrete steps to reach it. Students who see a clear path before them feel empowered and accountable. By contrast, students who cannot see a clear path toward a specific goal feel anxious. Combining a strength-based approach (see chapter 2) with an understanding of motivation (see chapter 4) provides a framework for goal-setting and progress monitoring.

Goal-setting is an inherently strength-based intervention for 2e kids. Students who are global thinkers and need to understand the reason for doing a task before they buy in benefit from recognizing the larger aim and breaking the task into manageable pieces. Logical and divergent thinkers alike will thrive when asked to brainstorm ideas for steps that can help them move toward self-improvement. When you work on student goal-setting using the model in this chapter, you integrate the three components necessary for intrinsic motivation as defined by self-determination theory: autonomy, competence, and relatedness.

If you are a teacher involved in writing IEP goals, you are already ahead of the game. IEP goals are very specific and relate directly to a student's needed area of growth. We're going to simplify this style of goal-setting just enough that teachers in all settings can use it daily and students can learn to self-monitor their progress.

Effective IEP Goals for 2e Learners

In chapter 1, we discussed the identification of 2e learners and the difficulties schools and families face in assessing them. The IEP team at a school may agree that a student needs additional support but may have trouble defining exactly what the goal should be for a student who is already performing at grade level. Special educators and administrators are trained to go strictly by the book when it comes to special education identification, due to the laws surrounding compliance. Meanwhile, gifted education facilitators often have little to no training in IEP development. Writing IEP goals for 2e learners requires some outside-the-box thinking and unique planning to determine how special education minutes can be best spent.

An IEP team should focus on the progress that can be made by a 2e student based on their established ability and achievement, rather than on bringing them up to grade level. A child with an IQ of 140 and a reading achievement standard score of 102 has a 38-point discrepancy between ability and achievement. Although the achievement number shows a child who is reading at grade level, the discrepancy shows an unrecognized and unsupported learning disability that can cause great frustration.

One of the biggest struggles faced by teachers and IEP teams is determining appropriate goals for 2e students. How do you set an IEP goal for a student with dyslexia whose reading skills are in the average range? It helps to look at the student's specific areas of struggle. Sometimes test scores don't paint the full picture. It can also help to be creative with what services might look like for the student. How many minutes of service do they really need? Who could provide those minutes? (In chapters 7 through 13 of this book, we will discuss possible IEP goals for 2e learners with specific diagnoses.)

Many 2e students, including students with an IEP based on an educational diagnosis of other health impairment (OHI), may specifically benefit from an IEP goal tailored for developing soft skills. Many 2e students who receive services under an OHI diagnosis have a medical diagnosis such as ADHD or ASD but don't qualify for services elsewhere. Their learning is significantly hindered by the deficits associated with their medical diagnosis, although they may not need a goal focused solely on academic skills. For example, a goal based on an executive function skill, such as response inhibition, might involve a student waiting their turn when they're playing a game or standing in line for an activity. Focusing IEP goals on these types of skills can not only give struggling students the skills they need, but also the supports provided through an IEP.

CAYDENCE'S STORY

Caydence excelled in her high school math and science classes. A 2e student with a diagnosis of ASD and SLD in written expression, Caydence and her parents opted not to enroll her in the honors English class. However, the general education English class was not a great match either. The reading done in the class was boring for her. Although the writing expectations were manageable for her skill level, she began struggling because she wasn't engaged in the content. Her strengths and struggles combined to hinder her success.

At her parents' request, the IEP team reconvened. What options existed to support Caydence based on her unique learning profile? The IEP team determined that Caydence's giftedness was keeping her from learning as expected in the typical classroom setting and wrote a provision into the IEP that Caydence would participate in an individualized program for her language arts class. Collaboration between her special education and language arts teachers resulted in a modified curriculum, providing appropriately challenging content with writing at a level appropriate for her needs. Caydence spent most of her language arts time in her case manager's classroom, working independently on her unique curriculum. She engaged in her own goal-setting and progress monitoring to assess how well she was learning. The IEP team's flexibility and creativity helped Caydence find individualized strength-based success. ■

Student-Led Microgoals

When I'm working with students and their parents or guardians, I typically ask them what their goals are. What do they want to work on? What do they want to achieve? The responses I get are often vague: "I want my kid to be a hard worker" or "I want to get good grades." These big-picture goals are an excellent starting point—they establish a vision—but they aren't actionable.

Even SMART goals (goals that are specific, measurable, attainable, relevant, and timely) are sometimes too broad for our purposes. While we will integrate several of these concepts into creating microgoals for students, SMART goals tend to be longer-term goals. Microgoals are the action steps that lead to achieving a SMART goal. They are the goals that students can complete in a single day or week. Microgoals use self-monitoring, self-evaluation, and self-regulation. They are fluid—if a microgoal is not working, we change it! We're constantly tweaking microgoals through the metacognitive cycle. This helps students understand that they are responsible for making their own progress. (See **figure 5-1**.)

Figure 5-1 Hierarchy of Goals

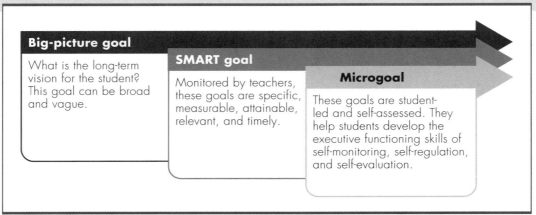

Big-picture goal
What is the long-term vision for the student? This goal can be broad and vague.

SMART goal
Monitored by teachers, these goals are specific, measurable, attainable, relevant, and timely.

Microgoal
These goals are student-led and self-assessed. They help students develop the executive functioning skills of self-monitoring, self-regulation, and self-evaluation.

Because students are going to be measuring their progress independently (or perhaps with a teacher as backup), we want them to be part of the goal-setting process. I find that framing all goals as a data-collection process is a great way to get away from the idea of succeeding or failing at a task. I say something like, "We're going to think of ourselves as scientists. We're going to try this method, collect some data, and see if it works." This reduces the fear of failing students may have. It also steers the conversation toward the idea of continual progress as the ultimate measure of growth and away from a black-and-white, pass-fail mentality.

Microgoals are:

- set collaboratively
- process oriented
- student tracked
- fluid
- intrinsically driven

Here are a few examples of microgoals:

- I can monitor and reduce the number of times I speak out in class without being called on.
- I will increase the number of minutes I stay on task during writer's workshop.
- I can track how often I volunteer to share during class discussions.
- I will reduce the number of errors made because I rushed and didn't check my work.
- I can improve my spelling grade by studying for ten minutes every night with my flash cards.

The Metacognitive Cycle

Metacognition is thinking about one's own thinking. Many gifted learners begin to do this at a young age compared to their peers. My own 2e daughter was asking at four years old what it would be like to live in somebody else's head and hear what they were thinking. She also asked why her own brain always made her worry.

Twice-exceptional learners will benefit from learning about metacognition as a skill. Metacognition is a natural process, but explicit instruction in what it is and how to use it can be a powerful change agent. The metacognitive cycle gives an opportunity to explore its usefulness in a variety of life's situations.

The underlying purpose of setting and working toward microgoals is to help students develop the skill of metacognition. Whether a student succeeds or fails at reaching their microgoal, they are engaging in metacognition. Metacognition is an executive functioning skill that is necessary for self-regulation.

When working toward reaching microgoals, I walk students through the metacognitive cycle. (See **figure 5-2**.) The metacognitive cycle focuses on three skills that are vital for 2e students: self-monitoring, self-evaluation, and self-regulation. When we work with students on changing behaviors and increasing success at school, we foster the growth of these three skills. Regardless of whether the microgoal is achieved, we are teaching students to think about what works for them, evaluate the effectiveness of their strategies, and modify their tactics.

Figure 5-2 The Metacognitive Cycle

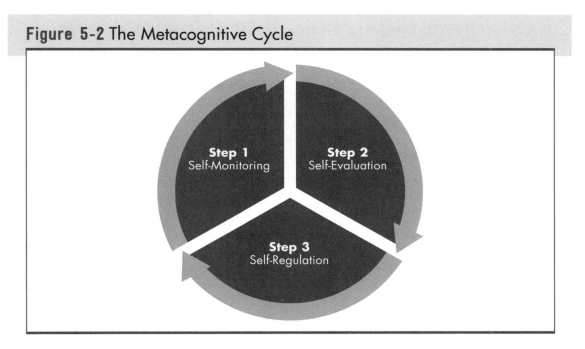

You may help a student track a microgoal by collaboratively monitoring progress with them, but microgoals are created by and for the students themselves. The first word of each of the steps is *self*. We want to harness self-determined motivation by including students intimately in the process. Setting a microgoal for a student and then evaluating the student based on your own observations takes away their autonomy. The most valuable aspect of a microgoal is the power it gives to the student. Microgoals teach students that they control their progress and they can monitor it on their own, judging their successes and struggles without adult approval.

STEP 1: SELF-MONITORING

Many of the microgoals that are helpful for 2e learners are related to their thinking and processing. Cognitive-behavioral interventions are based on awareness of our own thinking and the fact that we can shift and reframe our thoughts once we are aware of them. Building this awareness is an important step toward self-regulation. Some typical self-monitoring questions that may occur while brainstorming or revising microgoals are:

- How do I react when this happens?
- What else is happening when I do this behavior?
- How do I feel when I'm in this environment?
- When does this problem occur?
- How often does this happen?
- When I change the way I react, what happens?

STEP 2: SELF-EVALUATION

Self-evaluation is closely tied with self-monitoring. Students self-monitor when they reflect on their thoughts and behaviors and identify or quantify those thoughts and behaviors. Self-evaluation is taking it one step further and asking, "Is this working?" "What patterns do I see?" and "What can I do to make it better?"

Within the metacognitive cycle, there is always room for improvement. If a student is making progress toward their microgoal, we want to help them recognize what the next small step of progress looks like and how they can tweak what they are already doing to make it better. If they are struggling to meet the expectations they set, we can help them adjust the expectations to something more realistic. The self-evaluation step is essential to curtail goal vaulting. It also builds a sense of self-efficacy.

Here are some questions you can use to coach a student through self-evaluating a microgoal:

- Am I making the progress I expected?
- What is keeping me from making the progress I want?
- What changes should I make to my goal? Should I:
  - » raise or lower my expectations?
  - » modify the methods I'm using to achieve my goal?
  - » change my goal completely?

STEP 3: SELF-REGULATION

Humans are constantly self-regulating. We self-regulate our emotions, our motivation, our effort, and our interactions. All students need help learning how to self-regulate; 2e students generally need more help than their peers. Many of the struggles 2e students face are due to lagging executive functioning skills and asynchronous development. Self-regulation may not come as naturally to 2e kids as it does to other students.

Self-regulation is the decision-making step of the metacognitive cycle. After collecting data during the self-monitoring phase and assessing the effectiveness based on the data gathered during the self-evaluation stage, students determine the best way to change or regulate their patterns of behavior to move toward reaching their microgoal.

During the self-regulation step of the metacognitive cycle, a student may realize that the strategy they've been using isn't working and that they need to try a different method to reach their goal. They may realize that the specific skill being tracked during the first two steps is already going really well. Or they may realize that their microgoal isn't really the thing they need to focus on improving and change their microgoal entirely to focus more clearly on the area they wish to improve.

For some students, it may be beneficial to set a microgoal of tracking self-regulation. Tracking self-regulation is a basic step that helps students who aren't ready to track their progress on a more defined behavioral or academic goal. Think of this as step zero (before step one) for students who need it. This data collection helps students develop awareness of their levels of regulation.

Self-regulation data collection goals might include the following:

- tracking intensity of emotions at the beginning and end of a test

- tallying how often a student realizes they are off task during work time

- rating how much effort they put into a difficult assignment

- timing how long they are able to stay engaged with a task

Steps in Establishing a Student Microgoal

Have a coaching conversation with the student to gather the following information. Record it on the **My Microgoal** reproducible form (page 111). For a sample filled-out form, see **figure 5-3**.

This form can be used for all ages. For students who are too young to complete the form themselves, you can scribe for them as you coach them through the process. Another easy modification is to limit the number of ideas or responses you try to brainstorm with each step.

1. **Start with the vision.** What is the big picture goal we are trying to achieve?

2. **List the small skills integral to reaching this goal.**

3. **Choose the skill the student would like to improve first.**

4. **Brainstorm steps for self-monitoring.** What actions can be taken right away to move toward this goal? Make sure these action steps are things that rely only on the student, or the student with an adult as backup. A student's ability to self-regulate this goal is vital.

5. **Designate the first action step to monitor.** What does the student feel is the best first step? Where does the student feel competent to succeed?

6. **Determine how to measure progress and how often to do so.** Let kids be creative! Whether it is using emojis or complicated numerical rankings, bright kids love coming up with their own methods to track their progress. This step helps develop

relatedness and autonomy—both necessary for the child to feel motivated. Here are a few 2e-friendly ways to quantify progress:

- » emojis
- » rankings on scale of 1 to 10
- » letter grades
- » symbols
- » percentages
- » check marks
- » yes-or-no questions
- » qualitative descriptions

7. **Schedule check-ins during coaching sessions with student.** Facilitate reflection and self-evaluation to determine the effectiveness of action steps and desired changes.

8. **Guide student through the self-evaluation process.** Ask the student to evaluate their progress based on the benchmark they set. Identify any unforeseen obstacles.

9. **Plan a strategy for the student to self-regulate.** Based on the information gathered, help the student identify what they need to change or keep the same to continue moving toward reaching their microgoal.

Troubleshooting Microgoals

Problem: My student won't engage in the process of setting a microgoal. He feels down about his struggles and doesn't think there's any way for him to improve. He consistently blames his teachers or his disability.

Strategy: Have a conversation with the student about his strengths. This is a good starting point for developing self-efficacy. Perhaps the microgoal could be developed around a strength the child has, working to increase the frequency he uses that skill (instead of reducing the frequency of an unwanted behavior). It is especially powerful when you can connect the strength with the struggle. For example, a child with ADHD might be a strong divergent thinker and could self-monitor how often they are able to add a new and relevant idea to a discussion. This goal is inherently tied to the child's strengths but will also work to support a struggle of getting off topic.

Problem: I've asked a child's classroom teacher to help track her progress, but follow-through is inconsistent—almost nonexistent. The student is too young to do this all on her own.

Strategy: Some teachers struggle to maintain consistency for a variety of reasons, whether they are in the general, gifted, or special education classroom. This is one reason why self-evaluation is so vital to setting and tracking microgoals. Have a conversation with the teacher to brainstorm more efficient self-monitoring methods that might work better for their classroom. If that doesn't work, modify the tracking process for the child. Maybe you check in more frequently, so the student doesn't need to monitor progress on her own for an extended period. Or maybe you change the tracking method. For example, an index card taped to the child's desk might eliminate an obstacle like remembering to get a chart out of a folder in their desk at the end of each day.

Figure 5-3 My Microgoal Sample

1. What is my big-picture vision or long-term goal?	**I want to get more organized.**

2. What building-block skills will help me move toward my big-picture goal?	a. **Keep my backpack and binder cleaned out.**
	b. **Start using a planner every day.**
	c. **Check before I leave that I have everything for my homework.**
	d.
	e.

3. Which skill above will I choose to improve as my first microgoal?	**b**

4. Self-monitoring: What action steps can I implement and track?	a. **Make sure I have my planner with me.**
	b. **Ask my teacher to sign my planner at the end of each day.**
	c. **Write down my assignments at the beginning of each class.**
	d. **Use my phone to take a picture of the assignments on the board.**
	e. **Look at the online portal if I forget to write in my planner.**

5. Which skill will I monitor first?	**c**

6. How will I measure my progress?	Measurement unit/scale: **Check marks on an index card each time I remember to write down my assignment.**
	Frequency of data collection: **During every class.**

I'll know I'm improving if:	**I have check marks for 4 out of 6 subjects every day.**	
Do I feel like . . .	. . . I can improve and measure my progress on my own? ☒ Yes ☐ No	. . . this is a skill that I have the ability to improve? ☒ Yes ☐ No

7. Scheduled check-in	Date/time: **Friday afternoons**

8. Self-evaluation: What does the data show? Is this strategy working?	**I was able to write down my assignments for most classes and met the goal of 4/6 subjects per day. I notice I usually don't get it written down in algebra. I think this is because algebra is right after lunch and I am often late getting to class. This is also the class that is affecting my grade point average the most.**
9. Self-regulation: What do I need to change to keep moving toward my goal?	**I need to change my routine for writing down my assignment in algebra. I am going to continue monitoring how often I write down my assignments, but I'm going to set an alarm on my phone to remind me 2 minutes into algebra to write down my assignment.**

Problem: My student keeps wanting to change his microgoal. Every coaching session we have, he insists the current goal isn't really what is going to help him or that he already knows how to do it.

Strategy: Bring the conversation back to the vision and larger SMART goal. If the student agrees that these are goals worth reaching, there ought to be a way to find a microgoal that aligns with these. Sometimes a focus on the data collection necessary for the microgoal is a good start. You may suggest getting a benchmark of how often the student is able to do this skill and then analyzing where improvements can be made.

Problem: We are checking in on the microgoal, and although it looks like we're making progress on paper, overall it seems like little is changing in the classroom.

Strategy: Remember that the biggest benefit of setting microgoals is not necessarily achieving the goals themselves. Self-monitoring and self-evaluation facilitate change. Keep up the process and remember that change takes time.

Problem: I'm trying to work with a student in my class, but we can't get past her defiance and our poor relationship. Even after we've had a successful one-on-one conference, the microgoal goes out the window the minute she is expected to follow through on something. This leads to talking back or just ignoring basic classroom norms.

Strategy: It sounds like this student isn't ready for the goal that has been set and the focus needs to be on trust and understanding in the relationship. A more effective microgoal might be simply to track the frequency of outbursts and look for patterns of triggers or responses. Data collection in this situation may need to be more of a collaborative process, with the teacher gently guiding the process with nonjudgmental questions when her emotions are more regulated. For example: "Let's gather some data about when you were frustrated earlier. What did you notice?"

Problem: My student wants to know what they're going to get when they reach their goal. Should I give them a reward?

Strategy: Part of developing self-regulation skills is moving from extrinsic to intrinsic motivation. Giving rewards undermines any self-regulation the student is developing. Guiding the student to see progress as the reward itself is ideal. If a student wants to establish their own reward, which they implement independently based on their self-evaluation, this would be okay. (For example, if they feel they've reached a self-set benchmark, they put a sticker on their chart.) Any extrinsic component should be student-determined and student-implemented. If parents or guardians feel compelled to reward or punish based on the outcomes of the microgoal, remind them that regardless of whether students achieve their goals, they are building self-regulation skills.

Setting Up Self-Monitored Data Collection

Many 2e learners love complexity. For some, the more complicated things are, the better. Allowing free rein for students' creativity can help keep them motivated through difficult tasks.

Maybe a student wants to track their on-task time. They're happy to record that information on a T-chart, but they also want to enter the data into a spreadsheet to make a graph. Go for it! Let's say a student with anxiety needs help monitoring when their psychosomatic symptoms are increasing, to reduce the amount of time they're out of the classroom. Emojis might be a great way to help monitor mood and symptoms and look for patterns. The student might use a tally chart, a checklist, a Likert scale, or code made from Pokémon symbols. As long as you take the time when you're setting the microgoal to establish what measurement method will be used and how it will be documented, it's all good.

Data tracking can be kept in a shared online folder, in a binder on the teacher's desk, or in an assignment notebook. There are also free apps available, if a student has access to their own smartphone or tablet. (Daylio is one of my favorites because of its flexibility and data-tracking capabilities.) It is helpful to keep old documents so students can look back through them and see the progress they've made over time. Even if the goal changes, even if one of the goals is considered unsuccessful, recognizing how far a child has come can foster their drive to move forward.

Rewards for Reaching Goals

Generally, kids are motivated by the fact that through the goal-setting process, they have autonomy, they feel competent, and they feel connected to you. They buy into the process, and the progress is its own reward. Microgoals help them move toward independence. But let's say you're sitting next to a student and brainstorming microgoals, and the student asks, "So what do I get when I reach my goal?" The trick here is to help the student remember that the point of microgoals is not to receive an external reward. The point is to help them solve a problem they are having. Redirect them to their big-picture goal and ask them to identify why that is their goal and why it is important to them. If they aren't connected to their big-picture goal (for example, if it is something they chose because they think it is something *someone else* wants), they should choose something different. Some kids may be very direct with their big-picture goal: "I want to get my homework turned in so my parents quit bugging me." Give them freedom to choose something that is meaningful to them.

Some people may ask if letting kids use stickers to track their progress is an extrinsic reward. Because kids are determining their own methods of measurement and engaging in self-evaluation, this practice is more intrinsic than extrinsic. The student is in charge of setting and monitoring the goal on their own. Instead of distributing stickers to the student when they've earned them, give the student a sheet of stickers to keep with their chart. This gives the power back to the student and removes you from the role of extrinsic motivator.

For many students, it makes sense to keep their families informed about the goal-setting process. Have a conversation with parents or guardians to help them understand that the microgoals process is more important than the outcome. Give them tips about how they can talk

WHAT IF A STUDENT ISN'T MOTIVATED BY ACADEMICS OR PERFORMANCE?

You can't convince a student to set an academic goal they don't think is important. If you try to convince a student to set a goal *you* think is important without their buy-in, you take away their autonomy.

Maybe the student has a goal they'd like to work toward for an activity outside school. Or maybe instead of an academic or behavioral goal, they'd like to focus on something related to their social and emotional development. Whatever it takes to get their buy-in is fine. You can use any goal as a starting point. The ultimate value of this process is helping students realize they can set goals and make improvements on their own.

Once a student begins to feel both autonomy and competence, you must do your part to keep a relationship going with the student. Check in with them frequently and ask if they want to tweak their goals. Help them reflect on recent events and figure out if there is something they'd like to work on. Your consistent presence and support builds feelings of efficacy. In the future, they may choose to work toward a goal they weren't willing to address earlier.

to their child about progress without undermining intrinsic motivation. For example, when parents are checking in about microgoals, they can ask about what patterns the student is noticing or if they've found any strategies that are helping, while avoiding offering rewards for reaching their goal by a certain point in time. Parents want to be as helpful as possible when they talk to their kids about schoolwork, especially when it is related to classroom behaviors or motivation. It's easy for them to get caught up in wanting things to happen quickly, but for 2e students, parents can really help by using non-judgmental reflective listening. Reassure parents that the process of setting microgoals, determining how to measure them, and engaging in self-evaluation builds longer-term self-regulation skills that will help in all areas of a student's life—including academics.

Integrating Self-Advocacy into Goal-Setting

Self-advocacy is the ability to speak up for oneself—to request assertively that one's needs get met. We can coach students to overcome the impulse to be too aggressive or too passive in their requests. If a student needs help in developing self-advocacy, this could be a microgoal for them to work toward.

Appropriate self-advocacy skills are extremely important for 2e kids, but they often don't come easily. Students with specific learning disabilities may avoid self-advocating because they feel like they're supposed to be "the smart ones." Students with perfectionism often hate asking for help in any form. Some students may be able to advocate strongly for themselves; however, they may not do so in a socially appropriate way. Teaching kids self-advocacy skills can prevent them from becoming demoralized by a learning environment that is too challenging or not challenging enough.

We can't be with students every minute of the day. Eventually, a time will come when 2e students need to know what their needs are and how to get them met. Deb Douglas' book *The Power of Self-Advocacy for Gifted Learners* provides a framework for teaching gifted students how to recognize their needs and get the help they need.

Key Points

- When you're considering IEP goals for 2e learners, find ways to use the resources available flexibly and creatively. Traditional methods alone often won't meet the needs of 2e learners.

- Using a framework of motivation taken from self-determination theory, you can work with students to develop autonomy through goal-setting. Microgoals are student-led, focusing on metacognition, self-regulation, and self-evaluation.

- Microgoals empower students who lack feelings of autonomy and competence. Microgoals also help students develop self-advocacy skills.

My Microgoal

Name: _____ **Date:** _____

1. What is my big-picture vision or long-term goal?	

2. What building-block skills will help me move toward my big-picture goal?	a.
	b.
	c.
	d.
	e.

3. Which skill above will I choose as my first microgoal?

4. Self-monitoring: What action steps can I implement and track?	a.
	b.
	c.
	d.
	e.

5. What skill will I monitor first?

6. How will I measure my progress?	Measurement unit/scale:
	Frequency of data collection:

I'll know I'm improving if:

Do I feel like . . .	. . . I can improve and measure my progress on my own? ☐ Yes ☐ No	. . . this is a skill that I have the ability to improve? ☐ Yes ☐ No

7. Scheduled check-in	Date/time:

8. Self-evaluation: What does the data show? Is this strategy working?	

9. Self-regulation: What do I need to change to keep moving toward my goal?	

6 Executive Functioning

Executive functioning is a set of processes we use to manage ourselves and our resources so we can achieve our goals. Executive functions are brain-based skills involving mental control and self-regulation. They help us pay attention, switch focus, multitask, manage time, plan and organize, remember details and instructions, avoid saying or doing the wrong thing, and do things based on experience.

When I'm working with students and describing executive functioning, I like to use the analogy of an orchestra. An orchestra is made up of many musicians playing many instruments, each with its own sound and its own notes. Students can imagine a bunch of musicians tuning their instruments, playing their own notes, practicing their scales, and sounding chaotic. These musicians represent the knowledge and skills we each have. When the conductor raises a baton and begins directing the musicians to play their notes together, we hear music instead of chaos. If a few of the musicians aren't watching the conductor and are out of time with the music or off-key—or, even worse, if the conductor never showed up—that problem is like executive functioning struggles. We need our executive functioning skills to bring all our other skills together and keep everything working in sync. If one executive functioning skill, such as organization, task initiation, or sustaining attention, isn't working, that can throw off the entire system.

I have given executive functioning its own chapter in this book because many 2e learners struggle with executive functions. It's easy to imagine that a disorganized and disheveled student with ADHD might have weak executive function skills. But so do 2e learners with other diagnoses. A child who has dyslexia may struggle with emotional self-regulation due to chronic frustration. An autistic student probably struggles with cognitive flexibility. Mental health diagnoses such as anxiety and mood disorders can hinder a child's ability to sustain their attention or manage their time. This chapter offers interventions that can work for many 2e students, regardless of diagnosis. Accommodations and modifications to daily classroom activities (see reproducible on page 120) are generally easy to implement and can ease the impact of executive function struggles.

Working with students on executive functioning is not a simple or quick undertaking. Students may have some strong executive function skills and some weak ones. For example, a student may have decent organizational skills but falter when it comes to response inhibition or sustaining attention. Adults often misattribute such struggles to a lack of motivation or a behavioral problem, when executive function skills are directly related to brain wiring and development. Addressing weaknesses proactively can help students greatly as they progress. Holding these students to the same expectations as their neurotypical peers without helping them learn executive function skills is setting them up for failure. While educators don't want to enable bad habits, providing a little extra support can go a long way. As students get older and expectations rise, students may continue to need support. Students with a mental health diagnosis, such as anxiety or depression, may not need long-term support if their symptoms are under control.

It is tempting to use rewards and punishments to handle student struggles with executive functioning. Relationship building and coaching are more effective tools to help these kids. Because of the way their brains are wired, they need explicit teaching and structure to build the habits necessary for academic success. A student who has a row of zeros in the grade book may recognize the need to improve their work completion but may lack the skills to do so independently. Remember: kids do well if they can.

Executive Function Skills

Executive function skills fall into two main categories: decision-making skills and behavioral regulation skills. Decision-making skills require a person to process information, plan, and make decisions. Behavioral regulation skills enable a student to manage their actions in a way that allows them to learn.

Figure 6-1 Executive Function Skills

Decision-Making Skills	Behavioral Regulation Skills
planning	response inhibition
organization	emotional self-regulation
time management	sustained attention
working memory	shifting focus
metacognition	task initiation
	cognitive flexibility
	task persistence

Decision-Making Skills

Decision-making skills might be the ones you're used to thinking about when somebody mentions executive function skills. When these skills lag, students tend to fall behind in their work. They can't manage their time, remember what work they have to do, or plan enough in advance to get things done.

- **Planning:** In chapter 2 on strength-based instruction, we discussed how many 2e learners are holistic or global thinkers who see the big picture easily but get bogged down in the details. Planning can be difficult for these students. It requires figuring out all the steps that must happen and in what order, as well as estimating how long those steps will take.

- **Organization:** Some people are naturally organized—they effortlessly develop a system to maintain their stuff—and others are not. The latter benefit from establishing a routine and sticking with it rather than trying to design and use an elaborate organizational system.

- **Time management:** We all have that one friend who needs to be told to arrive at an event at least twenty minutes early, so they'll actually be on time. That friend probably struggles with time management. Time management involves accurately estimating how long certain tasks will take and using the time available as efficiently as possible. Understanding the importance of deadlines and prioritizing tasks to meet them also fall within this skill.

- **Working memory:** Working memory is the amount of information we can hold in our short-term memory while we manipulate the information. Students who leave a classroom and glance at the board to see what the assignment is, believing they will remember the task at the end of the school day—only to completely forget there was an assignment at all—need tools to help support their working memory.

- **Metacognition:** In chapter 5, we discussed the importance of a student's ability to reflect on their own thinking as it relates to goal-setting. A student who is unorganized or having trouble with peers can't find ways to solve those problems unless they are able to engage in metacognition and identify the areas they need to adjust.

Behavioral Regulation Skills

Behavioral regulation skills are also part of executive functioning, although many people don't realize it. Students who struggle with behavioral regulation skills are at risk of being labeled troublemakers or lazy. When we examine these struggles within the context of executive function, we can better understand their cause and support students' needs.

- **Response inhibition:** Response inhibition is the ability to pause, consider options, and make decisions before acting. A student who impulsively calls out the answer before the teacher is finished asking the question or tosses a pen across the classroom to a friend is having trouble thinking before acting.

- **Emotional self-regulation:** This skill is the ability to respond appropriately to situations that provoke intense emotions. A student struggling to regulate their emotions may get upset when group work doesn't go their way or become silly and out of control when something exciting happens.

- **Sustained attention:** This skill involves being able to focus on a task and maintain that attention for an extended time. Struggles with sustained attention often appear when a child is engaged in a nonpreferred activity. (So, for example, being able to focus for a long time while playing a favorite video game is not a sign that a student *doesn't* struggle with sustained attention.) This skill can be difficult to study because it is used internally. If a learner doesn't show other outward signs of executive function deficits, a struggle with sustained attention may be missed.

- **Shifting focus:** This is the ability to switch focus from one task to another. Many students who struggle in this area appear to be hyperfocused. They have trouble wrapping up a task and may resist putting aside work that isn't complete. They may not even be aware that you are asking them to transition to a new topic or task.

- **Task initiation:** A packet of math problems is distributed to the class. A student who has trouble with task initiation may sit there and stare at the packet or engage in other activities rather than begin the task at hand. Struggles in this area may also involve procrastination when working on a larger project.

- **Cognitive flexibility:** Shifting one's expectations when plans change or transitioning easily from one activity to the next requires cognitive flexibility. Struggles with cognitive flexibility can manifest when a student is a rule follower and other students bend the rules. Emotional regulation skills are also often directly tied to cognitive flexibility. Many perfectionists have a hard time with cognitive flexibility, although their struggles may be situation specific.

- **Task persistence:** Once a task has been initiated, a student needs the ability to persist until it is complete. Being able to work on a project or assignment until it is finished requires a student to be engaged with the task and resist being pulled away by other interests.

ELI'S STORY

In sixth grade, Eli began to struggle for the first time. A gifted student diagnosed with inattentive ADHD in elementary school, Eli had been pretty well able to manage his symptoms with medication and basic accommodations. Things changed when he got to middle school. The rapid pace, switching classes multiple times throughout the day, coping with the expectations of different teachers, and the increased workload were too much for Eli to manage. His grades and his self-esteem began to suffer.

It wasn't the content that was too difficult for Eli. His abilities could no longer compensate for his weak executive function skills. He resorted to carrying his backpack between classes. His backpack was stuffed with books, notebook paper, and handouts—with no rhyme or reason to them whatsoever. His organization was only one part of the problem, though. He had a skewed concept of time. This led to difficulty estimating how long certain tasks would take and how to use his time efficiently. When adults coached him on ways to overcome these problems, he had trouble being flexible about new strategies and beginning the plans once they were made. Overall, his awareness of the problem and possible strategies to overcome it was weak.

Eli was struggling with several executive function skills: organization, time management, cognitive flexibility, task initiation, and metacognition. He began working with his school counselor, who created a structured, regular check-in for him. During these check-in meetings, they sorted out Eli's backpack, set microgoals, and monitored his progress to support his executive function deficits. Eli continued to need the support through middle school, but the check-ins became less frequent as he got on more stable footing. ■

Coaching Students with Executive Functioning Struggles

If a neurotypical person's brain continues developing until they're twenty-five years old, the brain of someone who has executive function deficits can be expected to take a little longer. Gifted students who aren't 2e may have their own executive functioning deficits because of their giftedness. Research published in the journal *Nature* describes how the development of the cortical thickness varies based on an individual's intelligence (Shaw et al. 2006). Younger children with IQs between 121 and 140 showed a thinner cortex later into their childhood when compared to average- and high-intelligence children. A thin cortex is associated with increased neuroplasticity and the ability to learn new material rapidly. The thickening of the cortex is necessary for the development of executive functioning skills, but because of the extended period of neuroplasticity in gifted children when they are younger, executive functioning skills may come online later for them than for their nongifted peers.

Because the neurological differences of students with executive function deficits are at the core of their struggles, they often need educators to serve temporarily as their surrogate prefrontal cortex, or "brain CEO." Students who need support with executive function skills benefit from individualized coaching. If you are a 2e student's general classroom teacher, gifted education teacher, special education teacher, or counselor, you are a good candidate to be the student's executive function coach.

Ideally, you will involve parents in supporting a child's executive functioning struggles, but bear in mind that these students may have parents who are dealing with their own executive function difficulties. The parents may need your help to learn how to support their children. Parents also may be unaware of the nature of executive functioning difficulties and need your reassurance that their children's struggles are not something they can discipline away.

So, what is involved in coaching a student with executive function struggles? It involves rapport building, systematic and explicit instruction, goal-setting with consistent check-ins to assess current needs and update accommodations, and schoolwide support:

- **Rapport building:** Students who struggle with executive functioning are bombarded with the message that they are poor students, unintelligent, and lazy. Let them know up front that working with you to build skills does not mean they have a character flaw. It simply means their brain functions differently and they need different tools than other kids need to show their potential.

- **Explicit instruction:** Identifying a student's specific areas of executive dysfunction is the next step of coaching. At the end of this chapter, you'll find a reproducible **Executive Functioning Self-Assessment Tool** (pages 122–125) you can use to help students reflect on their strengths and struggles. You could also use this tool as a starting point to develop a student-led microgoal. Choose one area to improve and teach the student the specific steps involved in using that skill.

- **Goal-setting:** Once a student has gained awareness of the specific areas where they struggle, setting goals and tracking data about those processes can help them overcome their struggles. See chapter 5 for an in-depth discussion about the benefits and the process of goal-setting.

- **Schoolwide support:** It takes a village to support a student. The time that you take to meet with a student is important, but getting their other teachers on board is critical to the student's success too. If the student is working to improve but finds that teachers are grading them based on their lagging executive function skills, eventually they will give up.

Does counseling work to help kids with executive function problems? Counseling based on developing skills and learning strategies that will support areas of weakness is most effective. Typically, talk therapy alone is a less effective tool for kids with these deficits. Talk therapy requires a level of awareness and self-regulation that many students (especially elementary and middle school students) do not have. Talk therapy can, however, be helpful if a student is struggling with low self-esteem or friendship problems due to their executive functioning difficulties.

Goal-Setting to Build Executive Function Skills

Working with students through the goal-setting process of self-monitoring, self-evaluating, and self-regulating is necessary to help build the executive function skills necessary for academic success. **Figure 6-2** lists each executive function skill with a possible strategy that a student could use to self-monitor it. Narrowing a goal to a single executive functioning skill is important in the microgoal-setting process in order to be able to coach self-regulation skills; too many goals at once can be overwhelming and may confuse students about what specific behaviors to adjust.

Figure 6-2 Sample Self-Monitoring Strategies to Build Executive Function Skills

Executive Function Skill	Student Self-Monitoring Strategy
Planning	I can experiment with various planners to figure out which is most useful for me.
Organization	I can check my binder at the end of each day to make sure I have put my papers in the right folders.
Time management	I can estimate how long a homework assignment will take and track whether my estimate is over or under to develop an awareness of time.
Working memory	I can use an app on my phone to make checklists to help me remember steps in my daily routines.
Metacognition	I can look over my graded tests and identify areas of improvement and build study skills.
Response inhibition	I can keep track of how many times I feel the urge to speak without raising my hand but am able to stop myself.
Emotional self-regulation	I can track the trigger, intensity, and time of day that I get dysregulated to look for patterns in my behavior.
Sustained attention	I can time myself to see how long I can stay on task with an assignment before I have to take a break.
Shifting focus	I can rate on a scale of 1 to 5 how easily I can shift my focus when it is time to end one subject and move on to another.
Task initiation	I can start my schoolwork before the end of class.
Cognitive flexibility	I can identify when I'm stuck on my work and ask for help, even when I think I should be able to do the work on my own.
Task persistence	I can follow all the steps to turn in my work: write down the assignment, complete the work, and turn it in to the basket before class.

I used the tracking sheet in **figure 6-3** with an autistic gifted student who was struggling to manage his emotions, but wasn't sure what triggers were causing his dysregulation. He began tracking his emotions to see if he and I could spot any patterns. Then we could choose techniques to improve those specific situations.

Figure 6-3 Sample Goal Tracking Sheet for Emotional Self-Regulation

Managing My Emotions			
Date	Time of Day	Environment	Brief Description
	☐ Before school ☐ During school day ☐ After school ☐ Evening ☐ Other:	☐ Home ☐ School ☐ Car ☐ Cross-country practice ☐ Other:	

The tracking sheet in **figure 6-4** helped a gifted student with ADHD who was struggling with response inhibition on his assignments, leading to careless errors and sloppy work. To improve his awareness of how often this was happening, we met to go through the work sent home in his Friday folder each week. He used self-monitoring to individually assess each paper and used tallies on the chart to track how often his work showed that he was taking his time or, if he was rushing, if he could identify the rushing based on sloppiness or careless errors using criteria we had worked together to identify.

Figure 6-4 Sample Goal Tracking Sheet for Response Inhibition

Friday Folder Tracking		
Taking My Time	Rushing	
	Was it sloppy?	Did I make careless errors?

In **figure 6-5**, a gifted middle school student with ADHD was having a hard time with task initiation because she thought the work was going to take too long. She would waste a lot of time complaining about this, when the work really would take much less time than she thought. We worked on the time management skill of estimating the time would take on a task to help her improve her ability to accurately assess how long certain types of homework would take.

Figure 6-5 Sample Goal Tracking Sheet for Task Initiation

Time Management Tracking Chart					
Task	Estimate	Start Time	End Time	Total	Accuracy of Estimate
Math HW	25 min.	4:03	4:17	14 min	Over +11 min

Key Points

- Executive function struggles are common among 2e learners. Most diagnoses for 2e students affect an individual's executive function skills.

- There are two main categories of executive function skills: decision-making skills and behavioral regulation skills.

- Accommodations and modifications to daily classroom activities are generally easy to implement and can ease the impact of executive function struggles.

- The metacognitive cycle discussed in chapter 5 can be used to improve executive function skills for 2e learners.

BOOKS FOR SUPPORTING EXECUTIVE FUNCTION SKILLS

- *Executive Function in the Classroom: Practical Strategies for Improving Performance and Enhancing Skills for All Students* by Christopher Kaufman
- *Executive Skills in Children and Adolescents: A Practical Guide to Assessment and Intervention* (3rd ed.) by Peg Dawson and Richard Guare
- *Smart but Scattered: The Revolutionary "Executive Skills" Approach to Helping Kids Reach Their Potential* by Peg Dawson, Ed.D., and Richard Guare, Ph.D.
- *Teenagers with ADD, ADHD and Executive Function Deficits: A Guide for Parents and Professionals* by Chris A. Ziegler Dendy, M.S.
- *The Executive Functioning Workbook for Teens* by Sharon A. Hansen, MSE, NBCT

Accommodations and Modifications for Executive Dysfunction

Executive Function Skill	Student Difficulties	Possible Accommodations
Planning	• identifying multiple steps necessary to complete a task or project • remembering to bring home all components needed to complete the project at home	• organizational: using a planner or agenda with daily check-ins by the teacher • instructional: providing teacher-created lists of steps and materials needed for assignments or projects
Organization	• maintaining materials in a systematic way • accessing materials quickly and easily • distinguishing items that are needed from items that can be thrown away	• environmental: establishing location to keep materials in the classroom, reducing the need to bring them to and from their locker or home • organizational: using a uniform system for all students between all classes to keep materials organized
Time management	• estimating the amount of time a task will take • allocating enough time to complete a task or series of tasks	• behavioral: developing a system for student to self-monitor their time to stay on track • evaluative: allowing extended time to complete assignments or tests and turn in work • organizational: teaching student to work backward to accurately determine the amount of time necessary for an assignment or project
Working memory	• following a series of directions without reminders or visual prompts • successfully completing multistep problems	• instructional: providing visual lists on the board • instructional: allowing student to keep a list of steps necessary for completing problems or activities
Metacognition	• evaluating problem-solving strategies for effectiveness • self-monitoring and self-checking for both short- and long-term assignments or projects	• instructional: asking students to reflect on possible positive or negative outcomes prior to initiating a problem-solving strategy • instructional: providing opportunities to improve past work based on a student's own reflections
Response inhibition	• speaking before being called on or talking out in class • grabbing something from a peer's hands • fidgeting or other impulsive actions • pulling class discussions off track with unrelated or tangentially related comments	• behavioral: using self-monitoring tools to build student awareness of impulsive actions • behavioral: replacing disciplinary consequences for executive functioning struggles with proactive coaching
Emotional self-regulation	• emotional outbursts that look like anger or sadness • excitement or enthusiasm that can be disruptive • disproportionate emotional responses to stimuli	• behavioral: building awareness of physiological signs of dysregulation • instructional: integrating mindfulness activities throughout the school day to increase self-regulation

Executive Function Skill	Student Difficulties	Possible Accommodations
Sustained attention	• completing tasks in the expected amount of time • maintaining focus during passive learning • completing a single task from start to end without distraction	• environmental: collaborating with student to determine the best place for them to focus during work time • behavioral: implementing a signal to bring child's attention back to task without calling attention from peers
Shifting focus	• transitioning from one assignment to another • putting aside work that hasn't been completed • being aware that transitions are about to occur	• environmental: providing students with advance notice when transitions are about to occur (may include getting a student's attention directly) • organizational: developing a system for what to do when an assignment is incomplete and it is time to move on (like a special folder for work to complete later)
Task initiation	• not getting started on work in a timely manner • procrastinating on larger projects • paralysis due to perfectionism	• instructional: shortening assignments • behavioral: establishing system for student to self-monitor progress on assignments and projects and setting goals for quantity of work completed
Cognitive flexibility	• collaborating in groups when peers must agree on how to do the work or what a correct answer is • answering ambiguous writing prompts or questions that don't have a "right" answer	• evaluative: grading based on content created in group instead of group effort or collaboration • instructional: providing framework for essays and other assignments that don't have a "right" answer • behavioral: supporting student during interpersonal interactions to develop perspective-taking skills
Task persistence	• following assignments and projects through to completion • maintaining interest in a topic without wanting to move on to the next thing	• instructional: allowing students to study self-directed topics that fulfill process-oriented objectives • evaluative: grading based on process and work completed, even if final product remains unfinished

Executive Functioning Self-Assessment Tool
(Grades 4 and Up)

Name: _____ **Date:** _____

Executive functioning involves the part of your brain that oversees all the other tasks you have to do daily. Executive functioning helps you plan and carry out your daily responsibilities and manage your time effectively.

Rate yourself on each of the executive function skills listed below by marking the number that sounds right to you. Which do you feel are strengths and which do you feel are struggles? Skills marked with 1s and 2s are struggles. Skills marked with 4s and 5s are strengths. If you feel something is neither a struggle nor a strength, you can mark a 3.

Once you have finished the survey, work with your teacher or counselor to choose one or two skills that you'd like to work on improving and develop a plan to build that skill.

Executive Functioning Skill	How well do I accomplish this skill?				
	I have trouble daily.		I'm okay at this.		Easy for me!
	1	2	3	4	5
	STRUGGLES				STRENGTHS
Planning	I can plan all the steps necessary to complete a task or project.				
	1	2	3	4	5
	I remember to bring home everything I need to complete a project.				
	1	2	3	4	5
Organization	I keep my belongings organized so I know where they are.				
	1	2	3	4	5
	I often sort items and recycle those I don't need.				
	1	2	3	4	5
Time management	I'm good at guessing the amount of time a task will take.				
	1	2	3	4	5
	I usually give myself enough time to complete tasks.				
	1	2	3	4	5
Working memory	If someone tells me to do something, I can usually remember and do everything they said.				
	1	2	3	4	5
Metacognition	I can keep myself on track for assignments and projects. I adjust my strategy if I'm running short on time or it isn't working.				
	1	2	3	4	5

Executive Functioning Skill	How well do I accomplish this skill?				
	I have trouble daily.		I'm okay at this.		Easy for me!
	1	2	3	4	5
	STRUGGLES				STRENGTHS
Response inhibition	I don't call out in class unless the teacher calls on me.				
	1	2	3	4	5
	I never grab something from someone's hands without asking.				
	1	2	3	4	5
Emotional self-regulation	I can manage my emotions pretty well. I don't overreact.				
	1	2	3	4	5
Sustained attention	I can usually complete tasks in the expected amount of time.				
	1	2	3	4	5
	I can stick with one activity until it is finished, even if I don't really like it.				
	1	2	3	4	5
Shifting focus	Going from one activity to another doesn't bother me.				
	1	2	3	4	5
	I am usually ready to move to the next task when I'm told to move on.				
	1	2	3	4	5
Task initiation	I'm good about starting projects with enough time to complete them.				
	1	2	3	4	5
	When I get an assignment, I start on it right away.				
	1	2	3	4	5
Cognitive flexibility	I'm able to go with the flow during group work and let other people contribute, even if I don't agree with their ideas.				
	1	2	3	4	5
	I like assignments that are open-ended and have lots of possible answers.				
	1	2	3	4	5
Task persistence	I can complete long projects without losing interest or moving on to something else.				
	1	2	3	4	5

Executive Functioning Self-Assessment Tool
(Grades 1 to 3)

Name: _____ **Date:** _____

We all have a part of our brain that helps us get our work done and make good choices, but sometimes we need a little help with these tasks, called executive function skills. Which of these skills do you feel like you do well? Which are harder for you? Mark the answer that fits you.

Executive Function Skill	How often do I do this skill?		
	Not too much ☹	Sometimes 🙂	All the time 😀
Planning	I remember all my materials when I start an assignment or project.		
	Not too much ☹	Sometimes 🙂	All the time 😀
Organization	I can find my materials in my desk or backpack when I need them.		
	Not too much ☹	Sometimes 🙂	All the time 😀
Time management	I usually get my assignments done in the time the teacher gives me.		
	Not too much ☹	Sometimes 🙂	All the time 😀
Working memory	When someone tells me 3 or 4 things to do at once, I remember them.		
	Not too much ☹	Sometimes 🙂	All the time 😀
Metacognition	If something doesn't make sense or isn't working, I try to think of a new idea or solution.		
	Not too much ☹	Sometimes 🙂	All the time 😀
Response inhibition	I take my time on my assignments and make sure not to rush.		
	Not too much ☹	Sometimes 🙂	All the time 😀

Executive Function Skill	How often do I do this skill?		
	Not too much 😐	Sometimes 🙂	All the time 😃
Response inhibition	I am careful not to call out in class without raising my hand.		
	Not too much 😐	Sometimes 🙂	All the time 😃
Emotional self-regulation	My emotions aren't too big or too small for the size of a problem.		
	Not too much 😐	Sometimes 🙂	All the time 😃
Sustained attention	I can stick with one activity until it is finished, even if I don't really like it.		
	Not too much 😐	Sometimes 🙂	All the time 😃
Shifting focus	I can move easily to a new task, even if I'm doing something else.		
	Not too much 😐	Sometimes 🙂	All the time 😃
Task initiation	When I get an assignment, I start on it right away.		
	Not too much 😐	Sometimes 🙂	All the time 😃
Cognitive flexibility	I don't mind trying to do something in a new way, even if I'm used to doing it a different way.		
	Not too much 😐	Sometimes 🙂	All the time 😃
Task persistence	I can stay focused without getting distracted (thinking about something else).		
	Not too much 😐	Sometimes 🙂	All the time 😃

Part 2

INTERVENTIONS FOR
Twice-Exceptional
Learners

Part 2 breaks down the needs of 2e learners into three main types of diagnoses: academic, neurodevelopmental, and emotional and behavioral. Chapter 7 discusses academic diagnoses, often called specific learning disabilities in education or dyslexia, dyscalculia, and dysgraphia in medicine and psychology. Chapters 8, 9, and 10 address neurodevelopmental diagnoses, including ADHD, autism spectrum disorder, and processing disorders. Chapters 11 and 12 examine emotional and behavioral diagnoses, including various anxiety-based disorders, obsessive-compulsive disorder (OCD), depression, and bipolar disorder. Each chapter includes information about how to spot 2e learners with these diagnoses, specific social and emotional considerations for the population, and ways to accommodate their learning needs from a strength-based approach.

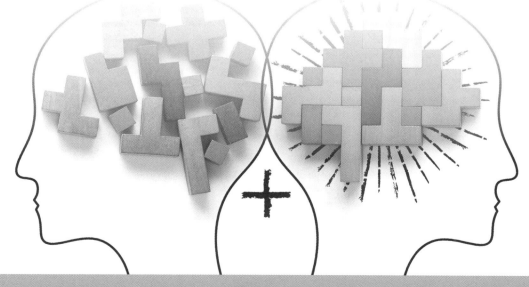

7 Academic Diagnoses: Specific Learning Disabilities

When awareness of twice-exceptional students began to grow in the 1980s, the first type of 2e students to be identified were those who had specific learning disabilities in the areas of reading (dyslexia), writing (dysgraphia), and math (dyscalculia). Students with these disabilities are struggling to master the academic skills necessary to succeed in the classroom. It is easy to understand why they get overlooked for gifted education services. Adults are tempted to think, "How can a student who struggles to read possibly be gifted?" But gifted students with academic diagnoses do exist, they need academic support, and they deserve gifted education services.

The Individuals with Disabilities Education Act (IDEA) identifies specific learning disability as one of the thirteen areas in which a student can qualify for special education services. Specific learning disability is an educational diagnosis. Technically, dyslexia, dyscalculia, and dysgraphia are psychological or medical diagnoses. A medical diagnosis may have different identification criteria than that of an educational diagnosis of specific learning disability. To further complicate matters, the terminology used to identify students may vary from state to state.

Gifted students who have learning difficulties in reading, writing, and math have unique learning profiles. Their achievement often looks like a series of peaks and valleys. Some areas are strong, and one or two areas show distinct weakness. The services provided through an IEP target those areas of weakness and teach skills to build strength. Within the IEP process, these peaks and valleys are referred to as "relative strengths and weaknesses" compared to a child's overall learning profile or cognitive ability.

Identifying Gifted Students with Specific Learning Disabilities

Few schools have a specific protocol to identify students who are gifted and learning disabled (GLD). This often leaves IEP teams trying to figure out how to fit the square peg of a 2e student in the round hole of typical special education identification. Both IEP and Section 504 laws include wording that says a student's difficulty must impede their access to the curriculum. When we're identifying 2e students with learning disabilities and looking at curriculum access, we must consider how much students are compensating for their struggles with their cognitive abilities. For example, a GLD student can compensate for their struggle to sound out and identify words while reading by pulling from their background knowledge or contextual clues. But this will only get them so far. Eventually, the content will become too difficult for them to compensate. Their grades will begin to show the effect of their disability. They may avoid taking advanced courses because of the amount of reading required, even though they have the cognitive ability to comprehend the subject.

Missing GLD identification can cause the following long-term negative effects:

- gaps in skills that should have been learned early on but were missed due to compensatory strategies

- frustration due to being placed in advanced courses while still lacking basic skills (such as math or reading fluency)

- boredom due to being placed in lower-level courses because of lagging skills but having the cognitive ability to quickly master complex content

- being blocked from future access to AP and honors courses

- inability to qualify for accommodations during standardized tests (such as ACT, SAT, and College Board exams) because disability and accommodations haven't been documented

- inability to access accommodations in college due to requirement that assessment was completed within the three years prior to requesting accommodation

- possibility of dropping out of high school or college

A gifted child with a learning disability is a student who is in the deep end of the pool and doesn't know how to swim. They've figured out how to keep their head barely above water, but eventually their strength is going to give out, and they won't have the skills necessary to swim to the side. Special education services teach 2e kids how to swim before they get too tired to keep afloat.

Assessing English Language Learners for Learning Disabilities

Just as language barriers can impede gifted identification among students who are English language learners (ELL), it is also difficult to identify specific learning disabilities in ELL students. Students whose native language is not used in their academic setting are often likely to go undiagnosed or be diagnosed much later, missing valuable instructional time and support.

Training for ELL teachers in the characteristics and needs of 2e learners is key to identifying GLD students in this vulnerable population. For example, a student who rapidly grasps verbal skills and vocabulary but struggles when asked to read phonetically may be a 2e learner. Progress that is dramatically uneven in different domains should be a signal for further investigation, including assessment for both giftedness and learning disabilities.

Assessment for learning disabilities in ELL students is typically done in both the child's native language and English. If a student reads very well in their native language but struggles to read in English, it's unlikely the student has a learning disability in reading; their struggles are likely related to language acquisition. Lagging skills in both their native language and English could indicate the presence of a learning disability.

Gifted ELL students are at risk of being unidentified. A gifted ELL student with a specific learning disability has a complex profile of strengths and weaknesses. A thorough evaluation with particular attention to areas of strength and weakness can identify both their gifted characteristics and areas that need support.

SPECIFIC LEARNING DISABILITY TERMINOLOGY

Normative scores are scores that are standardized for all students. An average score (or below- or above-average score) is determined based on all kids who took the test. It is most common for school districts to use normative scores to determine the presence of a specific learning disability.

Intraindividual scores are scores that consider only the context of an individual student. A student's strengths and weaknesses are viewed within the context of their own ability instead of compared to all other students.

Ability-achievement discrepancy refers to the difference between a student's cognitive ability (IQ) and their achievement scores in a specific subject area. When the achievement score is subtracted from the cognitive ability score, the resulting difference is the discrepancy. A discrepancy of at least 22.5 points is generally the cutoff for considering a possible learning disability.

Choosing to Use Normative Scores Versus Intraindividual Scores

The big question is whether we should use normative or intraindividual scores to determine whether a gifted student has a learning disability. Normative scores look at the scores across the entire nation and determine a baseline of what is considered average. Intraindividual scores look at the profile of strengths and weaknesses within a student's score report. Looking at scores using intraindividual differences allows educators to put a child's achievement into context with their overall ability, which is important when we are looking for a specific learning disability in gifted students.

Normative scores are generally used to identify learning disabilities. Students who show a discrepancy (a difference greater than 22.5 points) between their ability (IQ) and their achievement (in a specific subject) *and* have achievement scores below average (usually scores below 80) qualify for special education services with a specific learning disability. Using normative scores only would mean looking only at a student's overall achievement scores in each subject and comparing them to scores of all other students of the same age, without using overall ability level to contextualize a student's expected achievement. Using normative score criteria is the most rigid method of identifying a GLD student. This can be problematic for many gifted learners whose scores fall into the "average" range of achievement, which is anything between 80 and 120. (See **figure 7-1** for qualitative descriptors of scores.)

Intraindividual score discrepancy is similar to using normative scores, but the main difference is that a student's achievement scores need not be in the below-average range compared to all other students their age. Because gifted students' cognitive ability is above average, the discrepancy necessary to be identified with a learning disability based on the typical normative score process is often 50 points or more. The intraindividual score allows more flexibility to take into consideration that a student's achievement should approach their ability.

Using only intraindividual scores for identification can be problematic because many gifted students have a discrepancy between ability and achievement greater than 22.5 points; however, they do not have a learning disability. For example, if a child with a cognitive ability score of 140 has an achievement score of 117, it is difficult to say definitively that this child has a learning disability because the student is still performing above 85 percent of their same-age peers. One analysis of data showed that more than 92 percent of students with IQs above 120 met the criteria for having a potential learning disability if identified solely on having an achievement score at least 22.5 points lower than their ability score (Maddocks 2018). It is unrealistic to believe that more than 92 percent of gifted students also have a learning disability. There needs to be some middle ground that allows for gifted students to be identified with a specific learning disability that isn't limited by requiring an achievement score that is below 80, but also doesn't identify every single gifted student with a discrepancy of 22.5 points as GLD.

Figure 7-1 Distribution of Cognitive Ability Scores

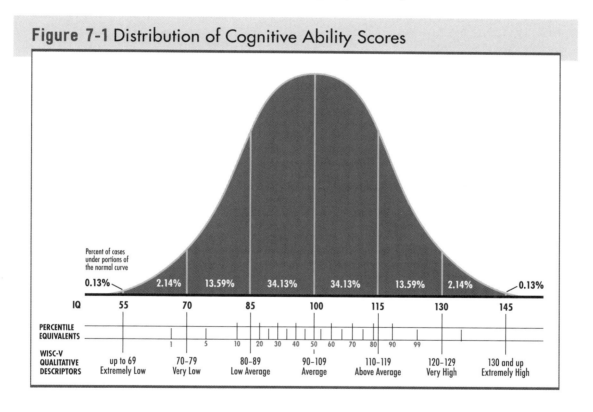

Figure 7-2 compares four students with varied learning profiles. Let's look at how they would fare within most commonly accepted SLD identification processes for an IEP.

Student A is easily identifiable as a student with SLD in reading. They have an average IQ and below-average reading achievement. Their ability-achievement discrepancy exceeds 22.5 points.

Student B also exhibits weakness in reading achievement, but it doesn't meet the normative or intraindividual score requirements for SLD identification. However, this student has a diagnosis of ADHD. The IEP team can determine that ADHD is impeding the student's achievement in the classroom and place the student on an IEP under an OHI diagnosis.

Figure 7-2 Sample Learning Profiles for SLD Identification

	Student A	Student B	Student C	Student D
Learning profile	nongifted with dyslexia	nongifted with ADHD	gifted reluctant reader	gifted with dyslexia
Ability score	105	105	130	130
Broad reading achievement composite score (including reading fluency, phonetic awareness, and comprehension)	79	86	105	90
Identify SLD based on normative scores?	Yes. Reading achievement is below average.	No. Reading achievement is in average range.	No. Reading achievement is in average range.	No. Reading achievement is in average range.
Identify SLD based on intraindividual scores?	Yes. Discrepancy exceeds 22.5 points.	No. Discrepancy does not exceed 22.5 points.	No. Although discrepancy exceeds 22.5 points, more information is needed. See **figure 7-4** for other considerations.	Yes. Discrepancy exceeds 22.5 points.
Notes	This is the profile of many students with an SLD diagnosis: IQ in the average range and below-average academic achievement.	ADHD diagnosis can allow special education services under other health impairment (OHI) diagnosis.	Based *solely* on intraindividual scores, this student appears to have a reading disability. Processing deficits or specific weaknesses in a skill area (such as phonetic fluency) may indicate special education services are appropriate.	Although the gifted student's normative score is in the average range, the extreme discrepancy (40 points) indicates a significant weakness.

Student C does not meet the normative score requirements for an IEP; their achievement score of 105 is solidly average. However, this student *does* have an intraindividual discrepancy of 25 points. Does this student have a learning disability? Student C is a reluctant reader; they've been attending reading instruction in the general education classroom for several years. The student's reading fluency does not appear to be a concern. Reading comprehension in fiction is a struggle, but in math word problems, comprehension struggles do not appear. Additionally, the student continues to show growth on benchmark testing. It appears this gifted student has a personal relative weakness in the area of reading but does not necessarily have a learning disability that requires special education services. This student's progress should be monitored and reevaluated in the future if it appears to stagnate.

Student D is also a gifted student. This student's achievement score of 90 is in the average range, so they do not meet identification criteria based solely on normative score. The intraindividual score discrepancy of 40 points, however, tells another story.

Using a modified ability-achievement discrepancy threshold for identifying 2e students for special education services allows this student to access those services.

If using only normative criteria is too rigid—and using only intraindividual scores is not rigid enough—to accurately identify GLD students, a modified identification model may be the solution. Montgomery County Public Schools in Maryland have a robust and forward-thinking model for meeting the needs of 2e learners. In their handbook for teaching 2e students, they suggest using the model in **figure 7-3** for identifying bright students with specific learning disabilities. This model recognizes that students' achievement in the average range can indicate the need for special education services if their ability is in the superior or very superior range (Montgomery County Public Schools 2015).

Figure 7-3 Montgomery County Public Schools GLD Identification Model

IQ Score Range	Achievement Score Range
130–139	≤100
120–129	≤94

The Influence of Processing Deficits

Another factor to consider when you're examining the learning profile of a student who may qualify for a GLD diagnosis is processing deficits. We'll talk more specifically about a variety of processing deficits in chapter 10, but during the identification process, it is important to understand how a child's processing abilities influence their learning profile. Visual and auditory processing deficits and generalized below-average processing speed are the deficits that most often directly affect a child's academic achievement.

When a gifted student shows signs of a processing deficit, consider how it influences the child's classroom performance and skill acquisition. A student may show average achievement on normative scales—but many of these scales are conducted one-on-one in settings with few extraneous sensory stimuli. In the busier classroom setting, a processing deficit may be impeding the child's progress.

Response to Intervention (RTI)

Many schools use an RTI model to help struggling students. Advocates of this system highlight the benefits of allowing all students to access specific targeted interventions for areas of struggle without needing to go through the IEP evaluation process. They also describe how the system provides services to students who may not otherwise qualify for special education services. For example, using the ability-achievement discrepancy model, many students with below-average cognitive abilities do not qualify for special education services because their ability and achievement do not show the necessary discrepancy; both are low. With RTI, any student who is struggling or below grade level can receive interventions, regardless of their special education status. Special education services are reserved for students who continue to perform below grade-level expectations despite the interventions provided through RTI.

The RTI model may, however, be ineffective at meeting the needs of 2e students. Because many 2e students are achieving at or above grade level thanks to their compensatory skills, they may not be assessed for interventions. Assessing a student through an SLD evaluation is often the only way to determine if a child's achievement is approaching their ability.

If your school uses an RTI model, it is important to develop an alternate identification process for 2e learners. To make sure these students get the support they need, train staff to recognize characteristics of cognitive giftedness even when a child's achievement is not well above average. Also instruct staff to watch for children who are cognitively gifted with high achievement in all subject areas except one. This can be a sign of an undiagnosed learning disability. Advocate for assessment to ensure that these students' needs are met.

Best Practices for Identifying GLD Students

■ Rely more on intraindividual scores than normative scores. Do not prevent gifted students from receiving services for specific learning disabilities because their achievement scores are in the average range.

■ Remember that many gifted students have achievement scores lower than their overall ability scores due to multiple factors. Discrepancies greater than 2 to 2.5 standard deviations (30 to 37.5 points) may be a better indicator of learning disabilities in gifted students than the commonly used discrepancy threshold of 1.5 standard deviations (22.5 points).

■ Look for peaks and valleys in achievement. For example, a student with strong reading comprehension but much weaker reading fluency should raise a red flag. So should a student with strong reading and listening comprehension and verbal vocabulary who has written expression skills at a much lower level.

■ Avoid relying only on composite or broad achievement scores when you're comparing achievement and ability. Gifted students with significant weakness in specific subject area skill sets often have composite scores that are higher—and therefore much less discrepant—due to compensatory abilities in other areas. Look specifically at subtest areas, like reading fluency or phonological awareness, for a better picture of the student's skill level.

■ Watch for slowed progress as children get older. A young student who seemed to be progressing as expected in earlier grades may begin to struggle as content gets more difficult in upper elementary, middle, or high school.

■ Consider mitigating factors. A mitigating factor is support that's already in place. Mitigating factors must be removed from the equation when considering whether a child should receive special education services. For example, perhaps a student is receiving tutoring outside school. They are achieving at grade level—but wouldn't be without that extra help. The extra help shouldn't work against them in the identification process.

- Consider compensation. If a student were not compensating with their cognitive strengths, how would they be achieving?

- Do not attempt to solve achievement issues by suggesting the student take lower-level coursework. Excluding a student from AP or honors courses based on a disability is against federal law.

- Do not rely on RTI to catch 2e students. Teachers should seek further investigation if a child shows underachievement compared with cognitive ability. Below-grade-level performance should not be the only trigger for an assessment.

Figure 7-4 provides a suggested alternative screening process for identifying 2e learners with a specific learning disability. It uses a multifaceted approach to look for signs of a potential learning disability and provides suggestions for screening and evaluation. One of the main factors it adds to the equation of determining if a student meets criteria for a specific learning disability is the presence or absence of processing deficits.

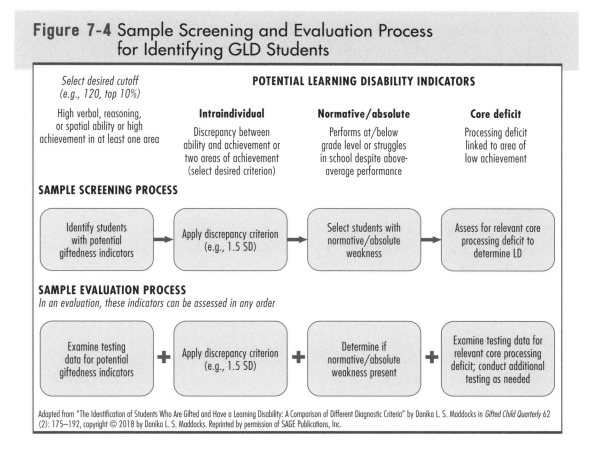

Figure 7-4 Sample Screening and Evaluation Process for Identifying GLD Students

Select desired cutoff (e.g., 120, top 10%)

POTENTIAL LEARNING DISABILITY INDICATORS

| High verbal, reasoning, or spatial ability or high achievement in at least one area | **Intraindividual** Discrepancy between ability and achievement or two areas of achievement (select desired criterion) | **Normative/absolute** Performs at/below grade level or struggles in school despite above-average performance | **Core deficit** Processing deficit linked to area of low achievement |

SAMPLE SCREENING PROCESS

Identify students with potential giftedness indicators → Apply discrepancy criterion (e.g., 1.5 SD) → Select students with normative/absolute weakness → Assess for relevant core processing deficit to determine LD

SAMPLE EVALUATION PROCESS
In an evaluation, these indicators can be assessed in any order

Examine testing data for potential giftedness indicators + Apply discrepancy criterion (e.g., 1.5 SD) + Determine if normative/absolute weakness present + Examine testing data for relevant core processing deficit; conduct additional testing as needed

Adapted from "The Identification of Students Who Are Gifted and Have a Learning Disability: A Comparison of Different Diagnostic Criteria" by Danika L. S. Maddocks in *Gifted Child Quarterly* 62 (2): 175–192, copyright © 2018 by Danika L. S. Maddocks. Reprinted by permission of SAGE Publications, Inc.

Implementing Special Education Services

Through the assessment process, it can be difficult to figure out exactly what services might look like for a gifted student with a specific learning disability. The IEP team may get stuck on what IEP goals and interventions look like for other students at the same grade level as the 2e student. In this situation, remember that an IEP is an *individualized* education program. What works for other students may work for the 2e student, but perhaps it won't. Identifying the distinct need of the student and developing interventions targeted to their specific struggle is the best approach.

Once the team has identified the child's IEP goal, it determines the type and amount of special education services. Special education services are often described as a certain number of minutes of service received per week. Chapter 1 discusses the various models of special education services, which vary depending on a child's specific needs. For example, a student may need to meet with their case manager only on a consultation basis for fifteen minutes a week (with additional time as needed). Or the team may find a student eligible for more than two hundred minutes per week and place them in a class within a class (CWC).

As students get older, more AP, honors, and challenge courses are available. Gifted students with specific learning disabilities should have access to both higher-level classes *and* special education services and accommodations. If a student still qualifies for services based on their most recent IEP assessment, it is against federal law to deny them access to either. Some schools may try to persuade students and their parents to remove the supports of the special education services. And some teachers of advanced courses may not be used to having 2e learners in their classes and may be unfamiliar with their needs. Elementary teachers are often comfortable with adapting their lessons to students with a variety of needs. Secondary teachers may need more support as schools move toward identifying more 2e students and placing them in more challenging courses.

Specific Learning Disability in Reading

Students who have a specific learning disability in reading may struggle with a variety of weaknesses. The weaknesses most easily identified and targeted through educational interventions are letter–sound knowledge, word decoding, reading fluency, spelling, and reading comprehension. Additional areas of reading difficulty are sequencing, left-right orientation, spatial perception, and eye movement control. Reading difficulties can also affect a student's ability to write or do math, since these skills are so closely related to reading skills.

Many professionals and parents in the 2e community describe dyslexia in gifted learners as "stealth dyslexia." This term refers to reading difficulties in bright students that fly under the radar. It highlights the fact that many GLD students are unrecognized and do not receive interventions because the signs and symptoms go unnoticed. It is important to recognize reading difficulties and provide interventions as early as possible because reading difficulties can snowball. The amount of time spent reading correlates directly with vocabulary acquisition and overall reading improvement. Students with poor reading skills find reading exhausting, frustrating, demoralizing, and unpleasant in various other ways—and therefore tend to read less than their peers. So 2e students whose reading difficulties go unrecognized gradually fall further and further behind.

CORINNE'S STORY

Corinne's dad knew something wasn't clicking. Corinne loved school and loved learning. School hadn't been a concern in kindergarten and first grade, although Corinne didn't enjoy learning to read. She much preferred listening to one of her parents read to her or listening to audiobooks. Then in second grade, students at Corinne's school began reading more difficult material and started spelling tests, which Corinne described as the worst part of her week.

Her dad worked with her to get more comfortable reading aloud. She seemed to read much more quickly in her head than when she read orally. Her teacher completed a running record of her reading fluency and noticed that she had trouble describing what she had read afterward. But when she had to answer multiple-choice comprehension questions about her reading, she did much better. Corinne was on grade level, so her teacher wasn't too concerned.

Corinne's dad described her concerns to Corinne's gifted education teacher during parent-teacher conferences, and the teacher mentioned "stealth dyslexia." Corinne's dad began to investigate this possibility.

When Corinne's dad asked the school to look at her reading difficulties, it convened an IEP team meeting but declined to move forward with testing because Corinne's academics weren't far enough behind. Her dad started looking for more help in the community. He found a dyslexia tutoring specialist who assessed Corinne and began a multisensory reading intervention specifically designed for students with dyslexia. The program helped Corinne rewire the way her brain read and interpreted written information and gave her the confidence to read independently and out loud in class.

Corinne's dad said, "I know if I hadn't done something, she would've gone the rest of her school years hating to read and avoiding it at all costs. The program her dyslexia tutor used is the same one the school had available. I wish she would've been able to get those services through her school. What about the kids whose families don't have the resources to find outside services?" ■

Reading struggles can morph as students get older. Younger students may struggle with letter or word recognition and decoding. As they get older, difficulties with reading fluency become more prevalent. Reading comprehension can also begin to suffer. Older students may learn to manage with only mild impact; you may notice trouble with reading or spelling unfamiliar words or through general avoidance of tasks that require reading.

Dyslexia or Specific Learning Disability? What's the Difference?

There's a lot of confusion around the terms *dyslexia, reading disorder,* and *specific learning disability in reading.* Do they all mean the same thing? Is dyslexia when somebody reverses letters when they read and write? What about if they struggle with reading comprehension or spelling?

The short answer is: it's complicated.

The 2004 federal IDEA law mentioned "specific learning disability" as one of the possible areas of disability that could qualify a student to receive special education services. It did not include the specific term *dyslexia*. Some educators interpreted this to mean that dyslexia could not be assessed or served under IDEA. Often parents would tell schools they believed their child had dyslexia, and confused school personnel would reply that they couldn't assess or support dyslexia. To help clarify this issue, in 2015 the Office of Special Education and Rehabilitative Services issued a Dear Colleague letter explaining, "There is nothing in IDEA that would prohibit the use of the terms dyslexia, dyscalculia, or dysgraphia in IDEA evaluation, eligibility determinations, or IEP documents" (Yudin 2015).

There continues to be general confusion about what dyslexia is. Is it a visual processing issue (it is not), a phonological issue, or something else entirely? This confusion is a result of a historical disconnect between the medical and educational fields. To address the confusion, in 2013 the *Diagnostic and Statistical Manual of Mental Disorders: Fifth Edition* (DSM-5) redefined *dyslexia*, *dyscalculia*, and *dysgraphia* as "specific learning disorders." But depending on which learning disability or psychological organization you ask, you will still find varied definitions of dyslexia. When used correctly, the term *dyslexia* refers to difficulties with the phonological processing of associating letter sounds with their symbols; however, the term is often (inaccurately) used more broadly.

Due to the lack of clarity surrounding its meaning, *dyslexia* has become the de facto term for a wide range of reading fluency, comprehension, spelling, and writing problems. Depending on an individual's role—parent, reading specialist, psychologist, or teacher—the word can mean different things. Taking time to clarify the specific struggles a student is having when someone uses the term *dyslexia* can help clarify the needs of the student. Understanding a student's specific skill deficits is what will drive instruction and interventions.

ONCE DYSLEXIC, ALWAYS DYSLEXIC?

Specific learning disabilities such as dyslexia are neurobiological in origin. If the skills we teach are successful and the student no longer qualifies for a diagnosis, it means our interventions have worked—not that the student no longer has dyslexia. Likewise, if a person is diabetic but controls their blood sugar by taking medication, exercising, and eating a healthy diet, it doesn't mean they're no longer diabetic. It just means that their interventions have worked.

So, if a 2e student qualifies for special education services, will they need those services throughout their academic career? Because 2e learners have advanced cognitive abilities, early intervention may mean that the student will need services only for a short time. (The longer we wait, the harder it is to catch up in lagging skills, and the longer services may be needed.) While they may not need long-term special education services, it's beneficial to continue documenting their needs, accommodations, and modifications.

Recognizing Reading Difficulties in Gifted Learners

Like many possible diagnoses in gifted learners, reading difficulties may remain unnoticed until students' struggles begin to outweigh their abilities. Here are some of the subtle signs of reading difficulties in gifted students:

■ **Struggles with reading aloud:** Bright students who struggle with reading skills may show improved reading comprehension and speed when reading silently but struggle and stumble when reading aloud.

- **Reading fatigue:** Most students without reading difficulties can read at a consistent pace, but students who have more trouble with reading will slow their pace as they read longer passages. You can assess reading fatigue by tracking the number of words a student reads correctly per minute for about four or five minutes. If the number of correct words drops noticeably each consecutive minute, this may mean the student is working hard to visually track and mentally decode the words.

- **Inability to complete work within expected time limits:** Students who struggle with reading often take much longer to complete assignments and homework than their peers do. For 2e students taking challenging courses, the demands of reading can be intense. If a student is taking a long time to complete in-class assignments, or their parent or guardian reports they are spending hours completing homework each night, consider the presence of a reading difficulty.

- **Discrepancy between spoken and written language:** Reading difficulties often appear in written work. If a student can orally describe their thoughts in intricate detail with impressive vocabulary, but their writing is simplistic, this may be a sign of reading struggles.

Teaching 2e Students with Reading SLDs

Twice-exceptional students with a specific learning disability in reading need support to reach their potential. Specialized instruction provided through an IEP is one way to meet this need. Other students may require accommodations and modifications through a 504 plan. Examine each child's learning profile and involve them in the process of determining the best way to meet their needs.

Instructional tools will vary based on the structure of the classroom. Twice-exceptional students may travel among general education, gifted education, and special education classrooms, and their needs may shift based on the format of each classroom. Teachers' flexible expectations and willingness to accommodate can make these transitions easier for students.

MULTISENSORY INSTRUCTION

Several reading programs have been developed specifically for students struggling with reading difficulties. The Barton, Wilson, and SPIRE systems, to name a few, were developed specifically to assist struggling readers, especially those with decoding and phonological issues associated with dyslexia. These reading systems are based on the Orton-Gillingham Approach, which is a "direct, explicit, multisensory, structured, sequential, diagnostic, and prescriptive way to teach literacy when

> " We tried for years to get my son an IEP for his reading troubles. He'd been diagnosed with dyslexia in first grade by a private psychologist, but the school kept saying he wasn't struggling enough. I knew how much he was struggling, though, because I saw him in tears at home every night, trying desperately to complete his homework. Finally, when he was in fourth grade, the school agreed to assess him. While we went over the results, the special education teacher spoke up and said that she'd received some new training on dyslexia, and she believed this system she'd learned could help my son rewire his brain to learn the skills necessary to become a confident reader. By the time my son entered middle school, he had built those skills and overcome his reading fluency struggles. Now he's in high school and actually likes school!
>
> —**Mallory,** mom of a dyslexic tenth grader "

reading, writing, and spelling does not come easily to individuals, such as those with dyslexia" (Academy of Orton-Gillingham Practitioners and Educators 2018).

For 2e students, these systems are as effective as they are with average-ability learners. Sometimes teachers or reading interventionists might think students who are gifted won't benefit from these methods because most of them require a student to "begin at the beginning," with very basic skills. However, most 2e students with reading fluency and spelling difficulties *need* to start with the basics so those phonological skills become automatic. When they learned to read, they missed these skills because they compensated with their other abilities. Without reintegrating these basic skills into their reflexive reading techniques, their struggles will continue to grow.

ASSISTIVE TECHNOLOGY

While many parents and educators bemoan technology as a detriment to children's academic development, apps and other tech tools do a lot to level the playing field for students with learning difficulties. Some educators may worry that assistive technology will create dependency, but the reality is that these resources are here to stay. If they help students reach their potential, we should embrace them.

Many of the tools listed here are available in a variety of formats. They are integrated within the operating systems of most desktop and laptop computers, plug-ins are available for a variety of internet browsers, and countless apps are available for mobile devices and e-readers. We can help all our students by making these tools available to them. If you don't have access to these in your classroom, check with the special education department; often assistive technology is made available through government funding for special needs programs. Here are some examples of assistive technology that can be used with students who struggle with specific learning disabilities:

- **Text-to-speech software** is helpful for students with reading difficulties who have strengths in listening comprehension skills. Students can use text-to-speech software to read audiobooks and text from websites or PDFs.

- **Speech-to-text software** can benefit students with strong verbal expression skills but weak writing abilities. If writing by hand gets in the way of a student's ability to produce work, speech-to-text tools can help them show their thinking. Most word processors and operating systems have some type of speech-to-text tools.

- **E-readers** may integrate text-to-speech software, and another benefit is that you can often adjust the size and contrast of the text on the screen. These simple changes can make lines of text shorter and easier to read for students with reading difficulties.

- **Electronic dictionaries** in e-readers help students who struggle with decoding or comprehension. Built-in dictionary tools allow them to click on a word and see its definition.

- **Word prediction software** allows students with poor spelling and writing skills to type the first few letters of a word, and the software predicts what word they are trying to write. Even for students with very weak spelling skills, these programs are getting better at predicting what word is being written based on phonetic sounds.

- **Smart pens** function in tandem with a tablet. For students who struggle with dysgraphia, writing with a smart pen digitizes their notes, making them easier to go back and read in the future. A smart pen also has recording functions in case the student falls behind during a lecture or group discussion. The pen syncs the notes with the recording, and the student can immediately access the portion of the recording missed by going to that portion in their notes.

THE CONNECTION BETWEEN WORKING MEMORY AND LEARNING DISABILITIES

Working memory can strongly influence a student's ability to learn the basic skills associated with reading, writing, and math. The connection between working memory and learning disabilities often goes unrecognized. Consider reading, for example. When children are beginning to learn to string together the sounds created by each letter in a word, they must be able to hold the information from each previous letter in their working memory. Students who struggle with working memory have trouble chunking that information and keeping it accessible in their working memory. Think about the process of sounding out a word like *school*. (See **figure 7-5**.)

Students with working memory deficits are at a distinct disadvantage. Poor working memory has a similar effect on the writing process as it has on reading. It is difficult to write a sentence, let alone a paragraph, if you can't remember what you were trying to write at the beginning of the sentence. Multistep math problems also require a student to have the ability to hold information in their working memory while completing the various steps. Multisensory methods can help students create permanent connections to chunk material together and maintain it in their working memory for longer periods of time.

Figure 7-5 Phonetic Spelling of School

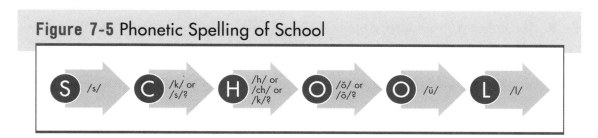

Specific Learning Disability in Writing

Students who have a specific learning disability in writing struggle to put their thoughts on paper or to accurately spell the words they are trying to write. Writing struggles are often intrinsically tied to reading difficulties.

Just as dyslexia typically refers to difficulties with the specific skills associated with phonetics and basic word decoding processes, dysgraphia typically refers to difficulty with fine-motor skills and handwriting. A specific learning disability in writing can also be related to difficulties with written expression. Written expression is the ability to put one's thoughts into words effectively, using vocabulary and grammar that is developmentally appropriate for the student's age.

Writing difficulties sometimes accompany other exceptionalities. For example, many autistic students have strong reading abilities and oral expression but struggle greatly with writing their thoughts. Slow processing speed, a common characteristic of ASD, impedes their writing. So do poor fine-motor skills associated with getting words onto paper.

Recognizing Writing Difficulties in Gifted Learners

The masking effect that often happens in 2e learners can make a specific learning disability in writing difficult to identify. Watch for subtle signs of struggle and frustration to help you know when a student might benefit from a referral for assessment. Here are some of the signs of writing difficulty in gifted learners:

- **Discrepancy between oral and written language skills:** Students who can explain their thinking in great detail but turn in writing at a far lower level may be dealing with an underlying learning disability in writing.

- **Poor spelling skills:** Spelling, or encoding letters into words, is essentially the opposite of decoding words to read. Students who struggle to spell often write slowly and choose simplistic words, rather than write with the vocabulary they use to speak. (Note: this can also be more directly related to a reading difficulty, instead of solely writing.)

- **Resistance to writing words students don't know how to spell:** Some schools de-emphasize spelling, pointing to the prevalence of typing and spellcheck in most academic and work environments. But for 2e learners, many of whom are perfectionists, difficulty spelling can be a huge barrier to successful completion of writing assignments. The frustration students feel when they can't put their thoughts into writing correctly may lead to unwillingness to try.

- **Discomfort with ambiguity:** Some gifted students may not show the same difficulty with writing in all situations. When asked to write simple responses to right-or-wrong questions, 2e learners can compensate for their writing struggles with their strong background knowledge in a topic. But when asked to craft a response to open-ended questions, students with an SLD in written expression may balk.

- **Illegible writing:** Students with poor handwriting, inconsistent spacing between words, or omitted letters or words may be struggling with writing fluency. This difficulty may be attributable to weak working memory or processing speed. Students with poor handwriting may benefit from an assessment for services. If they qualify for services, an occupational therapist (as opposed to the special education department) may provide them.

Teaching 2e Students with Writing SLDs

The following accommodations can allow 2e students with diagnosed learning disabilities in writing fluency or written expression to continue participating in their gifted programs and experiencing success in their general education classrooms:

- The easiest accommodation to use with students who struggle with writing is assistive technology. Learning to use a keyboard, using speech-to-text software, and using word prediction software can help eliminate the barriers to putting thoughts into writing.

- Graphic organizers are another beneficial tool. Many types of graphic organizers are easily available (just search the internet). Give students the opportunity to find graphic organizers that best match their thought process. Students may need help learning how to use graphic organizers. They may also benefit from having an adult scribe for them to get their thoughts onto the organizer without having to write their ideas on their own.

- Maximizing a student's strengths can also motivate students to push through the difficulty. Look for (or ask the student to find) ways to integrate their areas of passion into any writing that must be completed for class.

Specific Learning Disability in Math

Students struggling with math have trouble understanding the relationships between numbers and how to manipulate them to solve math problems. Although visual processing struggles can exacerbate both math and reading struggles, a learning disability in math (dyscalculia) and a learning disability in reading (dyslexia) are not the same.

Students with learning disabilities in math struggle with number sense, telling time, and recognizing and using mathematical symbols. Twice-exceptional learners can often understand the concepts and logic in mathematical processes, but they cannot use the necessary algorithms consistently to solve problems.

For gifted students, learning disabilities in math can cause frustration, especially as science coursework becomes more dependent on mathematical concepts in upper grades. Twice-exceptional students may not be placed in advanced math courses in middle school due to math struggles. However, these courses are often required for enrolling in upper-level science classes. Once a student is on a lower math track, it can be difficult to catch their math skills up. Students may end up struggling to complete the required math for courses like chemistry and physics.

Recognizing Math Difficulties in Gifted Learners

Students who are cognitively gifted but struggle with math concepts can develop learned helplessness and avoidance tactics to prevent feelings of inadequacy. Identifying a potential disability in math can help schools intervene to strengthen math skills. Here are some signs that may indicate a gifted learner also has a specific learning disability in math:

- **Mismatch between conceptual understanding of math and application of basic skills:** A student who is highly engaged during math activities (especially those that use multisensory manipulatives) but inconsistently applies skills on assignments may have an SLD in math.

- **Struggle with mental math or rote fact memorization:** Consistently calculating simple math facts instead of recalling them from memory can be a trait of dyscalculia.

- **Getting lost in word problems:** Difficulty understanding the steps necessary to solve a word problem when they can solve the straightforward algorithm using the same concept may indicate difficulty with math comprehension. Sometimes, older students with an SLD in math struggle to find options for solving multistep math problems because they lack a deeper understanding about how to use math strategies.

- ■ **Confusion about telling time or general sequencing of events:** Students with a math SLD may struggle to master concepts like elapsed time, dates, or appropriate sequencing of events.

Teaching 2e Students with Math SLDs

Direct instruction with a multisensory approach can help students struggling with math. Using manipulatives as tangible representations of numbers, drawing pictures to illustrate math problems, or using body movements (such as shifting arms to represent geometric concepts like angles) can help students create permanent neural pathways related to math concepts. The Barton System offers strategies and systems designed to help students with dyscalculia. TouchMath is another program that integrates multisensory tools to help students with math difficulties.

Twice-exceptional students who struggle with a learning difficulty in math benefit from a strengths-based approach to learning math skills. If a student is better at understanding the big-picture concepts of math but has a weakness in math fluency, focusing on application of the concepts in the real world will help them develop the skills. For students who are better at straightforward math facts but struggle with the application of these skills in word problems, help them use their strength in calculations with high-level math problems, but provide support to help them predict when to use certain algorithms with a short list of steps to solve a problem.

Working memory and processing speed are important factors to consider when a student is struggling with math. Many schools continue to rely on timed tests to increase math fluency. For students with slow processing speed, these activities are embarrassing and contribute to a lack of self-efficacy. If timed tests are necessary, shifting the structure can make a huge difference in how a student feels about their progress in math fluency. Instead of timing for five minutes and abruptly stopping when time is up, try this: Display a timer and have students work as quickly as possible to complete their page of math problems. When they complete their work, they write their time at the bottom of their page. They've successfully completed the work and can work to improve their time during the next test. Using this method eliminates the risk of failure, because every student succeeds at their own pace. For perfectionistic 2e learners, this cognitive shift can make a big difference in their feelings of self-efficacy.

Social and Emotional Needs of GLD Students

Tending to the social and emotional needs of GLD students helps them feel supported and successful. These 2e learners have cognitive abilities that help them understand complex topics and weaknesses that hold them back from showing what they can do. They feel frustrated by grades that don't reflect their understanding. If they have an IEP and receive special education services, they may feel confused about their true abilities.

Full disclosure is an excellent policy to help GLD students better understand their learning profiles, strengths, and weaknesses. Helping them recognize that each of us has very real things we are good at and things that are difficult for us provides a feeling of universality. Asking them to be an active part of determining how we can exploit their strengths to support their struggles helps them feel empowered. And involving them in progress monitoring lets them know their efforts are worthwhile.

Gifted students with unidentified learning disabilities struggle with anxiety and frustration. They develop poor work habits and learned helplessness. They believe they are in the gifted program by mistake.

What these students have going for them is their cognitive ability. Many students with a specific learning disability struggle, but with early identification and intervention, GLD students may not feel the impact of their disability for their entire academic career. Direct instruction methods to remediate their difficulties result in long-term positive effects across the curriculum. And simple accommodations allow them to excel in ways that work best for them, creating students who are aware of their strengths and weaknesses, but don't let anything stand in their way.

Chapter 5 discusses in detail how to work with 2e students to set microgoals. Microgoals help students experience autonomy as they make progress. For GLD learners, it's important to provide very specific feedback about their strengths and areas for improvement.

> **SOCIAL AND EMOTIONAL RISKS FOR UNIDENTIFIED GLD STUDENTS**
> - poor self-concept as a learner
> - attention difficulties in class or at home
> - low frustration tolerance
> - risk-avoidance behaviors
> - tendency to get discouraged
> - emotional dysregulation
> - outward anger or defiance

GLD students keenly feel the dichotomy of being 2e. The academic success of their gifted peers leads to upward comparisons and may make GLD students feel inadequate and unintelligent. If students receive special education services, they may feel confused. They may ask themselves, "Why do I need extra help if I'm supposed to be smart?"

Honesty about a child's learning profile followed with consistent and specific feedback about their strengths and progress is essential for GLD students. The benefit of understanding why some things seem easy and others seem hard contributes to their social and emotional well-being.

Key Points

- Gifted students with a specific learning disability often mask their struggles, but not identifying SLDs in gifted students can have long-term negative effects.

- Assessments for GLD students should consider both normative and intraindividual scores to determine the presence of an SLD.

- Assistive technology provides a wide range of options for students with specific learning disabilities.

Accommodations and Modifications for Specific Learning Disabilities

Major Life Activity	Possible Accommodation or Modification
Performing manual tasks	
Student with dysgraphia struggles to write legibly.	• Instructional: Let students use assistive technology to type or use speech-to-text. • Instructional: Provide a scribe to write student's oral responses. • Instructional: Modify or shorten expectations for taking notes. • Evaluative: Do not grade papers based on neatness.
Student struggles to keep up with writing notes or other written assignments with time constraints.	• Instructional: Allow student to record or use other assistive technology. • Instructional: Provide the outline for notes so students only need to write key phrases, reducing the overall writing load.
Reading	
Student has relatively weak reading comprehension compared to other skills.	• Instructional: Allow student to use audiobooks. • Evaluative: Read test and assessment questions aloud to student.
Student takes longer to complete assignments and tests.	• Organizational: Allow additional time for assignments.
Student has trouble following longer reading passages.	• Instructional: Provide colored strips for student to use beneath words to follow along.
Thinking	
Student has difficulty completing math calculations mentally.	• Instructional/Evaluative: Provide calculator to student to use on assignments and tests.
Effort required for longer assignments becomes overwhelming.	• Instructional: Break assignments into shorter pieces; give one page of a packet at a time.
Student struggles to follow multistep instructions in written form.	• Instructional: Use images along with written lists of directions; go over instructions orally.

Attention Deficit Hyperactivity Disorder (ADHD)

A 2018 report showed that 8.4 percent of all US children ages two to seventeen had a current diagnosis of ADHD as reported by their parents (Danielson et al. 2018). ADHD occurs at approximately the same rate in gifted kids as it occurs in the general population. Some in the field of gifted education have concerns about gifted students being misdiagnosed with ADHD, but this does not occur often. Research evidence shows that IQs are distributed in similar proportions among individuals diagnosed with ADHD as among the general population (Katusic et al. 2011). More often, 2e learners mask their inattentiveness, impulsiveness, and hyperactivity by compensating with their cognitive ability.

What Is ADHD?

The *Diagnostic and Statistical Manual of Mental Disorders: Fifth Edition* (DSM-5) describes three different types of ADHD:

- predominantly inattentive presentation
- predominantly hyperactive-impulsive presentation
- combined presentation

Sometimes you may hear inattentive ADHD referred to as attention deficit disorder (ADD). But technically, a standalone diagnosis of ADD is no longer made. For the purpose of this chapter, I'll use *ADHD* as a term that encompasses all three subtypes of the diagnosis.

ADHD is a neurodevelopmental disorder in prefrontal cortex functioning. The prefrontal cortex is the frontmost part of the brain. It plays a crucial role in regulating attention, behavior, and emotion (Arnsten 2009). Some people describe ADHD as less of an attention deficit and more of an attention overload. Kids with ADHD struggle to tune out the unnecessary stimuli in their environment and regulate their attention and behavior appropriately. Often, they are sensory seekers, whether that means fidgeting with something in their hands or jumping off the highest point they can find at recess. They may have trouble organizing their materials or managing their time. Many kids with ADHD face executive functioning struggles. (For more information on executive functioning, see chapter 6.)

One common misconception about ADHD is that individuals with this diagnosis are unable to pay attention. It is more accurate to think of ADHD as an inability to regulate attention on a nonpreferred activity. Families may note that they don't believe their children have ADHD because they can sit and focus on video games or Legos for hours at a time. A better measure would be whether the children can sustain focus on activities that don't interest them. Many of us have trouble focusing when we are unmotivated or

> When I'm working with my students who have a diagnosis of ADHD, I know my job includes more than helping them organize their backpacks or stay in their seats. I have to help them deal with their struggles to tolerate frustration and persist when things get hard. I try to balance guiding them to reflect before they make impulsive decisions with recognizing that the willingness to jump in with both feet can be valuable too.
>
> —Christy, middle school counselor

uninterested in a task, but we can regulate our attention to get it finished. People with inattentive ADHD have a lot more trouble with this.

Students who have hyperactive-impulsive ADHD may be chatterboxes, or always out of their seats, or constantly fidgeting, or struggling with impulsive actions. Generally, these kids don't miss instruction because they are able to maintain focus through their heightened psychomotor activity. Twice-exceptional learners with ADHD are often able to keep up academically even if they struggle to focus. Because of this, their families may rule out hyperactive-impulsive ADHD or may hesitate to seek a formal diagnosis or medication. I have found that when a student with ADHD begins to struggle academically, has trouble making friends, or loses self-esteem due to being called out frequently for behaviors or disorganization, it is time to consider formalizing a diagnosis and determining if the student would benefit from a 504 plan or IEP. Often students with ADHD benefit from easy-to-implement accommodations and can succeed without having to take medicine.

Identifying Students with ADHD

Students with ADHD may have any of the following characteristics (American Psychiatric Association 2017):

- **Difficulty regulating and sustaining attention:** A student who consistently makes careless mistakes on their work or is unable to sustain their attention to a nonpreferred task may be struggling with ADHD. The student may resist or avoid tasks that will take a long time or sustained effort.

- **Missing cues to transition to new activities:** Students with ADHD may not hear instructions if they are involved in another activity.

- **Frequently losing or forgetting things.** After receiving direct instructions or organizational strategies, a student with ADHD may have trouble remembering them.

- **Heightened psychomotor activity that is inappropriate for the environment:** Students dealing with hyperactivity and impulsivity struggle to stay seated or still for extended periods of time.

- **Talkativeness:** Students who have difficulty not talking during work time or who blurt out their responses before being called on might be exhibiting signs of impulsivity.

- **Trouble standing in line or waiting for a turn:** Situations requiring patience, such as waiting in line, can cause frustration or inappropriate behavior.

Difficulties Assessing for ADHD in Gifted Students

Identifying ADHD in gifted students can be difficult. Gifted learners with ADHD often perform better than nongifted students with ADHD on normative measures of ADHD symptoms. Their scores may be considered subdiagnostic (below the threshold for diagnosis). The tests that are used to detect ADHD were created for the typically developing population; when used with gifted learners, they may provide false negatives (Lovecky 2018).

On the flip side, when students are assessed for gifted education services, attention deficits and impulsivity can suppress a child's IQ score. Many screening tests that are used for gifted programs are administered in a group setting; some of those assessments many also be timed. These factors can work against accurate identification. The General Ability Index (GAI) on the Wechsler Intelligence Scale for Children (WISC) removes the emphasis on working memory and processing speed to get an appropriate measure of a child's general cognitive ability.

Young gifted students may exhibit symptoms of inattentive ADHD; however, their cognitive abilities allow them to show mastery of academic objectives despite being unfocused much of the time. Because their academics aren't suffering, teachers and parents may not recognize their struggle. Another factor that complicates recognizing traits of ADHD in gifted students is the way that inattention may manifest. Nongifted students with ADHD may show their lack of focus outwardly through excessive talking or psychomotor activity when they feel understimulated, while gifted students may prefer to entertain themselves cognitively (Zentall et al. 2001). A student who is engaged in imaginative thought is less likely to be recognized as off task in the classroom.

Many people in the field of gifted education express concern that some typical characteristics of giftedness—speaking out answers in class before being called on, frustration with repetition, and a need for novelty—result in an overdiagnosis of ADHD in gifted kids. Research on psychological testing and medical diagnosis of ADHD does not show this to be the case (Nicpon et al. 2011). Misinformed laypeople, however, may mistake traits of giftedness as signs of ADHD. Seeking information and assessment through qualified professionals in the community is the best way to determine the presence or absence of ADHD. ADHD is a "diagnosis of exclusion," meaning everything else needs to be ruled out before the diagnosis is given. The reproducible chart "Gifted, 2e, or ADHD" on page 158 gives examples of common characteristics associated with ADHD and how they may appear in a student who is solely ADHD, solely gifted, or 2e.

Another complicating factor in determining the presence or absence of ADHD is how often people with ADHD also have another diagnosis. Students with ADHD are likely to also have an anxiety disorder, obsessive-compulsive disorder, mood disorder, learning disability, oppositional defiant disorder, or autism spectrum disorder (Gnanavel et al. 2019).

Recognizing Giftedness as a Cause of Inattention

When provided with an anecdote about a hypothetical student showing inattention and boredom, many educators will lean toward labeling the symptoms as ADHD, rather than giftedness (Mullet and Rinn 2015). As educators, it's important that we recognize giftedness as a possible cause of inattention. In a 2000 revision of the fourth edition of the *Diagnostic and Statistical Manual of Mental Disorders* (DSM-IV-TR), the American

Psychiatric Association included a note about how giftedness should be a factor considered in assessing for ADHD. It stated, "Inattention in the classroom may also occur when children with high intelligence are placed in academically understimulating environments" (American Psychiatric Association 2000). When the DSM-5 was released in 2013, it did not include this note. However, inattention among gifted students remains an important factor to consider.

Reframing ADHD as a Strength

In chapter 2, we discussed the importance of looking for the strengths of 2e students when designing instruction for them. Two of their main strengths are big-picture thinking and strong divergent thinking skills. Students with ADHD are prime examples of these. In fact, educational psychologist C. Matthew Fugate has suggested that we should redefine ADHD as "attention divergent hyperactive giftedness" to help people see the diagnosis in a more positive light (Fugate 2018).

In many ways, students with ADHD show above-average creative and divergent thinking compared to their peers. Students with working memory deficits have an advantage when it comes to creativity: they aren't as tied to a linear thought process and are thus able to pull new and unique ideas into their problem-solving. Whether they are developing a list of possible solutions to a problem, engaging in creative writing, or making connections between abstract concepts, 2e students with ADHD have the advantage of unexpected thought patterns. Working with students to tune out the mental "noise" their ADHD may cause and to selectively filter their best ideas can help them reach their creative potential.

Executive functioning weaknesses in working memory and processing speed are strongly associated with ADHD. In these areas, a 2e student's giftedness is a protective factor and asset. Utilizing their cognitive ability and creative skills, many gifted students with ADHD can find new ways to compensate for their struggles. With specific skill training, they are often more able to generalize strategies they are taught. They may invent their own tools, such as mnemonic devices, to assist with their memory.

Gifted students with ADHD excel when they can explore their range of interests and abilities. Project-based learning and interest-based projects help them develop their own path for their learning. Breaking away from linear and hierarchal learning gives these kids freedom to show what they can truly do.

Social and Emotional Considerations for Gifted Students with ADHD

Gifted learners with ADHD are at a high risk of becoming underachievers and having low self-esteem. Many internalize the negative feedback received from their parents, teachers, and friends about disciplinary problems, poor grades due to missed assignments, or difficulties in social relationships. They also struggle because they recognize that their grades do not reflect their ability. Some schools may create roadblocks that prevent these students from accessing gifted education services based on their grades or missing work. The belief that gifted education services are a privilege disproportionately hurts students whose struggles seem to be behavioral. A supportive and understanding environment—one that recognizes that the struggles of gifted children with ADHD are a result of neuro-divergent brain wiring—goes a long way to help these kids reach their potential.

The asynchronous development sometimes seen in gifted children can be exacerbated by ADHD. Many gifted students with ADHD struggle with peer perceptions because their actions come across as immature or obnoxious. The way teachers treat these students can strongly influence how their peers see them. If we are patient and caring with these students, and do not treat their ADHD characteristics as disciplinary problems, we can help protect them from social rejection by their peers.

Emotional Regulation

Another core component of ADHD, beyond inattention and hyperactivity, is emotional impulsivity (van Stralen 2016). Emotional impulsivity is not considered one of the diagnostic criteria for ADHD, but those who study ADHD seem to agree that it is a common characteristic of the diagnosis. Emotional impulsivity is intense emotional reaction to a variety of situations; the reaction often seems to be disproportionate to the situation that caused it. Emotional outbursts are often the result of impulsive reactions to environmental stressors. The reaction may look like anger, disrespect, sadness, or moodiness.

Emotional impulsivity often gets interpreted as defiance, stubbornness, or another behavioral problem. With 2e students, their strong emotional response is often accompanied by a long, logical diatribe supporting their position. It may be caused by the student's strong opinions on what is right or wrong or by being questioned on a topic they know very well. When intense emotions combine with other common conditions, such as anxiety or low self-esteem, a student with ADHD might disengage or refuse to compromise. **Figure 8-1** provides suggestions on how to handle emotional impulsiveness in school.

> ❝ Hunter has always been a zero-to-sixty kid, going from calm to enraged or devastated before you can blink your eyes. We can't talk him down when he is in that heightened state. I just try to be patient and reassuring.
>
> —Paul, dad of a gifted/ADHD kid ❞

Rejection Sensitive Dysphoria (RSD)

Children who have ADHD are often hypersensitive to what other people say or think about them. They may get really upset if they think someone has criticized or rejected them, even if that criticism or rejection is imagined. This reaction is called rejection sensitive dysphoria (RSD).

Kids who experience RSD are more likely to be embarrassed if they make a mistake in front of the class or get a simple behavioral redirection from a teacher, a "bad" grade on a test, or an invalidating response when they ask for help. They experience anxiety in situations where they feel they may be judged. When they do receive negative feedback, they may react in anger and defensiveness, blaming others for the situation. Alternately, they may be devastated by the feeling that they are not accepted by their peers. They may break down in tears at being misunderstood.

RSD is associated with the emotional impulsivity and intensity seen in many individuals with ADHD. It can be difficult to deal with in the classroom. Kids and adults who experience this describe it as "spinning" or "spiraling." They engage in negative self-talk, repeating either aloud or internally statements that they are stupid, an idiot, or a failure. Students with RSD may avoid taking risks. The combination of not being understood as a gifted learner as well as showing the negative characteristics associated with ADHD makes it hard for them to find a like-minded friend group.

There may be times when the triggering event truly was a rejection, but other times a student may be interpreting an event through a lens of low self-esteem and negativity. Experts note that children with ADHD get many more negative messages about themselves than other kids their age get (Frye 2016). All that negativity can damage their self-esteem. Either way, we need to make sure we aren't accusing the child of seeking attention or drama. RSD is best handled with calmness, acceptance, and patience.

TIPS FOR HANDLING RSD

- **Provide support before the spiral begins.** Supporting a student with RSD before shame and disappointment spiral out of control is the best way to help them. Directly telling the student, "Don't worry. You aren't in trouble," followed by a suggestion or instruction, can prevent feelings of rejection.

- **Handle behavioral or disciplinary situations as discreetly as possible.** Shame due to an entire class knowing how a student messed up can magnify feelings of rejection. Avoid behavior modification systems that use public methods of designating success, such as colored cards, clip charts, ClassDojo, or point systems.

- **Explicitly teach strategies to promote direct and productive peer conversations.** For example, if a child's feelings are hurt by a friend making a teasing or sarcastic joke, they can self-advocate and resolve the situation by saying something like "When you made that joke, it sounded like you were saying you didn't want me to be part of your group. It would mean a lot to me if you would not make jokes like that anymore."

- **Normalize negative feedback and contextualize it within positive feedback.** If a student does poorly on an assignment or test, take a few moments to explain what they did well and the specific areas they can improve. Try to avoid handing back papers with poor grades without discussing or explaining it first. For older kids, writing clear and explanatory feedback on the assignment can also meet this need.

Internalizing and Masking ADHD Symptoms

Many gifted students with ADHD mask their symptoms by internalizing their distraction, rather than disrupting those around them. This internalization is generally a result of family, teacher, and societal expectations. Gifted students pick up on these expectations and learn to minimize the outward appearance of their symptoms in certain environments.

Because of internalization and masking, these students are often overlooked or diagnosed at an older age. They may not be offered the support that could help them. Their gifted characteristics are still a source of perfectionism, but achieving their goals

Figure 8-1 Handling Emotional Impulsiveness in School

Don't	Do
Punish the student for their reaction.	Recognize that emotional dysregulation is outside the student's control.
Minimize the child's emotions by saying things like "It's not that big a deal."	Help the student label their emotions. Finding the just-right emotion word is powerful.
Ignore the student.	Check in with your student. Ask them what you can do to help or give them options if they can't suggest solutions.
Try to force a student to talk while they are dysregulated.	If a child is dysregulated and unable to speak, help them communicate nonverbally. For example, ask yes-or-no questions and request a thumbs-up or thumbs-down. Or say, "I'll know you're ready to talk when you lift your head from the desk."
Repeatedly ask a student why they reacted the way they did. (Many students either don't know or don't want to talk about it because it brings up uncomfortable emotions.)	Help the student describe the situation by focusing on the facts. Many students find it easier to talk about a situation from an objective point of view.
Send the student to the hall or the back of the classroom when they are dysregulated.	If you know a student has trouble with emotional impulsivity, establish a plan for where they can go to calm down. When they use this tool independently, recognize their effort as a success.

seems impossible. The frustration and confusion caused by knowing their capabilities but not being able to fulfill them leads to low self-esteem and a lack of self-efficacy. Many of these students feel unable to ask for help. They get exhausted from the effort of appearing normal.

As teachers, we can help these students by checking in with them often and providing options for supports they may need. Offering discreet supports can make a big difference in a student's willingness to accept them. Frank discussions about how they are experiencing our classroom and what they notice as obstacles to their success can build self-advocacy skills while helping us make modifications that foster their academic success. For example, some students prefer not to be called on in class when they aren't expecting it; other students benefit from reducing the amount of redundant homework. Recognizing the subtleties of gifted students with ADHD who internalize their symptoms can help them excel.

EMILY'S STORY

I had a love-hate relationship with my ADHD diagnosis when I was a kid. On the one hand, I appreciated understanding why things that seemed easy for other people were hard for me, and that helped me self-advocate effectively. On the other hand, I didn't like other people pointing out that I was different or saying that there was something wrong with me.

In eighth grade, our gifted class was working on a group project. We were brainstorming ideas to design and construct a large model of a fictitious town. I was excited. We were all calling out our ideas as our teacher jotted them on the board.

I remember standing and describing my idea in detail to the rest of the class. I was probably more than a little verbose, and I've never been known for having a quiet voice. Right in front of my gifted class, my teacher asked me, "Emily, did you remember to take your medication today?"

"Yes," I told her, sitting down. I still remember my face getting hot and staring at my desk and remaining quite silent for the rest of the day. I wasn't really embarrassed by the fact that I had ADHD, and most of my friends already knew I did. But my teacher suggesting that my enthusiasm was something that should be medicated took the wind out of my sails. This vivid memory is part of the reason I became a teacher and counselor—to help kids know that they're more than their diagnosis. ■

Accommodations and Modifications for Gifted Students with ADHD

Many of the tools discussed in chapter 6 on executive functioning are effective interventions for students with ADHD. ADHD is essentially a constellation of lacking executive functioning skills. For 2e learners, certain interventions are more effective than others. The reproducible table at the end of the chapter (see page 159) provides a list of possible accommodations and modifications for writing a 504 plan or IEP, but many students won't qualify or won't require official documentation to support their needs. Teachers who can understand students' needs and modify their classrooms and instructional styles accordingly will help the students be successful.

Environmental Accommodations

Some students benefit from the opportunity to stay after school for a study hall or even have a study hall built into their schedule. For students with ADHD, unstructured study times often are not as effective as study times with parents or teachers available to help. Students with ADHD tend to struggle in unstructured environments. A guided study hall or other structured opportunities with frequent check-ins help students use their time wisely.

Students who are easily distracted benefit from an environment that is clear of clutter and extraneous visual stimuli. I've seen some adorable classrooms that have posters and decorations on all four walls and the ceiling. For a student with ADHD, this visual "noise" is difficult to tune out during class. Creating an environment that is truly quiet during work times is also essential. Some teachers like to play soft music, and some teachers don't mind if students chat quietly while they're working. But for a student with ADHD, the best setting for productivity is a quiet environment without sound pollution. This can be accomplished in a variety of ways. Instead of playing music in the classroom, students can be allowed to listen to their own music on headphones during quiet work time if they would like. If the class is unstructured and asking students for complete silence is unreasonable, students with ADHD (or any students with difficulty focusing) can work in an alternate environment, use noise-canceling headphones, or discreetly listen to white noise through earbuds.

Create procedures and routines for your class and explicitly teach those routines to your students. Procedures and routines help distractible students predict what is going to happen and prepare accordingly. Integrating frequent breaks in your routine gives students the opportunity to reset their brains and then get back to work.

JEREMY'S STORY

I attended a 504 plan meeting with Jeremy and his parents to speak to his high school teachers and administrators. Diagnosed with ADHD during elementary school, Jeremy had never been found eligible for accommodations because he could usually compensate for his struggles with his strong cognitive abilities. When he was a junior in high school, however, the workload was proving to be more difficult. The homework for his AP courses was taking him hours every night to complete. His family had already made the difficult decision for Jeremy to quit the high school swim team in order to focus on academics. Although he'd been swimming for years, his long-term goal of attending college to become an engineer depended more on his grades than his athletics.

The main accommodation Jeremy appeared to need was extended time for homework. He had begun a habit of robbing Peter to pay Paul. He would strategically choose what homework was the most important to complete, knowing that he wouldn't have enough time to complete all the work in a single night. This left Jeremy perpetually behind and frequently losing points for turning in late work. One additional day of grace would allow him to balance his work and occasionally have an additional weekend to catch up.

The meeting started off a little shaky. As Jeremy and his parents tried to explain the problem, the teachers, principal, and counselor asked why Jeremy was taking so many AP courses if the workload was too much. This response from school officials is common, but we gently reminded them that a student's disability cannot exclude them from content that is appropriate for their cognitive level. It was evident from Jeremy's test grades that the content was not too difficult. Through the discussion, we were able to separate Jeremy's cognitive abilities from his ADHD struggles. The school granted extended time for homework. Jeremy was even able to rejoin his high school swim team for his senior year after effectively using the extra time for homework when it was needed. ■

Instructional Accommodations

Students with ADHD benefit from wait time, so they have a chance to process questions and reflect on their own answers. Twice-exceptional students who struggle with processing speed or working memory also benefit. Giving students a way to record their answer during class discussions, such as on a whiteboard, allows all students to come up with an answer before it is given to the class. This strategy can also be helpful for students who have a hard time not calling out the answer as soon as a question has left the teacher's mouth.

Inquiry-based and problem-based learning offer excellent opportunities for 2e learners to spread their wings. However, long-term projects require a big commitment for students to follow through and may require accommodations. Big-picture thinkers with ADHD benefit from coming up with an alternate idea in case their original plan doesn't come together. Students who develop an alternate idea can learn to recognize that it's okay to self-monitor their progress and change course if necessary.

USING FIDGETS EFFECTIVELY

For many students with ADHD, using some type of fidget—such as a fidget cube, a stress ball, or doodling—can help them stay focused. ADHD is a misallocation of focus and working memory, and fulfilling sensory needs with a fidget can help students tune out extraneous environmental stimuli and focus on instruction. However, it can be difficult to tell if a student is actually benefiting from using a fidget or if it is causing more distraction.

I've found that explicit instruction about the purpose of fidgets and how to use them effectively can help students learn to self-regulate their attention. For example, many students like to draw or doodle when they are listening to classroom instruction. I encourage students not to get carried away with drawing an entire scene from the most recent superhero movie, but to doodle about the topic being discussed in class. Processing the information shared during class discussion and turning it into an image (for example, doodling a picture of a double helix while learning about the discovery of the structure of DNA by Rosalind Franklin) can help a student engage metacognitive thinking skills and solidify the concepts in their minds. Another way to teach students to doodle is to show them various patterns, such as polka dots, swirls, or crosshatches, that are repetitive and require minimal brainpower.

Students benefit from tactile sensory input when fidgeting. Tactile fidgets that do not require a student to look at them while using them are ideal, because they allow students to attend to what is going on around them. Some of my favorite tactile fidgets are fidget rings (a springlike ring that the student can roll up and down their finger) and marble fidgets (a small mesh tube containing marbles that the student can push back and forth). Both of these fidgets are inexpensive; having a class set gives all students access to this easy accommodation.

Share with your students these guidelines for using fidgets effectively:

- The fidget must help you focus, not distract you more.

- If the fidget is anything other than a normal tool used for school (such as a pencil used for doodling), you should be able to use it while keeping it out of sight.

- Your use of a fidget cannot distract other students from their work. If it makes noise or is visible to other students, it probably isn't an appropriate fidget.

Organizational Accommodations

Structured and consistent organizational systems allow 2e students to flourish. Establishing consistent routines for all classes reduces the need for students to shift gears for each subject. Regular check-ins on planners or agendas help keep students accountable. A single place for students and parents to check on assignments and missing work makes life easier for everyone. I've worked with some students who have six teachers, each of whom shares lesson plans and assignments in a different way—some have a blog, some use a reminder app, and others use the school's online grading system. Having to check multiple locations for assignments is inefficient and confusing, even for the most organized student. A cohesive plan for a school to keep this information in a single place is useful for all students and their families.

Once you establish a routine, stick to it for any procedures your class may have. Posting the procedure in an obvious place is helpful for students who don't remember what you said on the first day of school. Do the students know where to get make-up work if they've been absent? Where should they turn it in? If they've forgotten their materials, is there an easily accessible place for them to borrow materials for the day? Many 2e students struggle with self-advocacy; knowing they can count on the same procedures every day helps them stay organized on their own.

Key Points

- Gifted students with ADHD can show signs of inattention, forgetfulness, hyperactivity, impulsiveness, and heightened emotional reactions.

- Gifted students often mask signs of difficulty focusing and paying attention by compensating with their advanced cognitive skills.

- Gifted students with ADHD can draw many strengths from their diagnosis, such as increased creativity and passion for novel ideas.

Gifted, 2e, or ADHD?

Gifted	2e (Gifted with ADHD)	ADHD
Level of concentration		
Students who are gifted often can regulate their level of focus and concentration with minimal distractibility. They can maintain their attention for longer amounts of time. This could be mistaken for hyperfocus if the child is a perfectionist and resists transitioning to new activities if their work is incomplete.	High-interest activities and creative pursuits allow gifted learners with ADHD to thrive, and their inattention may not manifest in these situations. Shifting gears between one activity and another can be problematic. A 2e student's wide range of interests may also affect their level of concentration, if they tend to bounce from one activity to another.	External stimuli cause significant distraction, and the student is unable to regulate their level of focus during nonpreferred activities. Some students with more severe ADHD may be unable to regulate their attention even on preferred activities.
Repetitive tasks		
Gifted students are often frustrated with drill-and-kill assignments because they can master the content quickly and do not need additional practice to master the skill. Generally, gifted students without ADHD can show task persistence and complete the work, even if they find it boring or unpleasant.	Repetitive tasks are often met with significant resistance because of the anticipated difficulty regulating attention. Students may struggle with task initiation. Students may turn in half-completed work with the first portion completed accurately and the rest left blank.	Following routines and managing repetitive tasks is extremely difficult without prompting or support. Some level of repetition can be beneficial for students who need to practice rote memorization skills, such as math facts, to mitigate inattention when applying those skills in other situations.
Attitude about learning		
Many gifted learners have a positive attitude about learning and will engage in the academic environment easily.	Learning that isn't conducted in a preferred modality is difficult to engage in, even if the topic is interesting to the student. Gifted learners with ADHD may avoid tasks that seem too hard. They may show a low frustration tolerance.	Academic tasks, especially those requiring multiple steps, can be extremely frustrating. Students may learn to disengage in the classroom to avoid continued frustration.
Psychomotor needs		
Gifted children may experience mild heightened sensitivity to textures, sounds, or other sensory input. In general, it does not interfere with daily functioning, or it may be related to another diagnosis.	Gifted students with ADHD may benefit from being taught how to effectively use fidgets or doodling to enhance focus and reduce the impact of other environmental input.	Hyperactivity looks like the student is driven by a motor. Student is unable to manage their sensory-seeking needs without support or other tools.

Accommodations and Modifications for ADHD

Major Life Activity	Possible Accommodation or Modification
Performing manual tasks	
Lagging fine-motor skills result in poor handwriting and inappropriate spacing on written assignments.	• Instructional: Provide paper with extra lines to guide students' handwriting. • Evaluative: Do not grade papers based on neatness.
Concentrating	
Working memory deficits cause difficulty following multi-step instructions.	• Instructional: Give multistep instructions in written form. (Some students may require these to be on their desks instead of on the board.) • Instructional: Have student check in after each step is complete before moving on to next step.
Processing speed inhibits ability to complete work within typical time allowances.	• Instructional: Allow extra time on timed tests or assignments. (Providing supports and structure for this additional time can make it more effective.) • Instructional: Provide additional time to complete longer projects or homework without penalty.
Student struggles with inattention and distractibility.	• Instructional: Provide frequent check-ins to keep student on task. • Instructional: Give student a copy of any notes prior to class; fill-in-the-blank notes help students stay on track and focused.
Psychomotor needs impede ability to stay in seat and on task.	• Environmental: Allow student to pace or use wiggle chair, fidgets, or other sensory tools to meet psychomotor needs.
Student resists completing repetitive or mundane work.	• Instructional: Shorten assignments. • Evaluative: Allow pretesting to show mastery.
Impulsive behavior leads to class disruption and disciplinary problems.	• Behavioral: Set collaborative goals with student to improve specific behavioral regulation skills.
Thinking	
Difficulty with time management or response inhibition results in rushing through work.	• Instructional: Develop method for student to self-check assignments and check in with teacher prior to moving onto to different work.
Organizational deficits result in missing work and materials.	• Organizational: Develop process for frequent communication with parents. • Organizational: Allow student to keep class materials in classroom instead of in locker.
Student may become overwhelmed at large packets of information or tests.	• Instructional: Give student a single page of an assignment or test at a time.
Assignments and materials are left at school instead of taken home for homework.	• Organizational: Provide an additional set of textbooks for student to keep at home. • Behavioral: Require student to check in with teacher at the end of each day to double-check materials and planner.

9 Autism Spectrum Disorder (ASD)

Autism spectrum disorder is a developmental disability affecting an individual's social communication and social interaction skills. The *Diagnostic and Statistical Manual of Mental Disorders: Fifth Edition* (DSM-5) recognizes the following symptoms of ASD:

- **Difficulty with typical back-and-forth communication:** Conversations are often one-sided. The student has limited responses or responses that do not move the conversation forward, or they talk about their areas of interest without waiting for typical responses from their conversation partner.

- **Atypical verbal and nonverbal communication:** Autistic students may have difficulty regulating the volume of their voice or may speak without inflection. They may lack commonly expected nonverbal communication, like making eye contact when speaking, or they may struggle to interpret typical nonverbal communication from others.

- **Difficulty finding and keeping friends:** Autistic students may have trouble making friends and keeping them, especially as they get older.

- **Sensory processing differences:** Many autistic gifted learners process sensory information differently than their peers do. Autistic students may be very sensitive to sensory input, become overwhelmed and try to avoid it, or be underresponsive and engage in sensory-seeking behaviors.

- **Being overwhelmed by unexpected transitions or plan changes:** Substitute teachers, schedules changed for assemblies, or other unanticipated situations can be overwhelming when an autistic learner hasn't had advance notice.

- **Areas of intense interest or passion:** Autistic students may have areas of special interest that they pursue with passion. Given the choice, they will spend time researching, talking about, and engaging in this area of interest.

Identifying ASD in Gifted Learners

The DSM-5 states that symptoms "may not become fully manifest until social demands exceed limited capacities or may be masked by learned strategies in later life" (American Psychiatric Association 2017, 50). In gifted learners, ASD can be masked until late elementary, middle, or even high school because a child is able to get by. We may call what are really ASD symptoms "quirks," explaining away the signs of autism. Some characteristics of giftedness *can* mimic ASD, but rather than ignoring these signs, educators should be aware of them and investigate what needs the student may have. Gifted kids whose ASD goes undiagnosed miss the chance to proactively address concerns at a young age, when neuroplasticity is at its peak. At older ages, it can be extremely difficult to change rigid thinking patterns and problematic behaviors.

ABIGAIL'S STORY

Abigail was a breeze to care for as a baby. She slept through the night and was satisfied entertaining herself from an early age. Her parents noticed she was very particular about textures. Baby Abigail liked to be swaddled as tightly as possible. As a preschooler, she cried if she didn't have socks on her feet, and she refused to wear jeans. She was a picky eater. Her first favorite toys were Disney figurines. When Abigail played with them, she lined them up in various orders—first by color, then by story, then by size. Her parents noticed that her interests were intense and single-minded. After Disney princesses, it was superheroes, then sharks, then Justin Bieber.

By four years old, Abigail had taught herself to read. When she was in kindergarten, she began occupational therapy for concerns with textures, clothing, and food. Her parents noticed that these issues were causing a lot of stress at home, leading to hysterical crying meltdowns until Abigail chose her own clothing or got something different to eat. Her parents couldn't figure out why she never had any meltdowns at school. Her teachers described her as shy. Identified as gifted in kindergarten, Abigail was exceptionally well behaved, quiet, and bright.

In second grade, Abigail's pediatrician voiced concerns about her behavior and had her parents complete a screening questionnaire on Asperger's syndrome (now known as ASD). When the results of the assessment identified Abigail as having Asperger's syndrome, her parents dismissed them, feeling the concerns were not significant enough to warrant action and were likely better explained by Abigail's giftedness. They were reluctant to apply the Asperger's label to their daughter.

In third grade, the balance between Abigail's abilities and struggles began to shift. Standardized testing was a traumatic experience for her. Teachers stressed the importance of the statewide testing all year. When the week for standardized testing arrived, Abigail panicked. Her black-and-white thinking and perfectionism paralyzed her when it came to performing on the test. Her anxiety led to meltdowns, and Abigail was removed from the classroom. Her parents were called each day because Abigail was unable to regulate her emotions. Abigail's parents realized they needed to act.

Once Abigail had a medical diagnosis of Asperger's syndrome, her parents went to work advocating for support through the school system. The task was not easy. Abigail was above average academically, participating in the gifted program, and not a behavior problem at school. However, it was clear she needed support for standardized testing, social communication, and emotional regulation. With strong advocacy, Abigail's parents were able to secure an IEP for accommodations and speech-language services.

For Abigail, being a gifted student on an IEP has had its ups and downs. To receive the number of special education minutes required by her IEP, in middle school Abigail was placed in a CWC for math. This meant she couldn't take the advanced math class, even though she could have managed the work. At the time this seemed like a reasonable compromise with the special education team; however, it caused unanticipated problems when Abigail entered high school. She was able to take higher-level science courses, but she was at a disadvantage in these classes because she wasn't concurrently taking advanced math courses.

By the time Abigail was a junior in high school, she was playing on her school's tennis team and was passionate about social justice issues. She had a solid group of friends and a boyfriend and had found her stride as a gifted and autistic young woman. Abigail and I had been working together consistently since she was in fourth grade to help her understand the subtleties of language and build emotional regulation to handle anxiety. She learned to recognize when she didn't understand a social situation and built the confidence to ask for clarification when something was unclear. We worked on using the strengths of her giftedness to support the struggles of her ASD. ■

Abigail's story is one of success. Although it took several years working together at my office for her to overcome her intense test anxiety—for a number of years, she would refuse to get out of the car on standardized testing days—Abigail is now preparing to complete high school and go to college. She has chosen to disclose her diagnosis to a few close friends and school personnel who help her with her accommodations. The actions taken by her parents and school early on will allow her to enter adulthood with the skills she needs to manage her twice-exceptionality independently.

JILLIAN'S STORY

Jillian was identified as gifted in kindergarten. She never had a lot of friends and was rather aloof. Her brilliant mind showed her ability, but her grades never did. She struggled to understand the implications of completing and turning in work and had poor self-advocacy skills. As she entered high school and began showing signs of depression, her parents brought her to my office. During our sessions, I recognized that she had lagging social communication skills and rigid thinking patterns. Jillian was diagnosed with ASD and received an IEP, but she continued to struggle greatly. She often got stuck in patterns of black-and-white thinking. ■

Jillian's ASD is compounded by her depression. However, because her struggles weren't recognized at an earlier age, the beliefs she carries about herself are ingrained, and she is resistant to strategies that could help her. Counseling sessions are rough; Jillian has a deep sense of learned helplessness. She doesn't want to try to come up with new coping skills, and she struggles with perspective taking. If Jillian's needs had been identified earlier, we could have had years to work together and build her independence. Because her twice-exceptionality went unnoticed for so long, it is also taking a long time to unlearn the habits and beliefs she developed during that time.

The Language of Autism

The *Diagnostic and Statistical Manual of Mental Disorders: Fourth Edition* (DSM-IV), published in 1994, described four autism-related diagnoses: autistic disorder, Asperger's syndrome, pervasive developmental disorder, and childhood disintegrative disorder.

When the DSM-5 was published in 2013, the diagnostic criteria were modified based on research and clinical experience gathered over two decades. The DSM-5 describes just one diagnosis—autism spectrum disorder (ASD)—and no longer identifies four subdiagnoses. The DSM-5 also adds a new disorder that is not considered autism: social communication disorder (SCD). People with social communication struggles who don't show repetitive behaviors or restrictive interests may be diagnosed with SCD (Hyman 2013).

After the DSM-5 was released, many individuals originally diagnosed with Asperger's syndrome continued to use that terminology. Asperger's referred to a person on the autism spectrum who did not show the typical verbal delays in early childhood and who needed minimal support. The term *Asperger's* is being used less and less as the medical, educational, and neurodivergent communities grow in their understanding of autism. Some people use the term *high-functioning* to describe individuals with autism who need minimal support; however, this term is falling out of favor as well. Many autism advocates see using terms like *Asperger's* and *high-functioning* as ableist and divisive, preferring to discuss needs as mild or severe. Also, *high-functioning* is often mistakenly conflated with high cognitive ability; it's important to understand that students can have good verbal communication skills but still need significant support in school and at home. When I'm talking with families and they use autism terms based on functioning levels, I ask for clarification about what the terminology means to them. Beyond an official medical or educational diagnosis requiring certain terminology, educator awareness of historical and informal terms is important in building rapport with individuals and families in the autism community.

Misdiagnosis and Missed Diagnosis: Recognizing ASD

Common characteristics of giftedness overlap with symptoms of ASD. This overlap can lead to both misdiagnosis and missed diagnosis of ASD in gifted individuals. Understanding the nuances of this overlap can help educators ensure a child receives the appropriate services, whether they be gifted education services, social skills instruction, or special education services. Remember that with 2e learners, their gifts may mask their disability, or their struggles may mask their gifts. The reproducible chart on page 175 (**Gifted, 2e, or ASD?**), while not exhaustive, examines the diagnostic criteria of ASD and how each symptom could be mistakenly identified in a gifted child and might manifest in a 2e child. In addition to the masking common in 2e children, the layering of comorbid (additional) diagnoses can further complicate matters. The presence of generalized anxiety disorder, obsessive-compulsive disorder, or ADHD may also cause a delay in determining the presence of ASD.

The early recognition of ASD can make a big difference in the success of a student over time. Proactive interventions from a young age, including instruction in emotional literacy, social skills, and self-advocacy, can provide 2e students the skills needed for successful social interactions later in life. The stigma surrounding a diagnosis of ASD is strong, though, and many families may explain away symptoms by associating them with giftedness. The stigma is gradually weakening as awareness and understanding of the nature of ASD grows.

An official diagnosis is necessary to access both educational services through an IEP or 504 plan and to use medical insurance for services in the community. Early intervention can have a lifelong impact on a 2e child's self-image, social relationships, and academic success. The longer a child goes undiagnosed, the more difficult it can be to overcome rigid thinking patterns and struggles with appropriate social communication.

CADE'S STORY

Cade's mom brought him in for counseling when he was a fourth grader. He struggled with motivation and peer relationships. He'd been diagnosed with ADHD when he was in first grade. His mom reported that none of the medications Cade had tried had ever worked, and eventually Cade had stopped taking them.

Cade bounced on the couch throughout our entire first session. He jumped from topic to topic during the conversation and spoke very fast. I could see what looked like hyperactivity. However, I also noticed Cade kept returning to his favorite topic, which was wars—the Korean War, to be specific. After a few sessions with Cade, I asked his mom if anyone had ever suggested that he might be autistic.

Screening and assessment made it clear that Cade was indeed on the autism spectrum. Now it made sense that the ADHD medications had never worked. His hyperactivity was related to sensory needs; his inattention was a lack of social skills and awareness, not an inability to pay attention. We began focusing on building Cade's social awareness and cognitive flexibility to help him with peer relationships and academic success. By the time he got to middle school, Cade was succeeding with the help of a 504 plan.

Cade's mom reflected, "When we began looking into a diagnosis of autism, it made sense! We were looking at his problems from the wrong perspective—it wasn't inattention or hyperactivity at all. I'm grateful Cade's teachers have been able to accommodate his sensory needs and support his motivation with the 504 plan." ■

When ASD Looks Like ADHD

For many reasons, a child is more likely to end up with an ADHD diagnosis than an ASD diagnosis when problems first appear. There is a greater understanding of ADHD in the medical, educational, and parenting communities. ADHD symptoms are also often very visible, while ASD signs may be harder to spot. Here are three symptoms of ASD that can be misinterpreted as ADHD:

- **Inattentiveness:** An inability to focus and pay attention is a classic symptom of ADHD. Autistic children may also look like they can't pay attention. To figure out whether the cause is ASD, you could ask, "Is this inattentiveness better explained by not understanding the social expectation to focus in certain situations? Is the child motivated to engage only when the topic is within their area of interest?"

- **Impulsiveness:** Impulsive behavior is another symptom that often leads to a diagnosis of ADHD. When examined through the lens of ASD, impulsive behavior such as interrupting conversations could be caused by not understanding the norms of typical reciprocal conversation. Social norms and unspoken rules exist in game play and other interactions that autistic children don't pick up on; as a result, their behavior can look impulsive. Intense emotions and meltdowns associated with ASD may also be written off as the impulsive behavior of ADHD.

■ **Hyperactivity:** Hyperactivity is a third classic symptom of ADHD. It often looks like a child can't stop moving. But constant movement, bouncing, or pacing could be due to an ASD-related sensory need or stimming behavior instead of true hyperactivity. Hyperactivity can also look like a need to talk constantly. Autistic children or teens may talk about their areas of interest without pausing for feedback due to difficulty understanding the social rules of reciprocal conversation.

WHAT IS STIMMING?

Stimming is a term often associated with autism spectrum disorder. A stim is a stimulatory behavior; stimming is the act of using the behavior. Stimming is often a self-regulating behavior. For example, an autistic person might wave or flap their hands when they are excited, rock in their seat when they are worried, or pace around a room when they are concentrating. Stimming is related to both the sensory component of ASD and the repetitive or restrictive behaviors associated with the diagnosis. Some stims are visible and noticeable; other stims are more subtle, like a facial grimace. An autistic person who is attempting to hide their stimming behaviors may twirl their hair or pick at their nails, which are generally socially accepted behaviors. Sometimes, stimming behaviors can be self-injurious, like hitting one's head. Unless a stim has the potential to cause harm, we don't want to discourage autistic students from stimming. Stimming is an integral part of how their minds process information and regulate emotions.

Educational Diagnosis of ASD Under IDEA

Autistic gifted learners may struggle to receive services through an IEP due to a narrow reading of IDEA without contextualizing the needs of gifted students. IDEA defines an educational diagnosis of ASD as follows (US Department of Education 2017):

> *Autism means a developmental disability significantly affecting verbal and nonverbal communication and social interaction, generally evident before age three, that adversely affects a child's educational performance. Other characteristics often associated with autism are engagement in repetitive activities and stereotyped movements, resistance to environmental change or change in daily routines, and unusual responses to sensory experiences.*
>
> *Autism does not apply if a child's educational performance is adversely affected primarily because the child has an emotional disturbance. . . .*

Here are some reasons that autistic gifted learners may be wrongly denied a diagnosis or services for educational autism:

■ Many autistic gifted learners do not show clear evidence of struggles with communication or social interaction before age three due to their advanced cognitive abilities; their abilities mask their struggles until social demands exceed their capabilities.

■ The phrase *adversely affects a child's educational performance* can be interpreted to mean "academically below grade level," which many autistic gifted learners are not.

The term *educational performance* has a much broader meaning than just "academic achievement."

■ Many of the characteristics of an autistic gifted learner *do* appear to be an emotional disturbance; however, if the cause is directly related to deficits in verbal and nonverbal communication, social interaction, or other symptoms of autism, identification of emotional disturbance is a misdiagnosis.

To clarify the appropriate use of the educational autism diagnosis, in 2010 the US Department of Education's Office of Special Education Programs issued a letter stating that "a child with high cognition and . . . Asperger's Syndrome could be considered under the disability category of autism and the individualized evaluation would address the special education and related services needs in the affective areas, social skills, and classroom behavior, as appropriate" (Posny 2010).

It is important to note that symptoms of autism in 2e learners may not appear in assessments the same way they do in nongifted students. High-ability autistic children may not show elevated scores on some common screeners for autism because high-ability individuals were not included in the normative populations to create these assessments. ASD presents differently in gifted learners than it does in nongifted learners. On many of the basic measures used to diagnosis ASD, high-ability autistic children have stronger skills than nongifted autistic children in the areas of reciprocal conversation, social anxiety, and empathy. Symptoms of stereotypical behaviors, highly restrictive interests, and social pragmatics are more closely aligned with the normative autistic population (Cederberg et al. 2018). Unless individuals properly trained in the complexities of 2e learners examine a comprehensive evaluation, it is possible to miss ASD in gifted learners—along with the opportunity to provide proactive interventions to benefit them as they mature.

Once a student has been identified as needing special education services for ASD, appropriate placement can be tricky to manage. Instruction in social skills or pragmatic language may be appropriate; however, schools may find themselves struggling to find a suitable peer group for these 2e learners. It may work to place them with older students for this instruction. Integrating higher-level thinking skills into the special education instruction can meet the child's gifted needs while supporting the child's ASD needs.

If a child does not qualify for an IEP but has a medical diagnosis of ASD, families or educators can advocate for a 504 plan. Possible areas of accommodation and modification for autistic gifted learners are performing manual tasks, concentrating, communicating, and learning. The reproducible chart on page 177 (**Accommodations and Modifications for ASD**) provides examples of how each area may be affected in the school setting and possible accommodations and modifications.

Understanding Common Struggles for Autistic Gifted Students

Students who are identified as gifted and autistic face a variety of challenges in the school setting. Teachers and peers often do not realize these 2e learners are autistic and don't understand their unexpected behaviors or their struggles. The most frequent struggles I see in my autistic gifted students are related to black-and-white thinking and social relationships.

Rigid Thinking and Friendships

Black-and-white thinking often manifests in these students as perfectionism. Or it can look like defiance, even when it is not. Many autistic gifted students feel most comfortable when there is a clear right or wrong answer; they find the ambiguity of written assignments paralyzing. Some of these learners fall into habits of perfectionism and anxiety over completing work that is "just right." Others don't understand the implications of school and how grades fit into the big picture, and they become underachievers or selective consumers (students who engage only with material they deem interesting or valuable). It can be frustrating for students, teachers, and families when they see the disconnect between high cognitive ability and low achievement.

Because of these rigid thinking patterns, developing friendships can be difficult for autistic 2e learners. Inflexibility can cause struggles in interpersonal interactions. For example, if an autistic student wants to play only a specific type of role-play game at recess and attempts to enforce specific rules for this game, their peers may choose not to play with them. Opportunities to build relationships in class through shared projects or group work can be derailed by difficulties with social communication or expectations from group members to complete the work a certain way.

The asynchronous development of social skills in autistic 2e learners is complex, leaving these students vulnerable to bullying, isolation, or depression. Any person who tells you that autistic kids are loners or don't want friends is making a gross generalization. In most cases I've seen, that generalization is wrong. One of the hardest things I've had to help my young gifted and autistic clients through is the feeling of isolation—desperately wanting friends and having a very hard time finding them. Friendships for autistic gifted kids might look different from other friendships; they may be based on a common interest, or most of their interactions may take place online.

Problematic Behaviors

Many autistic students struggle with disruptive or other types of problematic behaviors in the classroom. These behaviors often result from stress, anxiety, and other uncomfortable feelings that arise when events do not align with expectations. Sensory overload can also lead to disruptive behavior.

I've seen students melt down in a variety of ways. Some completely shut down and cannot engage again until they become regulated. Others get angry at themselves and begin to self-injure. Still others show outward anger through aggressive actions or language. To put these incidents in perspective, try to remember the idea that students do well when they can. As psychology professor Ross Greene explains, "Kids with behavioral challenges are not attention-seeking, manipulative, limit-testing, coercive, or unmotivated. But they do lack the skills to behave appropriately. Adults can help by recognizing what causes their difficult behaviors and teaching kids the skills they need" (Greene 2008).

When a student is becoming dysregulated and needs support, there are several ways you can help:

- **Reframe behavior as communication.** The struggling student is not being manipulative or disrespectful. They simply don't have the language or emotional regulation skills to manage their emotions independently. Viewing their behavior as communication may prompt you to ask yourself what the child is trying to say without verbalizing. This situation is tricky for 2e kids, because adults often expect gifted kids' behavior and maturity to match the ability seen when they are not dysregulated.

- **Don't rush.** Try to avoid forcing a student to engage when they are shut down or to have a conversation when they are dysregulated. Rushing students to regulate can exacerbate their dysregulation and extend the time they need to recover.

- **Facilitate communication.** Simple statements like *I'm here when you are ready to talk* go a long way to build rapport and trust. Offering alternative ways to communicate—such as a whiteboard or hand signal—can help the student ease back into calm communication following a behavioral outburst.

- **Encourage microgoals.** Microgoals for behavior change that are set and monitored by the student are powerful ways to build feelings of self-efficacy. (See chapter 5.)

Not all problem behaviors are major disruptions. More often, you may face minor incidents that require redirection or support. For example, difficulty working in groups or managing other social interactions may interfere with the learning of the autistic student or other students in the class. Look for patterns among these incidents and engage the student's cognitive abilities to develop appropriate supports. Collaborate, collaborate, collaborate! The more engaged a student feels in a plan, the more successful the plan will be.

Sense of Duty

Some autistic gifted students struggle with any variation from their perception of the rules. For example, some students struggle to understand authority figures and hierarchies. They may not naturally internalize the social structures others take for granted. This can cause student behavior that appears disrespectful and power struggles between students and their teachers.

Autistic gifted students may not understand or agree with the social expectations we ask them to meet. They may not see the point of doing chores or homework because the consequences don't directly and immediately affect them. I've found that talking about developing a sense of responsibility, social justice, or duty is an effective way to help students with rigid ideas about the way things should be. Chris Wiebe, high school director at Bridges Academy, a school for 2e students, shares how he brings this philosophical point of view to his 2e students in episode twenty-five of *The Neurodiversity Podcast* (Wiebe 2019). Wiebe talks about how the larger order described in philosophy, with rules for ethical decision-making, can help kids who desire structure and consistency.

Pathological Demand Avoidance

Pathological demand avoidance (PDA) is an obsessive resistance to everyday demands and requests in some people with autism. It's driven by a combination of black-and-white thinking, anxiety, and difficulty with adjusting to unexpected situations and expectations. Students with PDA may refuse to comply with basic requests or assignments. If pushed too far, they may shut down or melt down.

Here are the best strategies I've found for helping these students:

- **Rapport:** Focus on your relationship with the student. Take time to get to know them, understand their quirks and preferences, and help them know they can trust you to be consistent and honest with them.

- **Preparation:** Give as much information as possible about the upcoming schedule of events (usually in writing or as a visual schedule, so students can refer to it as a reminder). This allows students to prepare for any upcoming transitions.

- **Agency:** Provide options and choices so students don't feel backed into a corner, and give lots of time for them to decide. If you don't apply too much pressure, quite often kids can wrap their heads around what is being asked and do it in their own time.

- **Acceptance:** Express unconditional positive regard for students, even when they have trouble complying. Many students with PDA have low self-esteem and feelings of inadequacy because they can't live up to their own or others' expectations.

- **Time:** Give kids with PDA the time they need to process what you're asking of them. Pushing them to try something they aren't ready to try will trigger a meltdown or more resistance.

- **Understanding:** Remember that resistance is not defiance. PDA is caused by anxiety and cognitive inflexibility.

Alexithymia

Alexithymia is the inability to recognize or identify one's own emotions. Many autistic students struggle with this. As a result, students may resort to clichés to describe their emotions, and these clichés can be misinterpreted. For example, I've had multiple clients who were extremely distressed or upset by something say they wished they were dead. This kind of language is concerning, of course—but upon further investigation, I found they weren't having suicidal ideation. Their statement actually meant, "I am having this really intense emotion that I don't know how to express to you, but I need you to know how big it is."

Helping students build emotional literacy is vital. Recognizing one's own emotions is key to self-regulation and self-advocacy. One tool you can use to help students build emotional literacy is an emotion wheel. You can find and print many emotion wheels online or use the reproducible on page 178. The latter asks students to engage their higher-level thinking skills to build emotional literacy because they must come up with words that suit them. I keep a laminated emotion wheel in my office and pull it out anytime a client is having a hard time finding the just-right word to describe their emotions.

AARON'S STORY

Aaron was a gifted middle school student with both ASD and ADHD. When Aaron was upset, you knew it. He often became dysregulated when he was frustrated, and he would use foul language. He said, "I like to use those words because I have a lot of really strong emotions and they show the person that I'm really passionate about what I'm saying." Although Aaron understood appropriate social skills, he had trouble using them.

One thing that often frustrated Aaron was what he interpreted as false praise. He didn't like teachers to be "too positive." He thought it was fake. It made him feel patronized, because he thought the praise was undeserved. It was often for something he felt he should be able to do without help. Aaron's outbursts toward people simply offering a kind word were difficult, although not impossible, to predict.

Through self-advocacy, Aaron and I worked on speaking to teachers and adults proactively, to set a norm for offering him feedback. Aaron preferred factual comments without hyperbole. Instead of "Great job!" he preferred "I like the way you applied the skill of foreshadowing in this writing piece." Neutral statements backed up with details helped this black-and-white thinker trust the speaker and use the feedback constructively. ■

Difficulties with Writing

Many autistic 2e learners struggle with writing. A variety of issues may cause this struggle. In some cases, it may be due to sensory needs or weak fine-motor skills. Slow processing speed is another obstacle. Or the student may feel paralyzed when faced with writing assignments, which tend to be open-ended rather than black and white.

When I've worked with autistic 2e students who struggle with writing, their problems usually boil down to trouble with ambiguity. As logical, black-and-white thinkers, they could answer multiple-choice and short-answer questions all day long. But when they were asked to make inferences about something they'd read, they were daunted by the fact that there was no single right or wrong answer. Choosing the just-right words to explain their thoughts seemed impossible. Additionally, inferencing often requires looking at things from someone else's point of view, which can be difficult for autistic people.

For students who struggle with writing in this way, we may need to scaffold writing assignments a bit more clearly. For example, taking time to brainstorm with a student all the possible responses is useful, but taking it one step further and scribing for them can help them see their choices concretely, instead of attempting to process them mentally and feeling overwhelmed. Providing options for graphic organizers also helps solidify their thoughts prior to writing them down. Graphic organizers that closely align with the task are most useful; try not to offer too many possible organizers, because that too can become overwhelming.

Encouraging risk-taking to overcome perfectionism can also help in the long term. A fun activity to build confidence with writing is to do a stream-of-consciousness journal entry—no erasers allowed! Ask students to write anything. (If needed, you can provide a few paragraph starters they can opt to use.) Even if they write only about how dumb they think the activity is, they will build confidence in their ability to get their thoughts onto paper.

PEYTON'S STORY

Peyton had participated in the gifted program since kindergarten. He seemed perfectionistic and was a rule follower. In third grade, when his struggles became more evident and began to outpace his abilities, Peyton was diagnosed with autism and placed on an IEP. The transition was difficult, but Peyton's mom was a tireless advocate. She worked with me and with the school to create a plan to support his needs. Ultimately, Peyton needed access to a self-contained classroom and resource teacher.

Tools that had worked with other students did not work with Peyton. He was a motivated learner, and when he couldn't complete the work to his standard, he shut down from frustration because he struggled to verbalize his emotions and ask for help. Both the general classroom teachers and the special education teachers viewed this behavior as noncompliance or defiance. Token systems, rewards, and punishments were useless with Peyton. He saw right through them, didn't care about them, or became paralyzed with fear that he wouldn't live up to the expectations set forth.

The things that were most effective for Peyton's success were:

- a relationship with his teacher, based on unconditional positive regard

- time to process decisions and prepare for transitions or changes to the routine

- thorough explanations to understand the nuances that didn't come to him naturally due to his black-and-white thinking ■

Social and Emotional Considerations for Autistic Gifted Learners

Autistic gifted learners need a different kind of social and emotional support than their peers need. As with all 2e learners, counselors and teachers must consider both the gifted nature of these children and the needs associated with their disability. Integrating higher-level thinking skills into solving social and emotional problems provides the greatest opportunity for growth for 2e students.

One common intervention used for individuals on the autism spectrum is applied behavior analysis (ABA) therapy; however, there is a lot of controversy surrounding ABA therapy in the neurodiversity community. Many autistic adults who experienced ABA therapy as children describe their experiences as traumatic based on the discrete trial reward and punishment methods used, such as removing a comfort item from the child until they complied with the specific skill (like stopping a stimming behavior).

Of the 2e kids I've worked with who've experienced ABA therapy, most of them don't gain great benefits from it anyway. They pick up on the habits that are required ("How many times are they going to tell me to look them in the eye?") but don't understand *why* these habits are important within the context of social relationships. Autistic gifted learners have a strong need to understand why something needs to be done a certain way. Relationship-based therapy and focusing on social communication skills is a much more effective (and humane) way to support autistic individuals.

ABIGAIL'S STORY, CONTINUED

Sitting in a counseling session, Abigail told me about an incident that occurred with her parents. They had just arrived home after a run on a hot day. Abigail noticed her parents smelled sweaty. She said, "Can you guys open the window? You kind of stink." Her parents obliged, but they also explained how it's poor manners to tell people they stink. During our conversation, Abigail struggled to understand the nuances of the incident. She felt she'd asked her parents to open the window politely and had simply stated a fact when she said that they stank. She stored the rule away for future reference, but she still didn't quite understand why her parents had made a fuss. After all, Abigail said, she would *want* someone to tell her if she stank! Like many autistic gifted kids, she wasn't satisfied just knowing the rule. She also needed to know the *why*. ■

Autistic gifted learners need to understand the context of the social and emotional skills they are learning. With these students, it's more effective to build emotional regulation and social skills through higher-level thinking, problem-solving, and creativity. These activities develop both social skills and flexible thinking skills.

Creativity is a useful tool for developing social skills because gifted children can often come up with a variety of possible solutions to social problems. Dramatic arts work especially well. Instead of talking about the "right" way to interact with another person (which many 2e students already know), improvisation and acting build theory of mind skills (the ability to anticipate what another person is thinking), empathy, communication, and in-the-moment social processing (Lerner and Girard 2018). Brainstorming a variety of creative solutions to certain situations and learning through the reactions of others helps these students understand the "why" of social expectations. Students who struggle with acting may find that cartooning allows them to visualize what other people are thinking and feeling more easily. Students who have an interest in a television show or video game can use that as a starting point for elaborative creativity.

KENZIE'S STORY

Kenzie, an autistic fourth grader, struggled with problem-solving in social situations and frequently had feelings of retaliation against peers whom she felt had wronged her. Kenzie had an intense interest in My Little Pony stories and characters. We used this area of interest as a starting point for solving problems creatively in social situations. Kenzie could look at the situations through the characters' eyes. This was easier than discussing her own emotions and was a step toward implementing social skills appropriately and using perspective-taking skills. ■

The reproducible activity on page 179 (**Improvisation and Role Play [Grades 2 and Up]**) provides a creative opportunity to build social awareness. This activity can be helpful for all students, not just 2e students. All kids need practice building empathy and social skills.

Building Dialectical Thinking for Cognitive Flexibility

Dialectical thinking is considering that two things that seem opposite can both be true at the same time. For example, "I am doing my best" *and* "I can try to do better" can both be true. So can "I messed up on this assignment" *and* "I am a good student." Any student who struggles with black-and-white thinking can benefit from learning about dialectical thinking. It can help students find gray areas and middle ground. Dialectical thinking is also crucial to building empathy in students. You can use the reproducible activity on page 180 (**Two Truths**) to introduce this concept to older students (grades 4 to 8). Younger students (grades 1 to 3) can practice cognitive flexibility through the reproducible activity on page 181 (**What Are They Thinking?**).

Understanding Empathy in Autistic Students

There are two types of empathy. Cognitive empathy, or theory of mind, is the ability to anticipate what another person is thinking. Affective empathy is the ability to feel another person's emotions. It is closely aligned with acts of compassion.

You may have heard or read that autistic people lack empathy. Some people believe a child who shows empathy could not possibly be autistic. This is untrue. Autistic individuals may have difficulty with cognitive empathy but show affective empathy intensely and often. Autistic gifted kids have keen awareness of others' feelings and are driven by compassion to help those in need. Many are passionate about social justice and are fervent antibullying advocates.

Empathy is much harder to show when one's own emotions are involved. For example, if I'm angry at someone and feel strongly that I'm right and they're wrong, it is hard for me to empathize with that person because my emotions are heightened. However, if I weren't personally involved, I could look at the same situation objectively and easily see the viewpoints of both people involved.

When autistic gifted learners become dysregulated, their emotions may blind them, and they may be unable to understand another person's point of view even after the situation has been resolved. Building emotional literacy so children can talk about and share emotions is integral to emotional regulation. The **Emotion Wheel (All Ages)** activity at the end of this chapter (page 178) integrates higher-level thinking skills as students create their own hierarchy of emotions; it can then be used as a tool to improve understanding and sharing emotions. Additionally, many apps can help students build emotional literacy. (See the sidebar on page 174 for more information.)

To support the social and emotional needs of autistic gifted learners, it's important to be aware of their tendency to focus on rules. If their self-advocacy skills are not yet well established, these students may need specific permission from the authority (you) to "break a rule." Typical accommodations may not seem fair to their logical minds. I've seen these learners refuse to accept extra credit or retake a test because they believe it would be "cheating." I've also seen students ask to go to the nurse or bathroom and be told no, then return to their seats with disastrous results because they felt they couldn't ask again. Consider how social communication struggles affect daily interactions. Because these students are so bright, it is easy to forget that they miss the small things, and that can cause emotional distress.

APPS AND GAMES TO BUILD EMOTIONAL LITERACY AND SOCIAL SKILLS

- **Discovering Emotions with Zeely:** This app helps autistic kids five years and older learn to recognize and interpret a variety of facial expressions. The app is game-based, which makes it engaging for users.

- **Mood Meter:** Developed by the Yale Center for Emotional Intelligence, this free app helps users from elementary school through adulthood track their emotions, develop their emotional vocabulary, look for patterns in emotional reactions, and understand the relationships between various intensities of emotion.

- **Social Adventures:** For users three to thirteen years old, this app focuses on building social skills and making friends.

- **Zones of Regulation:** This app, for kids four years and older, supplements the Zones of Regulation curriculum. It helps students identify their level of regulation based on physiological signs and react appropriately.

- **Wisdom—Kingdom of Anger:** This free app for kids four to eight years old is a role-play game that allows players to win superpowers as they learn to control their anger.

- **Zoo U:** In this web-based game, students seven to twelve years old work through scenarios to build skills in communication, cooperation, emotion regulation, empathy, impulse control, and social initiation.

Key Points

- Autism in gifted students can be difficult to identify. Autistic gifted learners are often good at masking the symptoms of their diagnosis and are thus identified later than their nongifted peers.

- Autistic gifted students struggle with social communication, developing strong and healthy friendships, and black-and-white thinking.

- Many of these 2e students struggle with writing due to slow processing speed and paralysis when there is no "right answer."

Gifted, 2e, or ASD?

Gifted Characteristics	Possible Manifestations in Autistic Gifted Learners	Characteristics of Autistic Children and Teens
Differences in expressing emotions		
The affective memory and emotional intensity of gifted children may make it difficult for them to talk about emotions. Sharing emotions verbally can cause the emotionally intense gifted child to relive strong emotions, which may be uncomfortable. They may resist talking about feelings because those emotions can be so big. Generally, when given the opportunity, they are able show both cognitive and affective empathy.	Autistic gifted children and teens may easily explain or repeat the emotions of fictional characters in books they enjoy. They may also understand and talk about the emotions they see others experiencing. However, they struggle to verbalize their own emotions, especially when in an emotionally heightened state, and can lack cognitive empathy to infer what others are feeling. For example, they can empathize with and show compassion for a child who is bullied at school (affective empathy), but completely miss the other person's feelings when disagreeing with the right way to complete a project.	Autistic children struggle greatly to identify and share their own emotions, either verbally or nonverbally. Predicting others' emotions can be a very difficult task. When asked to share emotions, autistic children and teens may shut down and be unable to speak at all, or they may simply be unable to provide a specific reply.
Differences in reciprocal communication		
Peer groups that are not an appropriate fit for a gifted child may make it difficult for the child to engage in age-appropriate back-and-forth communication due to mismatched interests and verbal ability that exceeds that of same-age peers. This child may easily engage in back-and-forth communication with older peers or adults.	Autistic 2e learners may engage easily in back-and-forth conversations about topics of their interest and when they take the lead in the conversation. Struggles happen when the child is asked to engage in a conversation about a different topic or guide a conversation that is focused on their conversation partner's interests or experiences.	Struggles with back-and-forth communication in autistic individuals are common and hamper their ability to develop relationships. They may have conversations with other children about shared interests; however, these conversations often look more like parallel play because the two individuals are sharing their own thoughts but not really engaging or responding to the other person. When you're engaging an autistic student in conversation, it may feel like you are conducting an interview; the response from the student answers the question but does not carry the conversation forward; you must lead the conversation forward.
Differences in using and interpreting nonverbal communication		
In general, gifted learners accurately interpret and use nonverbal communication. They may have an advanced understanding of sarcasm or other communication skills, which could cause difficulties communicating with same-age peers.	Autistic gifted learners may struggle to interpret tone of voice or facial expressions, even when they are able to use these tools themselves. Their tone of voice may lack inflection, or their face may not express their emotions. They may easily pick up on specific nonverbal skills they have been taught, such as making eye contact when listening to another person; however, they may not understand why this is important to communication and relationships.	Autistic individuals struggle to use and interpret gestures, facial expressions, tone of voice, sarcasm, and other types of nonverbal communication. When communicating, they may lack typical voice inflection or facial expressions. It is important to note that making eye contact is only a single nonverbal skill; it does not rule out the possibility of ASD.

Gifted Characteristics	Possible Manifestations in Autistic Gifted Learners	Characteristics of Autistic Children and Teens
Differences in preferred social relationship styles		
There are many reasons why gifted children may struggle to develop or maintain relationships. They may have an introverted personality. They may have different interests from those of their same-age peers. They may have trouble connecting with peers because of divergent ability levels in vocabulary and comprehension. Gifted children are able to develop and maintain appropriate relationships with individuals who are at their cognitive level.	Lagging skills in developing and maintaining relationships may not be evident until the 2e student is in late elementary or middle school. For example, they may have some long-term friends they made at a young age, but developing new relationships is a struggle. One of the best ways for an autistic 2e learner to build relationship skills is through a peer with similar interest and ability.	Autistic individuals struggle to make and keep friends, may misinterpret the level of friendship they have with a peer, or may unknowingly engage in behaviors that damage existing relationships. They may prefer to withdraw or isolate rather than engage with peers. They may not understand when to back off from social interactions.
Repetitive psychomotor activities		
While gifted learners may show some sensory sensitivities, these sensitivities generally don't appear as repetitive movements, like hand flapping, grimacing, and so on, unless they have a diagnosis such as OCD or Tourette's syndrome. If a gifted child does engage in such behaviors but it is a habit instead of a stimming behavior, the habit can be broken and is not substituted with another behavior.	2e students may recognize that certain types of stimming behavior are unexpected in certain environments and find ways to engage in these behaviors discreetly or do them only in certain environments where they are very comfortable. For example, a 2e learner may resist waving their hands unless they are with trusted individuals and feeling very excited. They may show embarrassment when others notice these behaviors.	Stimming behaviors may include hand flapping, finger tapping, face wiping or rubbing, running hands through hair, blowing air through pursed lips, and more. These behaviors may change over time, with one behavior replacing another. Stimming behaviors are generally used to self-regulate emotions, which may range from excitement and joy to stress and overwhelm.
Preference for consistency and routine		
Almost all children thrive on structure, but most can transition from one activity to another without major emotional dysregulation. Gifted children often thrive when new experiences are presented and with support can manage most transitions. Gifted kids can be extremely logical and may get frustrated when situations don't adhere to their version of "right." Gifted kids also tend to be sticklers for rules.	2e learners may struggle with inflexibility in certain situations. For example, an autistic gifted learner might learn how to manage change and transition in a classroom on a daily basis but become extremely dysregulated when a substitute is there for a day. Some 2e learners may resist trying new things, such as reading a new book series, due to the comfort associated with an established routine.	Unexpected changes in routines can cause significant emotional dysregulation in autistic individuals. Parents and teachers may observe a pattern of behavior that looks almost like OCD.
Areas of interest		
Areas of passion can appear as perseverative interests. Gifted learners may have several areas of passion. Their ability to converse on topics outside this area of passion is within the range for expected behaviors with same-age peers.	This is one of the most difficult areas in which to distinguish typical gifted behaviors from ASD symptoms. Many 2e learners have interests that are abnormal in intensity or focus. How long the fixation lasts and whether the child has other interests can give clues as to whether this is a gifted or ASD characteristic.	An autistic individual may have a single area of interest to the exclusion of all others. It may be difficult to get them to engage in social interactions that are outside this area of interest.
Sensory sensitivities		
Gifted children may experience mild heightened sensitivity to textures, sounds, or other sensory input. In general, it does not interfere with daily functioning. It may be related to another diagnosis.	Autistic gifted students may have heightened sensitivity to textures of clothing or food, sensitivity to loud noises or bright lights, or sensory-seeking or -avoidant behaviors. The 2e child may be able to manage or hide these sensitivities in certain situations.	Significant impairment associated with unpleasant sensations or a constant need to seek sensory stimulation is a common characteristic of autistic individuals.

Accommodations and Modifications for ASD

Major Life Activity	Possible Accommodation or Modification
Performing manual tasks	
Sensory-avoidant students may struggle with stamina for handwriting. Fine-motor skills may lag.	• Instructional: Allow scribing for homework and longer assignments. • Instructional: Use recording device to dictate thoughts before writing them. • Instructional: Offer occupational therapy services. • Environmental: Allow use of preferred writing utensil.
Concentrating	
Students with specific perseverative interests may struggle with concentration and motivation on topics outside their interest areas.	• Instructional: Segment assignments into shorter tasks and provide teacher check-in between segments. • Instructional: Allow child to modify assignment to include area of interest.
Lagging social skills may cause difficulty concentrating when working in groups.	• Instructional: Assign groups instead of allowing students to self-select groups. • Instructional: When students are working in groups, give student specific role to provide structure for social communication and focus during group activity.
Sensory issues cause difficulty with concentration and attention.	• Environmental: Allow student to listen to self-selected music or white noise through headphones or use noise-canceling headphones to reduce auditory distractions. • Environmental: Provide alternate materials if student is unable to use materials provided due to sensory concerns. (For example, avoid scented markers or certain types of paper.) • Environmental: Allow student flexible seating for comfort or proprioceptive needs. • Environmental: Designate a pacing area. A piece of tape on the floor can be a "pacing strip" so students needing sensory input by pacing don't disrupt others' learning.
Communicating	
Slow processing speed can slow down verbal or written communication. Trouble identifying and sharing emotions can increase emotional distress and anxiety. Struggles with language can cause struggles with interpersonal relationships or understanding implications of conversations.	• Instructional: Allow extra time during class discussions and for written assignments. Remember that with 2e kids, slow processing may not be equally evident in all environments. • Instructional: Provide scaffolding to give structure for writing activities without a "right answer." Give narrow topics for writing prompts. • Behavioral: Allow the student to share emotions and thoughts when they are ready. Do not attempt to force a conversation before the student is ready. • Instructional: Teachers should use clear, concise language and avoid sarcasm. A 2e student might be good at using sarcasm when they are speaking but may have a difficult time understanding when it is used by others. • Instructional: Autistic gifted learners may need permission to access accommodations or specific tools available to them. Because these students may be black-and-white in their thinking, a teacher may need to expressly tell them they have permission to use an accommodation.
Learning	
Motivation in autistic gifted learners can lag when a topic isn't within their area of interest.	• Instructional: Provide opportunities for learners to create their own projects within their areas of interest to show mastery of learning objectives. • Behavioral: Give immediate positive reinforcement when the student completes a task. Provide opportunities for self-evaluation.

Emotion Wheel (All Ages)

To gain control of our emotions, the first step is to recognize the emotions we have in both comfortable and uncomfortable situations.

An **emotion wheel** is a tool that can help you identify emotions beyond the basic ones. The center circle is already completed for you with basic emotions. Fill in the remainder of the circle with emotions that get more specific you move outward.

For example, the word *happy* is in the center circle. One emotion that might name a kind of happy is *excited*. On the outermost circle, two emotions that might be different kinds of excited are *delighted* and *hysterical*.

Note to teachers: If older students need help coming up with words, encourage them to use a thesaurus. With younger students, brainstorm a list of emotion words as a class and let them use it as a word bank. The activity can also be modified for younger students by having them complete only the middle circle.

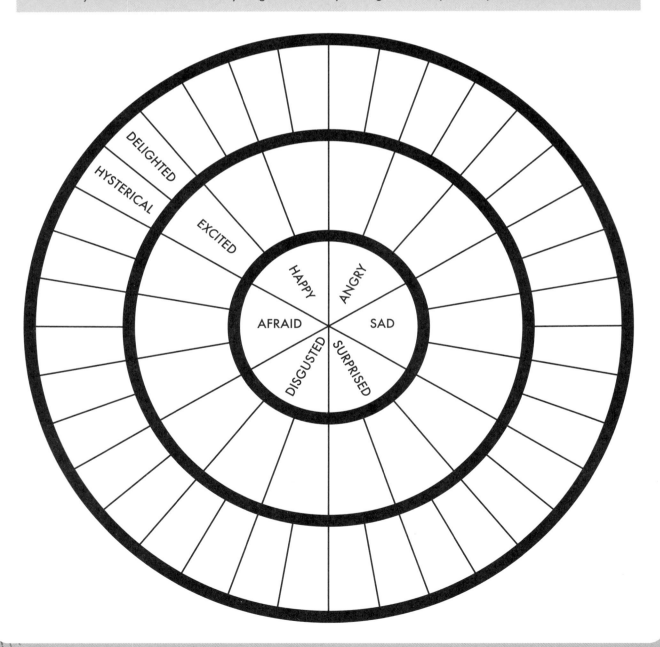

Improvisation and Role Play (Grades 2 and Up)

If you've ever frozen in the middle of a social interaction, you may have felt like an actor who forgot their lines. You can think of social conversations and interactions as a play where each person is an actor. This can help you build your confidence with social situations. Imagine the perspective of an actor in your role and the point of view of the other actor.

Use scissors to cut the scene starters below into cards. One person should select a card. You may briefly plan the content of the scene with your partner. For a bigger challenge, try to truly improvise, with the first person starting the scene without preparation. Try to keep your scene going as long as possible. Be sure to follow these improvisation rules:

- **Add to the story.** When you are improvising, you are building on what the other person says. Listen to what they say and add to the story. For example, if your partner says he has been out working in the garden all day, you can add that you would love to garden but are afraid of bugs.

- **Ask questions.** If you aren't sure what to add to the story, ask a clarifying question. "Oh, you were gardening? What types of plants do you have?"

- **Reflect and react to emotion.** If your acting partner says something that indicates an emotion, make sure your response addresses it. "You seem exhausted after being outside in the garden all day. I know I'd feel tired after that hard work too."

- **Stay on track.** Try not to take the scene off course. Imagine that the topic of each scene is like a highway, and while you can shift between lanes, you don't want to take an exit to a totally different topic. Jumping from gardening to bugs, plants, or weather is okay; talking about trains or video games would be off topic.

- **Use nonverbal communication.** Don't forget gestures, facial expressions, and tone of voice to help get your point across.

Scene Starters

"So, did you find out about the results for the team you tried out for last week?"	"My friend said he would call me this afternoon, but he still hasn't! I think he probably is mad at me."	"If that kid runs into me or pushes me in the hallway again, I'm going to make him pay."
"Are you ready to give your presentation in social studies today? I practiced for an hour last night."	"I leave tomorrow for vacation! I can't wait!"	"I spent all weekend camping with my parents. Do you ever camp?"
"I am taking a cooking class. We are learning how to make cakes from scratch."	"We just got a new kitten! She is so cute!"	"I got grounded from video games yesterday. I can't play them for two weeks!"
"Can you believe Mr. Jansen talked for the entire class period?"	"I think my friends forgot that it is my birthday tomorrow."	"I got to meet my favorite YouTuber yesterday. I even got her autograph."
"I have to go to watch my brother's basketball game tonight. It is going to be so boring!"	"I have to go to the dentist tomorrow. I hate going to the dentist."	"I want to take horseback riding lessons, but my mom won't let me. She says it costs too much."

Two Truths (Grades 4 to 8)

Empathy is using your imagination to feel the emotions of another person. Some people call this "taking a walk in someone else's shoes." When you read a book and you have emotions because you can relate to what the characters are experiencing, you are experiencing empathy!

Why is using empathy such an important skill in real life? If you are able to understand another person's **emotions**, when you have a conflict with someone, you will be able to compromise and find solutions that satisfy you and the other person. Plus, when others see you showing empathy, they will feel that you are trustworthy and a good friend. One of the hardest parts of using empathy is that you must **infer (guess)** what the other person is feeling based on their words and actions.

The **Two Truths** chart gives you an opportunity to show that there is more than one point of view in every situation. Read the following story and complete the chart to understand how each character is feeling. You can also use this tool in situations where you need or want to show empathy and understanding to another person in real life.

Jenna and Malachi are sitting next to each other at lunch and talking about the upcoming math test. Malachi is speaking quickly about the test, talking about how much he studied and how if he gets a good grade, his mother is going to take him out for dinner at his favorite restaurant. Jenna begins to look down toward the table and doesn't say much to Malachi.

Malachi finally notices that Jenna isn't responding to him. "What's your problem?" he asks her.

Jenna stands up and grabs her backpack and mumbles, "Nothing. I've got to go study," and walks away without saying goodbye. Malachi watches her leave, trying to figure out what is wrong with her.

Two Truths		
	Malachi	**Jenna**
What is this person's truth?		
Using empathy, what feelings do you imagine this person has?		
How does this person's truth affect the other person's emotions?		
What does the other person need to say to help this relationship get back on track?		

What Are They Thinking? (Grades 1 to 3)

People in the same situation can have different thoughts and feelings about what is happening. When we predict (make a good guess about) what another person is thinking, we can use **empathy** to understand why another person is feeling or reacting the way they are.

Below, read about each situation and read what the first person is thinking. Predict some thoughts the second person could be having. Write those thoughts in the empty bubbles. The first situation is done for you as an example.

While working on a group project, Malia was working really hard. Yuan kept getting distracted and wasn't getting much work finished.

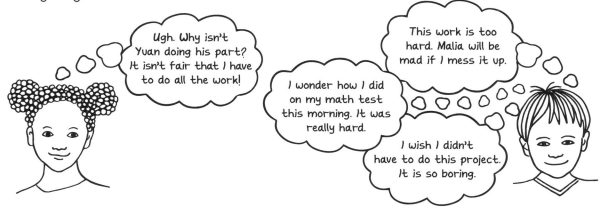

The class was lining up for lunch. When they were in line, Josiah felt Terrence bump into him.

Sera wanted to play with Jenae at recess, but Jenae was already playing with other friends.

Processing Difficulties

Processing difficulties such as central auditory processing disorder (CAPD), visual processing disorder (VPD), and sensory processing disorder (SPD) can affect twice-exceptional kids in many ways. With all processing disorders, information received through the senses is somehow scrambled when it is interpreted by the brain. For example, the ear hears sounds, but the brain can't differentiate between noise and words; or the feel of the fabric of a sweater is interpreted by the brain as sandpaper on the skin.

Some individuals struggle only with processing issues, but processing disorders often accompany other diagnoses. The most common overlap occurs with SPD and autism spectrum disorder. (The DSM-5 lists hypo- and hyperreactivity to sensory input as a possible symptom of ASD.) Students with ADHD and anxiety may also have auditory, visual, and sensory processing difficulties.

Of the three processing disorders, CAPD is the only one delineated as its own diagnosis by the medical community. VPD and SPD are descriptions of a variety of symptoms that may be noticed by medical professionals. When another diagnosis does not fit, the professional may describe the symptoms seen as a visual or sensory processing disorder. The status of these labels should not affect the overall ability of a student to receive services or accommodations, because the US Department of Education Office of Civil Rights says the term *disability* should be defined broadly and should consider the overall impact of struggles. This gives latitude for schools to provide services and accommodations when sensory processing symptoms substantially affect a student.

This is good news for 2e students who are assessed by professionals unfamiliar with the ways many diagnoses manifest in gifted learners, because the symptoms of a processing disorder may be obvious even when other symptoms are considered subdiagnostic. A student may not meet the threshold requirements for a diagnosis of ADHD, ASD, or dyslexia—or the disability may be missed by an examiner unfamiliar with the masking effect of giftedness—but the characteristics of a processing disorder are more evident and can help families and teachers advocate for services or accommodations.

Central Auditory Processing Disorder

Students with CAPD do not have a physical condition that impedes them from hearing. Rather, they have difficulty distinguishing certain sounds, like spoken words, from other noises and interpreting them. For students with CAPD, understanding what a partner is saying or a teacher's instructions in a noisy classroom can be difficult. Twice-exceptional students with CAPD may be identified later than their peers. Most students with this diagnosis are already in fourth grade or older before adults notice the impact of their difficulties.

ARE PROCESSING DIFFERENCES ASSOCIATED WITH GIFTEDNESS?

Many people describe gifted kids as being very aware of sensory experiences, like noticing the seams of their socks are misaligned, disliking certain sounds, or having heightened awareness of visual aesthetics. Although sensory differences are not seen in all gifted individuals, there is discussion in the field of gifted education about whether processing differences are a part of the neurological makeup of giftedness. Some professionals point to Kazimierz Dabrowski's theory of overexcitabilities to explain why some gifted individuals experience heightened sensory sensitivity. Dabrowski's theory discusses five areas in which gifted people experience increased sensitivity or awareness: intellectual, emotional, imaginational, psychomotor, and sensual. Within this theory, sensory sensitivities can be attributed to both psychomotor and sensual intensities. However, the wider psychological community has yet to reach consensus on this point.

Research does point to a correlation between sensory processing difficulties and ADHD, ASD, and anxiety (Little et al. 2017; McMahon et al. 2019). Gifted learners with sensory processing difficulties may have these diagnoses, but they are not yet identified due to masking. Or perhaps gifted people have neurological wiring that causes them to process and experience sensory stimuli differently from their nongifted peers. As the body of neurobiological research grows, we will learn more about why some people experience sensory processing difficulties.

An audiologist can assess students for CAPD. Feedback from a speech-language pathologist may also help determine its presence. They generally screen for features of language disorders, due to overlapping symptoms with CAPD.

Gifted students with CAPD may mask their struggles when they are younger, but later may end up with academic and social difficulties due to their difficulties. These students may appear to have trouble focusing in class because they miss key components of lectures or instructions. In peer relationships, they may be so focused on processing what was said, the conversation has moved forward by the time they've developed a response. Giftedness can support their skills because they can guess the intent of instructors or friends, but the effort required is difficult to maintain for the long term without other supports.

A frequency modulation (FM) system can be a useful tool and accommodation in the classroom for students with CAPD. An FM system involves a teacher using a wireless microphone that transmits and amplifies the sound either to speakers in the classroom or to an earpiece the individual student uses. The amplification helps make the teacher's voice less disrupted by ambient noise.

HENRY'S STORY

Henry was a multi-exceptional learner in sixth grade. In addition to being highly gifted, he had diagnoses of ASD and CAPD. During our counseling sessions, he asked me to turn off the white noise machine in my office so he could focus on our conversation more easily.

One of Henry's main concerns was a desire for friends. He wanted to connect with his peers and build relationships. Watching his classmates chat easily between classes or at lunch left Henry flustered and confused. He never felt like he could keep up with the conversation. The few times he did interject a comment, he got reactions that suggested he'd said something that didn't make sense, and he felt embarrassed. The loud environments where school socializing took place made it hard for Henry to make out what was being said. The din of the cafeteria was nonstop, and Henry couldn't understand the kids at his table unless they were right next to him.

In class, Henry struggled in group work. He ended up doing the work for his groupmates. Discussing ideas with them while the rest of the class was making noise was too difficult to manage. ■

Here are the key characteristics of CAPD:

- **Trouble ignoring background noise:** Understanding what is said amid a lot of background noise requires auditory figure-ground discrimination, or the ability to pick out important sounds and filter out unimportant ones. Students with CAPD cannot distinguish spoken words from environmental noises.

- **Difficulty distinguishing various sounds:** Auditory discrimination involves noticing subtle differences in sounds and words. CAPD causes students to misunderstand words that sound alike, such as *copy* and *coffee*.

- **Poor auditory working memory:** Working memory skills are closely related to CAPD. First, auditory sequencing involves understanding and recalling the order of sounds and words. Someone with weak auditory sequencing might mix up the order of sounds in *chicken* and *kitchen* and be unable to tell these words apart. Second, auditory memory requires someone to remember what they've heard (immediately or in the future). Students with CAPD can struggle with multistep instructions that are provided verbally.

Visual Processing Disorder

Students with VPD do not have any physical cause for their vision difficulty. If they use corrective lenses, like glasses or contacts, that is unrelated to their visual processing skills. Visual processing difficulties can hamper activities that require hand-eye coordination (such as sports) and academic skills such as reading and writing. Visual processing difficulties often accompany other neurological differences.

Learners struggling with reading may be assessed by an ophthalmologist or optometrist, who looks for physical impediments to vision. Alternatively, parents and teachers may initiate an assessment at school to look for a specific learning disability. If a student does not have a vision problem or an identifiable learning disability but continues to struggle with reading, parents may seek further evaluation, leading to a referral to a behavioral optometrist. A behavioral optometrist can assess for problems that benefit from vision therapy.

Vision therapy was developed to improve several visual processing problems. Eye tracking skills are one area vision therapy can address. These skills include being able to consistently look at a stationary or moving target or shift smoothly from focusing on one item to focusing on another. Eye teaming is another common problem addressed through vision therapy. Eye teaming is when the eyes work together to follow a point of focus. If someone struggles with eye teaming, they are likely to have blurred or double vision. Two types of eye teaming issues are convergence insufficiency, in which the eyes turn outward when attempting to focus on an image, and convergence excess, in which the eyes turn inward.

ANISHA'S STORY

Anisha was an elementary student. As a young girl, she loved learning and would ask question after in-depth question about any topic that came to her mind. She was imaginative and loved creating dramatic recreations of her own invented stories.

As Anisha entered late elementary school, she became a more reluctant learner. She got emotional when she was asked to read passages that she felt were too long. Writing was tedious and laborious for her. Anisha's parents and teachers were concerned that her progress had slowed from its once-rapid pace. The school tested for learning disabilities, but the testing did not qualify her for any special education services.

Undeterred, Anisha's parents kept looking for answers. Eventually they found an optometrist who recognized visual tracking and teaming issues. Anisha often needed to refocus on the words on the page, and she had trouble keeping her place each time she moved on to the next line of text. After several months of in-office and at-home vision therapy, Anisha's ability to read for extended periods of time improved greatly. When the therapy was complete, Anisha told her mom she "never realized that this is what it is like for other people to read." ■

Figure 10-1 VPD or Dyslexia?

VPD and dyslexia may appear similar, but they are quite different from a neurological perspective. The easiest way to clarify the difference is to remember that dyslexia is primarily a difficulty with *language*, while VPD is a difficulty with *interpreting what is seen*.

Visual Processing Disorder	Dyslexia
Has difficulty interpreting visual input	Has difficulty processing language
Has trouble with copying from a book	Has trouble sounding out words
Struggles to write neatly	Leaves letters out when spelling
Doesn't notice math symbols	Is confused by sequencing directions

Here are the key characteristics of VPD:

■ **Difficulty scanning and pulling out certain information on a page:** When a student attempts to skim a page to look for specific information, lagging skills in visual figure-ground discrimination can prevent them from easily finding the information. Visual figure-ground discrimination is the ability to pick out an important form or object within a busy field and filter out unimportant ones.

- **Trouble copying information from the board or from a book:** Processing visual stimuli and recreating it in written form requires strong hand-eye coordination.

- **Reversals of letters and numbers when reading and writing:** When reading or writing, students with VPD may read or write letters as their mirror images (for example, *b* as *d*) beyond the age when this is common. Typically, children outgrow this pattern by about seven years.

- **Poor visual working memory:** Trouble remembering what they've read, like a list of instructions, or remembering how to spell certain words can be related to VPD.

Sensory Processing Disorder

SPD is a difficulty with processing and integrating information received by the senses. SPD is not limited to tactile sensory experiences. Students with SPD can also be sensitive to visual, auditory, olfactory, or gustatory stimuli. They may have extremely high or low tolerance for sensory input; they may seek or avoid sensory experiences outside the range that's typical for maintaining comfort and sensory regulation.

In addition to the five senses most people are familiar with, there are also the vestibular, proprioceptive, and interoceptive systems, which help us process information from our bodies. The vestibular system relates directly to the way our body moves. It helps us maintain balance and understand where our body is within space. The vestibular system lets us know if we feel off balance, whether we are stationary or moving, and whether we are moving forward or backward. The canals in our inner ears are vital to our vestibular awareness. The proprioceptive system has to do with our awareness of our bodies, especially how we navigate the space between ourselves and the world around us. For example, we use proprioceptive awareness when we bring a spoon to our mouth or tie our shoes. The interoceptive system interprets the messages our brain gets from our internal organs. If our stomach feels uncomfortable, our interoceptive system helps us decipher whether we are hungry, have to go to the bathroom, or are about to vomit.

An occupational therapist usually addresses sensory processing struggles. Occupational therapists can develop a "sensory diet" for students who are struggling with sensory integration. A sensory diet involves frequent and regular sensory experiences that either help a sensory-avoidant person become gradually more comfortable with sensory stimuli or help a sensory-seeking person fulfill their need for sensory input before becoming dysregulated.

The connection between sensory regulation and emotional regulation is strong. Have you ever felt hangry? This humorous word refers to the irritability people experience when they are hungry. Similarly, when we feel too hot, cold, or tired, or our muscles are exhausted, these physical sensations greatly influence our mood. Students who are more

HYPERSENSITIVITY VERSUS HYPOSENSITIVITY

- **Hypersensitivity:** Student is oversensitive to sensory stimuli. This can lead them to avoid experiences in which they may feel overwhelmed by sensory input.
- **Hyposensitivity:** Student is undersensitive to sensory stimuli. This can lead them to seek sensory experiences to fulfill their needs.

sensitive to sensory stimuli are often perched at the edge of emotional dysregulation, and they have diminished ability to regulate those emotions.

Here are the key characteristics of SPD, organized by sensory system:

Visual (Sight)

- easily bothered by bright, fluorescent, or flickering lights (hypersensitive)

- distracted in environments with a lot of visual stimuli (hypersensitive)

- loses interest in visual activities or does not notice items in surroundings (hyposensitive)

Auditory (Hearing)

- overwhelmed by noisy and crowded environments (hypersensitive)

- significantly disturbed by loud noises, like fire drills (hypersensitive)

- distracted by subtle noises unnoticed by those around them (hypersensitive)

- appears to ignore or miss verbal communication (hyposensitive)

- does not modulate volume of voice based on environment (hyposensitive)

Olfactory (Smell)

- avoids strong smells, like strong perfumes or pungent foods (hypersensitive)

- has heightened ability to notice and identify subtle scents (hypersensitive)

- strong positive or negative reaction to "smelly stuff," like scented markers or oil diffusers (hypersensitive)

Gustatory (Taste)

- avoids eating foods with certain flavors or textures (hypersensitive)

- seeks spicy or strong-flavored foods with minimal sensory reaction (hyposensitive)

- hesitant to try new foods; prefers to eat the same foods all the time (hypersensitive)

Tactile (Touch)

- refuses to wear certain types of clothing that are deemed uncomfortable; insists on cutting out tags or wearing socks inside out (hypersensitive)

- seeks pleasurable tactile feelings, like fuzzy or silky fabrics, to reduce anxiety

- does not like unexpected touch, hugs, or cuddles (hypersensitive)

Vestibular (Body Movement and Balance)

- enjoys spinning, rocking, or jumping movements (hyposensitive)

- frequently fidgets with fingers, hair, or other objects (hyposensitive)

- avoids experiences like roller coasters (hypersensitive)

Proprioceptive (Body Awareness)

- does not recognize amount of pressure being used (hugs too tightly, rips paper when erasing, stomps feet or tiptoes when walking) (hyposensitive)
- feels calmed by using weighted blankets or other deep pressure/"heavy work"
- poor endurance and posture; clumsiness

Interoceptive (Internal)

- very sensitive to temperatures, either hot or cold (hypersensitive)
- unaware of intensity of pain (big reaction to small injury like paper cut; minimized reaction to large injury, like sprain or broken bone) (hyposensitive)
- has difficulty interpreting body signals related to physical or emotional well-being

Impact of Processing Difficulties on Gifted Learners

Twice-exceptional learners with processing difficulties may also have another diagnosis. Some 2e students undergo therapies and treatments for processing difficulties and then receive another diagnosis when they are older and their compensatory skills no longer mask their other struggles. Gifted learners with various processing struggles may learn to hide or minimize their difficulties in environments where their concerns are dismissed or misunderstood.

Screenings for admission into gifted education programs may miss students with processing disorders. For example, students with VPD who struggle with visual figure-ground differentiation may perform below their ability on visual-spatial tasks in screening tools that involve matrix reasoning and pattern analysis. Schools that use standardized testing administered in group settings as an initial benchmark to identify students for gifted services may find suppressed scores for students with processing disorders.

Many gifted education classrooms offer environments that are less structured than traditional classrooms are. This can be a blessing or a curse for students with processing difficulties. Flexible seating can help students who have vestibular and proprioceptive needs; frequent peer discussions and group projects can cause students with CAPD to struggle. To meet the various needs of all learners in a classroom, provide options and help students know what options are available and how to access them.

Qualifying for Services and Accommodations for Processing Disorder Symptoms

Because of the nuances and complexity of processing disorder symptoms, it's easy to see how these symptoms might be misinterpreted or misdiagnosed. It's understandable that parents and professionals working with gifted students hesitate to choose a label for a constellation of symptoms that could have a variety of causes: ADHD, ASD, anxiety, dyslexia, depression, and more. Often, simply recognizing the symptoms of students' processing difficulties can allow schools to meet the needs of these 2e learners without applying labels that may not fit.

Many students with processing difficulties benefit from occupational therapy services. These services are usually associated with special education. However, if the services help a student access the curriculum, there is no legal standard that prevents a school from offering them through a 504 plan.

Key Points

- Twice-exceptional students often have processing difficulties that stand in the way of their academic success. These struggles can involve auditory, visual, or sensory processing.

- In addition to the five senses most people are familiar with, students with SPD may also have needs related to their vestibular, proprioceptive, and interoceptive senses.

- Providing options and tools for students with processing difficulties is the best way to meet their needs.

Accommodations and Modifications for Auditory, Visual, and Sensory Processing Disorders

Major Life Activity	Possible Accommodation or Modification
Performing manual tasks	
Proprioceptive sensory struggles cause fatigue and lack of endurance for writing.	• Instructional: Provide paper with extra lines to guide students' handwriting. • Evaluative: Do not grade papers based on neatness.
Hand-eye coordination weakness causes difficulty copying from board or book.	• Instructional: Shorten written assignments or allow students to write incomplete sentences or print or type their work.
Visual processing difficulties cause poor handwriting and spacing when writing.	• Instructional: Provide a copy of the notes to students in advance of lecture.
Concentrating	
Sensory integration difficulties impede student ability to focus and concentrate during class.	• Environmental: Provide alternatives to reduce exposure to sensory triggers.
Auditory processing difficulties cause distraction when listening to class discussion or group work.	• Environmental: Use FM system when instructing class to increase volume of instruction. • Environmental: Provide alternate setting for group work. • Instructional: Check frequently for understanding.
Sensory needs impede ability to stay in seat or concentrate on task.	• Environmental: Allow student to pace or use wiggle chair, fidgets, or other sensory tools to meet sensory needs.
Poor visual or auditory working memory skills make following multistep instructions difficult.	• Instructional: Use multisensory methods to provide instruction involving both spoken directions and directions written in list format.
Thinking	
Visual processing difficulties necessitate additional time to read, comprehend, and write.	• Instructional/evaluative: Allow additional time for completion on assignments and tests involving extensive reading.
Visual or auditory processing difficulties lead to weak spelling and writing skills.	• Evaluative: Do not grade for spelling; shorten spelling lists for tests.
Communicating	
Difficulty interpreting body signals about emotions or physiological needs reduces student ability to identify and self-advocate for needed breaks or assistance.	• Behavioral: Provide an "anytime" pass for student to leave classroom as needed. • Environmental: Establish system for communicating nonverbally with student if their needs are not being met.

Anxiety and Related Disorders 11

Some twice-exceptional learners may have mental health diagnoses that hinder their ability to succeed in school. There's a pervasive belief that gifted people are prone to mental illness, but lengthy reviews of data show little support for the claim that gifted learners are more susceptible to mental health concerns than the rest of the population (Cross and Cross 2015). Gifted students are, however, prone to stress from being placed in situations that are neither developmentally appropriate nor adequately supportive.

Emotional and Behavioral Diagnoses

In the process of writing this book, I considered whether to include students with emotional and behavioral diagnoses like generalized anxiety disorder (GAD), major depressive disorder, and obsessive-compulsive disorder (OCD) under the umbrella of 2e learners. On one hand, they are not neurological disorders that involve differences in brain development and structure, like specific learning disabilities, ADHD, autism, and processing disorders. On the other hand, they are biochemical disorders that influence brain functioning and well-being. Ultimately, I opted to include emotional and behavioral diagnoses because gifted students with these diagnoses are adept at masking their struggles and often need identification and support in the schools.

When a gifted learner *is* diagnosed with an emotional or behavioral disorder, it is important to explore how environmental factors may be affecting the student's well-being. Being in a classroom with same-age peers who do not have similar interests can cause feelings of isolation. Lack of academic challenge leads to confusion and boredom. Although the diagnoses we discuss in this section are related to the lack of certain chemicals and receptors in the brain, much relief can be found when a student is placed in an appropriate academic setting.

These diagnoses are less likely to require an IEP than the diagnoses discussed in chapters 7 through 10. Often, accommodations and modifications through a 504 plan are adequate to meet the needs of 2e students with emotional and behavioral disorders. If a student does require specialized instruction and support through an IEP, the educational diagnosis under IDEA is emotional disturbance.

Anxiety-Based Diagnoses

The category of anxiety disorders is large and varied. In the United States, 7.1 percent of children ages three to seventeen are diagnosed with an anxiety disorder (Ghandour et al. 2019). Medical anxiety diagnoses include generalized anxiety disorder, social anxiety disorder, separation anxiety disorder, and selective mutism. Obsessive-compulsive disorder is not technically an anxiety disorder as specified in the *Diagnostic and Statistical Manual of Mental Disorders: Fifth Edition* (DSM-5), but because 2e students who receive accommodations or services for OCD may have educational needs similar to the needs of those with anxiety disorders, OCD is included in this chapter.

Recognizing Anxiety as a Common Factor in 2e Learners

Twice-exceptional students often suffer from clinical anxiety along with another diagnosis. Anxiety is generally triggered by an environmental stressor or situation.

Twice-exceptional kids struggle daily with a mismatch between their ability and achievement. The stress caused by this struggle may cause symptoms that meet the clinical threshold for anxiety diagnosis. A gifted learner with ADHD may experience anxiety if they are constantly getting in trouble for not turning in their work. An autistic gifted learner may experience anxiety when a plan is changed without warning. A gifted learner with a specific learning disability in writing can experience anxiety when they are accused of not trying hard enough on writing assignments. Environmental factors are a key reason educators need to support 2e learners without judgment and use a strength-based approach. Providing support proactively reduces the risk that anxiety will become debilitating.

Qualifying for Services or Accommodations

When a 2e student has a medical diagnosis of an anxiety disorder that hampers their ability to participate and learn in the classroom, they may need to be considered for special education services, accommodations, or modifications. IEPs are uncommon for students with only an anxiety diagnosis, because such students are usually able to access the curriculum without specialized services. If a student with anxiety is identified for an IEP, the educational diagnosis is emotional disturbance. A student with anxiety this severe would likely have a lot of trouble regulating their behavior and successfully navigating the school day.

Twice-exceptional students with anxiety disorders can more easily qualify for a 504 plan. Accommodations and modifications through a 504 plan offer the emotional

CONSIDERATIONS FOR STUDENTS WITH TRAUMA

Students who have experienced significant trauma in their lives are often in survival mode, constantly assessing for need to fight, flee, or freeze. Whether a child has experienced chronic food insecurity or they have experienced the trauma of a single large event, like a natural disaster or domestic violence, trauma responses are often like anxiety responses. Many of the strategies that are useful for students with clinical anxiety can also be helpful for kids with trauma. We can help them by focusing on developing a safe place for them to take risks and seek help. One factor to be aware of when working with students who have anxious thoughts and feelings is that students whose anxiety responses are caused by past trauma are facing fears based on experiences they've had in real life. We need to be cautious not to invalidate or minimize their experiences when we work to help them overcome their fears.

support necessary for a student to manage daily classroom expectations. To determine eligibility, educators must consider the impact of anxiety on the student when no mitigating measures, such as medication or other supports, are in place.

Generalized Anxiety Disorder

Students with GAD suffer worry and stress related to a real or perceived threat. The level of worry is usually higher than the likelihood of a negative outcome. Some children with GAD may begin experiencing such worry at a young age. For others, anxiety may begin during a time of increased stress. GAD can be episodic, meaning it may appear for a limited period in a person's life, may come and go in waves throughout a person's life, or may be a chronic condition with little to no relief from symptoms for long periods of time.

GAD can be difficult to identify in children because its symptoms overlap with those of other diagnoses (such as ASD and ADHD) and because young people are less able to verbalize their thoughts and describe how they are feeling. If students say they are feeling "on edge" or having trouble paying attention, these symptoms are easily misdiagnosed. Anxiety in a child may not be obvious and may go unnoticed by adults. One symptom that adults *do* often notice in children is increased irritability. Irritability is often outwardly visible, but many adults chalk it up to a child being spoiled or picky or high maintenance, instead of seeing it as a sign of a potential emotional problem.

Some characteristics of giftedness can resemble anxiety symptoms. For help distinguishing between them and understanding how both might appear in 2e students, see the reproducible on page 205 (**Gifted, 2e, or Anxiety?**). Here are the key characteristics of GAD:

- **Frequent worry about a wide range of topics that the student can't control:** Students who anticipate negative outcomes about daily events may be dealing with an anxiety disorder.

- **Psychosomatic symptoms of worry:** Although many students won't associate their physical symptoms with anxiety and worry, they may feel tired or sick to their stomach.

- **Low frustration tolerance:** One of the most easily visible signs for a child or adolescent dealing with anxiety is a sudden increase in their level of irritability. Underlying anxiety can lead to being annoyed easily or having little patience for people and situations.

- **Increased off-task behavior and difficulty paying attention:** When a student is spending a lot of time thinking about other worries, they may have a hard time regulating their attention.

Impact of GAD on Gifted Students

Everyone feels anticipatory anxiety at some time during their lives. Waiting for the results of a big test or realizing that a friendship is in turmoil can cause worry and stress. Recognizing the difference between normal anticipation and clinical anxiety is important when determining whether a gifted student has GAD and requires accommodations or modifications.

Gifted learners tend to be overthinkers. They are analyzers. They see patterns and connections that others don't see. When you combine this cognitive tendency to overthink with a biochemical predisposition for an anxiety disorder, the result can be overwhelming.

The environmental stressors that gifted students face can be unique compared to those faced by their nongifted peers. High expectations from teachers, parents, and peers result in feelings of inadequacy and failure if the student comes up short. Multipotentiality (the potential gifted students may have to be talented and successful in a variety of domains) and overcommitment to multiple activities lead to less time for self-care. A gifted student who ends up with a diagnosis of clinical anxiety may have a difficult time finding ways to balance the stressors in their life to try to improve their mental health.

As with other types of exceptionalities, gifted learners may mask their anxiety until it reaches a breaking point. Because of their advanced cognitive ability, they're able to hold it together even when they are on the cusp of fight-flight-freeze response internally. They have a white-knuckle grip and are hanging on for dear life. How does this masked anxiety manifest? Here are a few possibilities:

- seeking reassurance by asking many questions, especially ones that are redundant or on topics or skills the student has already mastered

- hypervigilance on assignments and tests; spending a lot of time repetitively reviewing information or answers

- resistance to group work due to inability to manage others' efforts and work production, or bossiness during group work, insisting they do all the work to avoid errors made by their groupmates

- extreme distress at perceived failure; perception may not reflect commonly accepted benchmarks of failure (for example, seeing a 92 percent as a huge disappointment)

- pushing back on tasks or expectations that appear difficult or unfair

- negative comments, especially self-critical ones ("Ugh, I'm so stupid!")

Cognitive-behavioral skills can relieve the impact of GAD. Skills like reframing and challenging negative thoughts can be developed through direct instruction and coaching. Noticing the subtle presence of GAD in gifted learners who are adept at masking their struggles makes the process of building coping skills quicker and easier.

COLTON'S STORY

As an elementary student, Colton loved school. He had several good friends and was generally well liked. Colton's parents described him as shy. But after he entered sixth grade, Colton's quiet demeanor became more than just shyness. It began to hinder his academics.

As content progressed in difficulty, Colton began to struggle with self-advocacy. Unwilling to ask for help, he did his best to appear busy during work time and took all his schoolwork home to complete there. It then took him hours to finish the work that most of his peers had completed during the school day. He meticulously went over his homework and never felt comfortable that it was good enough. Tests had always been easy for Colton, but now he began to overthink every answer and had trouble completing tests within the allotted time. He obsessed over the spelling of words, even when teachers told the students that spelling was not a factor in their grades.

Colton's anxiety began to escalate to avoidance. He became paralyzed when faced with the task of completing his schoolwork but couldn't face the idea of going to school with his work incomplete. He began to refuse to go to school. He made it there only two or three days a week.

Colton's teachers were perplexed and concerned about the change in his behavior and grades. His performance as a sixth grader would influence his ability to enroll in challenge-level courses as a seventh grader. The school counselor, his gifted education teacher, and his general education teachers collaborated with Colton and his parents to find accommodations that mitigated the effects of his anxiety on his school performance. ■

Social Anxiety Disorder (Social Phobia)

Kids dealing with social anxiety have intense anxiety about social interactions. Fear of being judged, meeting unfamiliar people, or performing in front of a group are common in people with social anxiety disorder. Test anxiety is closely related to social anxiety, due to the fear of being graded.

Introversion is more common in gifted individuals compared to the general population (Sak 2004). Introversion is often confused for anxiety in social situations. However, introversion and anxiety are unrelated. Many people who are introverted are not anxious in social situations. A gifted child who is quiet or prefers introspection over socialization does not necessarily have social anxiety disorder.

Gifted students who have social anxiety disorder are likely to experience significant stress when they are asked to work in groups. Asking these kids to "find a partner" is like asking them to enter a lion's den. Putting them in front of the class to do a presentation can be paralyzing. Many gifted and advanced-level courses emphasize group learning and public speaking. Forcing kids with social anxiety disorder into situations that exacerbate their anxiety can make them choose to drop the challenging curriculum they need. Accommodations to alleviate the stress from these situations are simple. For example, teacher-selected groups for projects eliminate the need for a student to find a partner. Allowing students to record an oral presentation on video or present it to the teacher with no other students around can reduce the social anxiety associated with performances or public speaking. It's important for teachers (especially in middle and high school) to understand the importance of implementing them.

Here are the key characteristics of social anxiety disorder:

- **Intense fear and worry about being judged by others:** Whether they are meeting new people in different situations, performing in front of a group, or taking a standardized test, students with social anxiety disorder assume they will be judged and that people will think poorly of them.

- **Avoidance of social situations:** Even though students dealing with anxiety about social situations want friends and want to socialize, the idea of participating in a group or event can be paralyzing.

Impact of Social Anxiety Disorder on Gifted Students

Expectations are high for gifted students in social situations. Others often expect them to be the leaders in their groups, to have social skills aligned with their cognitive skills, and to take advanced classes that rely on presenting projects and research frequently. Social anxiety can make gifted learners who are perfectionists even more afraid of making mistakes. Peers who declare that a gifted student who makes a mistake is "supposed to be the smart one" can exacerbate fear of scrutiny.

Many gifted programs focus on collaborative projects. A gifted student with a social phobia may dread these projects. Even the first step, finding a group to work with, is petrifying for them. Once in a group, advocating for their ideas is difficult. They go along with the rest of the group's ideas because they don't want to rock the boat. Or they end up doing all the work themselves because the other students expect them to and they don't want to make anyone mad.

A gifted student with social anxiety may gradually withdraw from social situations in order to feel secure. Twice-exceptional students with unsupported social anxiety may experience the following negative consequences:

- **Dropping gifted education classes:** Leaving class for a pull-out program feels awkward and brings unwanted attention.

- **Strategic underachievement:** Whether choosing to not enroll in advanced courses or "dumbing down" around other students, it is easier to appear average than to deal with the expectation of intelligence. Reduced expectations are less intimidating.

- **School refusal:** Bright students may fly under the attendance-tracking radar because they mask their struggles by maintaining acceptable or above-average grades even while missing a lot of school.

EVA'S STORY

Eva's transition to high school was rocky. Prior to the school year, Eva had visited the school five times for various events—and still had not managed to leave without crying. She was paralyzed with fear that people would realize she didn't know her way around the building. This left her unable to explore the school, build confidence, and feel more comfortable there.

Once the school year began, Eva got familiar with the routes between her classes. But in class, she sat silent, hoping the teacher wouldn't call on her. The possibility of making a mistake in front of the teacher and her classmates kept her frozen in her seat, staring downward. Eva had a heavy load of advanced classes, exacerbating her fear of judgment from older students. Lunch was agony. Eva assumed nobody liked the little freshman in all the smart-kid classes.

The worst part for Eva was group work. Whenever a teacher said, "Find a partner," Eva was terrified. She could never gather the courage to ask to join a group, and nobody asked the quiet girl to join them. Eva always ended up with whatever other student didn't have a partner. Or, even worse, a teacher forced her upon an unwilling group: "Oh, you can join so-and-so's group."

Eva's anxiety began to lead to school refusal, which prompted the school to begin the process for a 504 plan. Asking teachers to intentionally place Eva with selected peers for collaborative assignments eased her anxiety about group work. Arranging an in-person meeting with each teacher before the semester for a five-minute get-to-know-you helped Eva feel safe and believe that she wouldn't be judged by the teacher for being quiet or not volunteering. Eventually, Eva got to know more of the students in her classes, and although she still experienced social anxiety, she became more comfortable and better able to learn. ▪

Other Anxiety-Based Disorders

Other anxiety-based disorders that can affect the academic lives of gifted learners include separation anxiety disorder and selective mutism. Although these diagnoses don't typically affect gifted learners differently than nongifted learners, I've included them here to address how they may appear in the classroom and to suggest additional accommodations that can help gifted learners succeed.

Separation Anxiety

For most people, separation anxiety is a stage of development in early childhood that is part of healthy attachment to caregivers. It becomes a disorder when it is no longer developmentally appropriate based on a person's age and ability. There may be a specific triggering event (such as trauma) that initiates the separation anxiety, but not always. When the separation anxiety is focused on a parent, the child may refuse to attend school or request frequent check-ins with the parent throughout the day. A supportive teacher or counselor can help ease the transition from home to school and help the student feel safe.

Occasionally, a student with separation anxiety may become attached to a teacher. This is most likely in the elementary years. If it is the student's general classroom teacher, the student may become distressed about and avoid going to special classes, such as physical education or music. They may also ask to drop their gifted class to prevent separation from their classroom teacher. Transitions before longer school breaks or weekends can be difficult.

Students can gradually overcome separation anxiety by collaboratively building a plan with the school counselor to improve independence and feelings of security. Using the steps for setting microgoals (see chapter 5) can be effective with these students.

Selective Mutism

Selective mutism occurs when an individual is consistently unable to speak in certain social situations, and the inability is not related to any type of language delay. The person can speak clearly and fluently in other situations, usually with people they know well and are comfortable with. For an inability to speak to be considered selective mutism, it must be present for at least one month—and not just the first month of the school year. Typically, students with selective mutism also have a diagnosis of social anxiety disorder. They may outgrow the symptoms of selective mutism, but as they get older, the social anxiety often continues.

Gifted students with selective mutism may struggle to adjust to various classroom environments, like attending a pull-out program. Presentations, class discussions, or reading aloud may be situations that require accommodation for students with selective mutism.

AMBER'S STORY

Amber joined my gifted classroom as a first grader. She seemed quiet and always sat next to her best friend, Kendra, who traveled to our gifted center from her home school. The first few days, Amber talked to Kendra when they were working together but avoided sharing with the class. When we talked as a group and it was her turn to share, she looked down and shook her head, or she quietly spoke to Kendra, who relayed Amber's message to the rest of the class. When I asked Amber a question individually, she whispered her response softly in one or two words.

After a couple of weeks, we were talking in small groups. I asked Amber about her thoughts, and she turned to whisper to Kendra. "It's okay, Amber," I prodded. "Why don't you tell us yourself?" She looked at me. I waited, attempting to reassure her with my expression and patience. Kendra started to answer for her. I interrupted, "It's okay. I think Amber can speak for herself." After several more agonizing moments, tears filled Amber's eyes. "Okay, don't worry, Amber," I conceded, and I moved on.

Soon afterward, I visited Amber's home school. I spoke to her classroom teacher, who told me Amber had selective mutism. Amber was quiet and shy but functioned moderately well because she was familiar with her peers, and she knew her classroom teacher from the previous year. The school also made undocumented accommodations for her, like placing her with Kendra and arranging for her to meet her teacher before the school year began. There was no documentation, such as a medical record or a 504 plan, anywhere in Amber's file that would have indicated to me that Amber needed accommodations. The school hadn't felt it was necessary to put anything in writing, because the accommodations were made easily without an official plan. But when she began attending the gifted program, the unofficial accommodations fell short.

Several months later, Amber had blossomed in our class. One day at recess, she sat next to me and talked nonstop for the entire twenty minutes about her family and dance classes. Although everything worked out okay for Amber, I found myself wishing somebody had put a 504 plan in place for her. Such a plan would have made clear that her success relied on accommodations her home school had implemented. It would have helped Amber's transition to a new environment go much more smoothly. ■

Obsessive-Compulsive Disorder

OCD occurs when a person has a pattern of thoughts (obsessions) and behaviors (compulsions) they cannot control and that cause significant distress. Obsessions are repetitive and may include specific thoughts, fears, images, or urges. For example, a student may experience repetitive thoughts about an intruder and have to check on every noise they hear to feel safe. Compulsions are repetitive behaviors or mental acts. For example, a student may have the repetitive thought that their handwriting must be perfect or the teacher will be mad at them, so they erase and rewrite any letter that appears imperfect multiple times, causing simple work to take hours to complete—or to never get completed at all.

OCD is not technically an anxiety disorder, but 2e students with OCD may have educational needs similar to those of students with anxiety disorders. Like other types of 2e learners, gifted students with OCD mask their symptoms. They often recognize that their behaviors are more harmful than helpful and try to hide or minimize them. OCD in high-achieving students can also appear as intense perfectionism, although the impact on daily life and functioning is much greater than that of perfectionism.

Here are the key characteristics of OCD:

- **Intrusive thoughts that are hard to ignore (obsessions):** Kids with OCD have thoughts enter their mind that they can't control. These thoughts might be about a fear, about a pattern or ritual, or about images.

- **Urge to perform an action to alleviate anxiety about intrusive thoughts (compulsions):** Many people with OCD cannot relax or reduce their anxiety without performing some type of behavior.

Impact of OCD on Gifted Students

Gifted students with OCD need support in the classroom to make sure their symptoms don't impede their achievement. Some characteristics of giftedness may look like OCD behaviors at first glance. Gifted students are prone to perfectionism, they like to play with numbers and patterns in their minds, and they have an awareness of their environment that may spark questions and a need for reassurance. The difference between these characteristics and OCD is the level of impact on daily functioning.

Symmetry OCD (or "just-right" OCD) is the type of OCD I see most often in gifted learners. They are labeled meticulous or perfectionist students. As content grows more difficult, grades begin to drop. Students with this type of OCD may turn in work late (or never) because they are continually checking and rechecking it, and it never feels complete or good enough. Some students may write a word that doesn't look "right" and erase it multiple times (or perhaps a prescribed number of times) to reduce their anxiety that it isn't right.

Finding the right accommodations for gifted students with OCD can give them the structure and support they need to continue their academic success. Depending on the student's level of insight, they may be able to self-advocate for their needs. Most often, students with significant OCD benefit from structured cognitive-behavioral treatment. Collaboration between therapist and teacher has a huge impact on the success of such treatment. For example, if a student is tasked with reducing the number of times they wash their hands in a day, helping the student track and control their progress is an integral part of their treatment.

SUBTYPES OF OCD

- **Contamination obsessions:** Students with contamination obsessions worry about germs or infections. They may ask to go to the bathroom often to wash their hands, may avoid touching items in the classroom (especially shared materials), or may dislike working in groups or near other students.

- **Harm obsessions:** Students with harm obsessions are afraid of harm coming to themselves or others. They may be very concerned about the possibility of intruders, fire, or severe weather. Sometimes people with harm obsessions worry that even thinking about an event makes it more likely to happen. Students may need frequent reassurance about their safety or find other ways to check in to alleviate their obsessive thought.

- **Obsessions without visible compulsions:** Kids with this type of OCD experience intrusive thoughts and engage in mental rituals, such as praying or counting, to reduce anxiety caused by obsessive thoughts. These students may appear unfocused in class and may avoid situations that trigger their obsessive thoughts.

- **Symmetry obsessions:** Often referred to as "just-right" OCD, students with this subtype experience compulsions related to ordering, arranging, and counting. A student who rewrites an assignment because the spacing was incorrect or who must clean their desk on a daily basis may be struggling with a symmetry obsession.

- **Hoarding:** Although hoarding is technically its own diagnosis in the DSM-5, it is related to OCD. It involves the compulsion to collect items or the inability to get rid of items that seem useless or seem like trash. A student may collect scraps of paper off the floor or refuse to throw away old assignments; desks and lockers may be overwhelming to the student, and they may have a hard time organizing their materials. Hoarding can be missed in gifted children because many emotionally intense gifted students form strong attachments to material belongings and keep them because of this attachment or for future projects.

Social and Emotional Considerations for Gifted Students with Anxiety Disorders

To be fair, this section really doesn't need the word *disorders* in its heading. The tools and skills herein will benefit any gifted learner who experiences the emotion of anxiety, whether they have an anxiety disorder, a different exceptionality, or no label at all other than giftedness. Building skills of mindfulness, understanding perfectionism, and learning about the psychosomatic symptoms of anxiety are useful life skills that can help anyone overcome feelings of being overwhelmed when they occur.

Overcoming Avoidance

Anxiety makes a person want to avoid the thing that is causing it. When I work with kids dealing with anxiety, we label the anxiety as a "worry bully" or a "worry monster." We talk about how the anxiety is trying to push them around and keep them from doing the things they want or need to do. Avoidance in gifted kids with an anxiety disorder can look like the following:

- not enrolling in advanced courses or dropping gifted education classes
- refusal to try a task that appears difficult
- disobedience or defiance when confronted about avoidant behaviors
- always choosing to work alone
- never raising their hand in class
- asking to eat lunch in the classroom or skip recess

When you are working with students who have anxiety, provide support along with gentle nudging toward the task or activity they are avoiding. This helps them overcome the fear associated with the task or activity. Avoid putting anxious students in a sink-or-swim situation. Even if they are successful, the fear experienced in the process can keep them from trying again, instead of building their confidence.

Psychosomatic Symptoms of Anxiety

You may notice a student experiencing anxiety before they even realize they are feeling uncomfortable. Helping students get in tune with the psychosomatic symptoms of their anxiety is a first step to helping them learn to help themselves. Here are some common psychosomatic symptoms of anxiety:

- flushed face
- fidgeting
- increased heart rate
- rapid breathing
- sweaty palms
- racing thoughts
- tearfulness
- furrowed brow
- stomachache or nausea

Gifted students often appreciate learning about the neurology behind anxiety and how the stress hormone cortisol triggers their emotions and their "body signs" of anxiety. Students can track how often they experience symptoms or emotions and the possible triggers. Many times, simply tracking the occurrences helps reduce their frequency and intensity by building awareness, which allows the student to use logic and self-talk to calm themselves and persist through the situation.

Teaching Mindfulness

I often tell clients that anxiety is borrowing worry from tomorrow. Worry is expecting that the outcome of a future event or situation will be negative. The cycle of worry is hard to break because the brain perceives worrying as doing something to fix a problem, although in reality worry does nothing constructive. Our self-talk focuses on the possible negative outcome: "What if something happens? I wonder if I should change my plans?" The brain interprets the self-talk as action, and although no decision has been made and no action has been taken to address the situation, the brain feels a slight sense of relief because we are, at least, thinking about it. But since there has been no resolution, we have to keep thinking about it. And the worry cycle continues.

Mindfulness moves us from the future into the present. Mindfulness is a metacognitive skill—stepping back and observing our thoughts, emotions, and body sensations objectively. For 2e students with an anxiety disorder, mindfulness is an essential, multifaceted skill that can be developed over time and implemented in most situations.

Building on the awareness developed about their psychosomatic anxiety symptoms, students can learn to use basic mindfulness skills independently. Additionally, many teachers are beginning to use mindfulness as a skill in their classrooms on a daily basis. Coaching all kids in the methods of mindfulness helps develop a safe and calm learning environment.

Here are some of my favorite mindfulness activities to help students reduce stress:

- **Counting breaths:** This easy and effective breathing technique can be done in any environment, and most people will not notice the student is doing anything out of the ordinary. Breathing deeply in through the nose and out through the mouth, the student mentally counts to ten with each inhale and exhale: (inhale) *one*, (exhale) *two*, (inhale) *three*, (exhale) *four*, (inhale) *five*, (exhale) *six*, (inhale) *seven*, (exhale) *eight*, (inhale) *nine*, (exhale) *ten*. When they reach ten, they simply start over and continue as many cycles as needed to feel calmer.

- **Body scan:** Imagining some type of scanning device, the student visualizes the scanner slowly processing their body from head to toe, noting any bodily sensations, discomfort, or signs of stress. If muscles are tight, they can relax them. They can also take note of bodily signs, like hunger or needing to go to the bathroom, that can increase distress.

- **5-4-3-2-1:** This grounding activity helps students become focused and aware of their surroundings. They focus on each of their senses, making a mental note of each sensation: five things they can see, four things they can hear, three things they can feel, two things they can smell, and one thing they can taste.

Many kids experience frustration with mindfulness. Sometimes they try it in a moment of intense dysregulation, and it doesn't make the anxiety evaporate. This leads to the logical (but usually erroneous) conclusion that mindfulness doesn't work for them. I like to help students understand that mindfulness is a skill like anything else. It has to be practiced often in order to work well.

Some mindfulness activities call for a person to close their eyes. However, this is never a necessity. The focus is on awareness of the body and our thoughts. For some learners who have an anxiety diagnosis, who've experienced past trauma, or who have sensory problems, closing their eyes can be extremely uncomfortable. If you are coaching students to learn mindfulness techniques, give them permission to either close their eyes or focus on a spot on the ground or wall.

Social Anxiety and Scripting

Kids with social anxiety worry about navigating social interactions and recognize that they can't always predict or control the flow or topics of conversation. Group work or think-pair-share activities trigger this fear. Some gifted kids with social anxiety do not experience performance anxiety; they excel at public speaking because it allows them to plan in advance, or script, what they will say.

Scripting is an easy tool you can use with your whole class or one-on-one with students. Scripting is just what it sounds like: creating a script for certain situations or activities. You can use scripting for some classroom activities, to help students with social anxiety feel comfortable. For simple think-pair-share types of activities, providing the questions (or even a fill-in-the-blank answer) in advance to the class or the student can allow them to prepare before it is necessary to share. For less structured activities, taking a few minutes to prepare a student with social anxiety on what to expect and what topics may be addressed can ease distress.

Test Anxiety

Gifted students tend to take high-stakes tests more often than other students do. Between AP tests, finals for challenging courses, and taking the ACT or SAT, a gifted student with severe test anxiety will need to find coping strategies in order to do their best work. Test anxiety is a type of performance anxiety in which the student feels exposed and fearful of doing poorly. Students with test anxiety can benefit from a 504 plan with accommodations for extra time or an alternate testing environment. While these accommodations may help, they are unlikely to eliminate the test anxiety.

Relaxation strategies, reducing negative self-talk, and mindfulness are all internal processes students experiencing test anxiety can use. For classes that take standardized tests, mimicking the testing environment for practice tests can help desensitize the student to the experience. Beyond strategies to help reduce anxiety during test-taking, overcoming the fear of failure or the perception that they will be harshly judged based on their performance is key to overcoming test anxiety.

Perfectionism

Perfectionism is common in gifted learners. Gifted students with anxiety are especially prone to developing harmful, chronic perfectionistic habits. These habits are most likely associated with a diagnosis of GAD or OCD.

Students with anxiety-based perfectionism often believe the pressure to be perfect is coming from sources outside themselves, such as their parents, teachers, or society. Some students may identify the source of perfectionistic anxiety as coming from within themselves but do not know how to temper the expectation that their work must always be perfect. Other times, perfectionism is others-oriented, meaning the student exhibits their perfectionism toward other people. They get frustrated and uncomfortable when others make mistakes or when someone does something that could be embarrassing.

Providing an environment for 2e learners where they feel comfortable attempting tasks, knowing the risks of true failure are minimal, is essential to supporting these learners. Focusing on process instead of outcome is also a useful framework for students dealing with perfectionism.

Key Points

- Gifted students may need accommodations and modifications due to an anxiety disorder, such as generalized anxiety disorder or social anxiety disorder, or for obsessive-compulsive disorder.

- Providing consistent expectations and routines can reduce the impact of anxiety.

- Perfectionism and test anxiety are both common manifestations of anxiety in gifted learners.

- Learning about the psychosomatic anxiety symptoms and how to use basic mindfulness skills can help students manage their anxiety.

Gifted, 2e, or Anxiety?

Gifted Characteristics	Characteristics of Gifted Learners with Anxiety Disorders	Characteristics of Anxiety Disorders
Thought patterns		
Gifted learners are often described as "overthinkers" or "little professors." However, these thinking patterns do not necessarily indicate an anxiety disorder. Gifted learners may occasionally have some worries, but they do not obsess over them, they are able to keep them in perspective, and their worries are generally over topics that appear to be of realistic concern.	The thought patterns of gifted learners with anxiety may be focused on perfectionism, grades, or ability-achievement discrepancies. The worries cause significant disruption in mood or behavior. These 2e learners may be able to mask their thought patterns and feelings of anxiety through their verbal and logical thinking skills when rationalizing thought patterns to others, but these thought patterns may still strongly affect their well-being and overall performance.	Kids and teens with anxiety disorders feel uneasy in a variety of situations. They may be unable to control their thought patterns, which focus on sources of stress or worry.
Social relationships		
Gifted students are often able to keep healthy relationships with like-minded peers. Difficulties in social relationships are often related to the student being in an environment that is a poor match for their ability and interests.	Gifted students with anxiety may struggle with social relationships due to others-oriented perfectionism. Frequent collaborative projects in both gifted and general education classes may cause heightened anxiety due to fears that others will not complete their portion of the project or because of social anxiety.	Anxiety that manifests as irritability can cause difficulty in social relationships. Students may also struggle with social anxiety; this fear of judgment from other students can inhibit a child's ability to make friends.
Emotional responses		
Intense emotional reactions and passionate responses are common in gifted learners but are not persistent and intense enough to cause interruptions in daily functioning. Perfectionism is generally within the realm of striving for excellence.	Gifted students with anxiety may try to hide their emotional responses to conceal worry. Their fear about performance may result in perfectionism. Avoidance or hypervigilance may be signs of anxiety in these 2e learners.	Generalized anxiety can cause increased irritability, emotional meltdowns, and avoidance of anxiety-provoking situations. It may appear that students with anxiety have very low levels of tolerance for distress.
Academic expectations		
Gifted learners tend to have high academic expectations for themselves. This may be fueled by an internal or external drive. Gifted learners may struggle with temporary feelings of anxiety at a new school if they've been accustomed to being the highest-achieving student in their previous school.	Gifted learners with an anxiety disorder are likely to have anxiety compounded by the fact that they have diverse learning needs and skills that don't match their abilities. They are susceptible to perfectionism.	Anxiety disorders affect school performance, preventing students from focusing, self-advocating, and learning.
Obsessive thoughts or compulsive behaviors		
Gifted learners can be interested in numbers or patterns and like to look for them in their environment or repeat them mentally. They may also have an area of passion that appears outwardly as almost obsessive. None of these traits causes significant impairment in functioning.	Symmetry OCD can look like perfectionism in 2e learners, with students focusing on redoing work multiple times. OCD related to performance or schoolwork can result in incomplete or missing work because the student is unable to complete it to their own exacting standards.	Students with OCD struggle with repetitive, unwanted thoughts and the irrepressible urge to complete some ritual to relieve the anxiety of these thoughts.
Test anxiety		
Gifted students may feel stressed or worried about taking a test, but their level of stress does not affect their performance and is manageable while taking the test.	Test anxiety may be heightened due to the frequency of high-stakes tests experienced by high-ability learners.	Test anxiety is a type of performance anxiety under the umbrella of social anxiety disorder.

Accommodations and Modifications for Gifted Students with Anxiety

Major Life Activity	Possible Accommodation or Modification
Performing manual tasks	
Obsessions and compulsions lead a student to write and rewrite assignments until they are "just right."	• Instructional: Use technology to avoid writing by hand. • Evaluative: Emphasize grading based on content instead of appearance or neatness.
Concentrating	
Constant focus on worries causes distraction, inability to keep up with note taking, and severe test anxiety.	• Instructional: Provide copy of notes to student. Have student complete fill-in-the-blank notes or outlines. • Environmental: Offer preferential seating. • Environmental: Offer an alternate testing setting and extended time to complete tests.
Learning	
Social anxiety prevents students from engaging productively and successfully in group work. Separation anxiety leads to difficulty with a substitute teacher. Student's anxiety leads to school refusal.	• Instructional: Intentionally place students in groups with peers who are a good fit. • Environmental: Use cluster grouping to ensure appropriate peers are available for group work. • Instructional: Provide advance notice when a substitute will be in the classroom. • Environmental: Provide an alternate safe learning setting for days when teacher is absent. • Environmental/instructional: Use a partial-day schedule or homebound education.
Thinking	
Student has difficulty transitioning to an anxiety-provoking activity. Student feels intense anxiety and fear in certain situations.	• Instructional: Provide advance notice about upcoming transitions in activities or environment. • Behavioral: Provide an "anytime" pass for student to leave classroom to relieve anxiety as needed.
Communicating	
Performance anxiety complicates reading aloud in class or making presentations to a group. Anxiety appears as irritability or defiance.	• Evaluative: Allow student to record and submit presentations on video or audio, or complete in a one-on-one setting with teacher only. • Behavioral: Avoid disciplinary responses for anxiety-based behaviors.

Depression and Other Mood Disorders

You may have students in your classroom who are dealing with depression or another mood disorder that you aren't aware of. Or there may be a time when a child in your class has a drastic change in mood, and the fact that they are experiencing an episode of depression is obvious and concerning. Some students with mood disorders can cope through the school day; some have good days and bad days. Research does not indicate that gifted students experience depression at higher rates than their peers, but it does recognize that cultural, societal, and environmental factors can influence their well-being (Cross and Cross 2018). The experience of being a twice-exceptional student can make one more likely to suffer from other personality characteristics associated with depressive disorders, such as low self-esteem (Martin, Burns, and Schonlau 2009; Mueller 2009).

This chapter will address major depressive disorder (MDD), which is the most well-known type of depression. It will also address disruptive mood dysregulation disorder (DMDD) and bipolar disorder (BD). Bipolar disorder is not classified as a depressive disorder in the *Diagnostic and Statistical Manual of Mental Disorders: Fifth Edition* (DSM-5), but many of its characteristics appear similar to those of depressive disorders in the classroom, and interventions align as well.

Risk Factors for Depression in Gifted Learners

Depressive disorders are often triggered by environmental stressors. Experts generally agree that people who end up with depression are predisposed to it in some way. Some risk factors common among gifted learners are:

- perfectionism
- difficulty connecting to same-age peers
- feeling of being different
- feelings of isolation
- asynchrony between existential awareness and emotional maturity
- societal pressures to achieve
- impotence to influence or change perceived injustices
- career indecisiveness due to multipotentiality (talent across a variety of domains and the fear of forgoing one to pursue another)
- stigma of giftedness

Gifted students who are 2e may be in environments that don't meet their needs and cause chronic feelings of inadequacy. Providing an environment that supports the needs of 2e learners can insulate these students from situations that might trigger a mood disorder.

RIAH'S STORY

Since elementary school, Riah had been acutely aware of all the inequities in the world and had been passionate about social justice issues. As a middle school student, she couldn't wrap her head around how there were people in some countries who were starving and had next to nothing, when the kids at her lunch table were throwing half their meals away. It wasn't fair, and she wanted to do something about it.

She started by trying to talk to her friends about her concerns. They agreed with her that it was sad but didn't understand her drive to change things. Riah spent hours searching the internet for information on various local, national, and global charities addressing hunger. She came up with ideas to try to help—fundraisers or food drives—but got stuck when it came to implementation. She couldn't find adults who understood how important this cause was to her and who would help her get things off the ground. Suggestions to scale back some of her big ideas fell flat because Riah felt that the scaled-back versions wouldn't make enough change.

Riah's existential awareness of injustice led her down a path of questioning her own value. Why was she was born in a prosperous country to a family living comfortably, when other people were starving? The lack of support from others fostered a sense of helplessness. Riah began to shut down and cycle through thoughts of guilt and worthlessness. Her level of existential awareness and inability to initiate real change exacerbated and accelerated symptoms of clinical depression. ■

Qualifying for Services or Accommodations

Gifted students with mood disorders may need temporary or long-term support to reach their academic potential. Students with a diagnosis of MDD, DMDD, or BD may be eligible for special education services under IDEA with an educational diagnosis of emotional disturbance. DMDD and BD diagnoses are prone to intense emotional dysregulation, and an IEP can provide resources to help support building regulation skills or safe spaces in the school for when the student needs to leave the classroom.

Gifted students with milder forms of depression may benefit from accommodations and modifications through a 504 plan. If a student takes medication for their diagnosis and appears to be managing the academic environment appropriately, they can still qualify for a 504 plan because the plan must be developed based on the child's needs without any mitigating factors.

Major Depressive Disorder

Students experiencing an episode of MDD show a significant shift in their mood and their ability to manage the daily expectations and stresses of life. This shift in mood is present for at least two weeks; however, it may be present for a longer period of time. MDD can be tricky to identify in kids. First, the outward appearance of their mood may look like irritability instead of sadness or low energy. Second, kids are more likely to have periods of apparent engagement or activity, masking depression symptoms. As children grow into teens, their symptoms become more obvious and more like those of adults.

In addition to a depressed mood, you may notice that a child seems to have lost interest in activities they previously enjoyed. Changes in activity levels that are outwardly visible, like an increase in restlessness or decrease in overall movement, can also be an indication of depression. Teachers may notice students making frequent negative statements about themselves indicating a feeling of worthlessness or having difficulty making decisions. In more serious cases, thoughts and talk of death or even suicidal ideation can occur.

Here are the key characteristics of MDD:

- **Increased sadness, irritability, or hopelessness:** Students may talk about the changes in their emotions, or you might notice an increase in tearfulness or withdrawal from peers.

- **Losing interest in preferred activities:** Children may have difficulty motivating themselves to engage in activities they previously enjoyed. A gifted student who was a highly motivated learner may be unable to muster the energy or interest to complete work.

- **Increase in negative thinking and negative self-perception:** Students may begin making uncharacteristic statements, indicating they feel like they aren't good enough or aren't worthy of others' approval.

- **Struggle to focus, complete work, or make decisions:** Students may be unable to complete work in an expected amount of time or make even small decisions.

- **Noticeable increase or decrease in levels of psychomotor activity:** Students with depression may exhibit uncharacteristic restlessness or lethargy.

- **Recurrent thoughts or statements about death:** Thoughts or statements about death or dying indicate it is on a student's mind and should be taken seriously. Evidence of self-injury should also be addressed.

Impact of MDD on Gifted Students

The word *depressed* is thrown around today rather casually. We've all felt sad, we've all been lonely, we've all experienced disappointment—but these feelings are not necessarily depression. Clinical depression is much more serious than someone lamenting that they are "*so* depressed." Students who are depressed may not mention or even recognize what they are experiencing. It may take an adult who is in tune with the child's typical behavior to notice the change. Gifted students typically have an advanced vocabulary, but they may have trouble describing their painful emotions in a way that tells adults how much pain they're in.

Gifted students who suffer from MDD need support from the school, even if their grades continue to be satisfactory. The compensatory skills of giftedness can mask the outward appearance of symptoms in students with depression. Grades may drop, but not significantly. Students involved in extracurricular activities may still manage to attend practices or meetings. What does masked depression in a gifted learner look like? Here are a few possibilities:

- Gifted students develop existential awareness about life, death, and their place in the universe much earlier than their same-age peers do. A gifted student with depression may avoid making statements that disclose suicidal ideation, but an increase in nihilistic existential commentary about the value of life (or lack thereof) can indicate a need for further investigation.

- Gifted students who are high achievers may begin to do just enough work to get by. Their work may be late, incomplete, or of lower quality. Depending on the structure of classes and their ability to maintain decent test scores, their overall grades may not be obvious indicators of a problem.

- Perfectionistic gifted students may show an increased level of negativity surrounding perceived failures. Dysregulation characterized by negative self-talk or extreme black-and-white statements can offer a glimpse into the students' thought processes.

- Because depression in children and adolescents can outwardly look like irritability, gifted students with high verbal abilities may come across as overly sarcastic or disrespectful.

VICTOR'S STORY

Most kids with an upcoming birthday would be excited and making a wish list of gifts. As Victor approached his tenth birthday, he had other things on his mind. He realized that getting older meant more responsibilities. It meant more homework. It meant only one more year at his elementary school before moving on to middle school.

Victor's mom noticed that he had recently become withdrawn. He had always been a pretty quiet kid, but he had liked to play video games with his brother and shoot baskets with his neighborhood friends. Recently, he'd begun spending more time alone in his room. Victor's mom also noticed that he seemed more sensitive about things, easily becoming tearful or angry.

At school, Victor's teacher noticed some changes too. He was taking a book out to recess and sitting alone instead of playing with his friends. His work quality, usually thorough and detailed, seemed rushed, with frequent careless errors. He wasn't volunteering during class discussions, and his teacher noticed him sneaking a book under his desk to read instead of listening to instruction.

After a particularly tough morning when Victor had to be prodded out of bed, had gotten in trouble for reading during class, and had gotten an assignment back with a C- grade, Victor refused to go to recess. He sat with his head down on the desk while the teacher dismissed his classmates. When she went back to talk to him, he started crying and talking about his fear of getting older. "If life is this hard when I'm turning ten, how will it ever get easier when an adult?" he asked. "Sometimes I wish I could just die."

Victor's teacher reached out to the school counselor and Victor's mom. Outside school, he was diagnosed with MDD and began counseling. In school, Victor was given a 504 plan to allow him revisions on his work and a safe place to go and talk to someone if he felt sad. His teacher set a microgoal with him to stay on task in class and self-evaluate his work before turning it in.

Victor's MDD was episodic. His mom and teachers learned to watch for signals of recurrence. They recognized that the approach of his birthday could be a trigger. ■

Disruptive Mood Dysregulation Disorder and Bipolar Disorder

Disruptive mood dysregulation disorder and bipolar disorder occur less often than major depressive disorder. DMDD is a diagnosis that was added to the DSM-5 because many children were being diagnosed with BD without evidence of a true manic episode. Usually, BD manifests with an initial manic episode in the teen or early adult years.

DMDD is a depressive disorder characterized by a persistent irritable or angry mood and frequent temper outbursts that are either verbal or physical. The driving emotion behind these outbursts is often described as rage, and the episodes are disproportionate to the triggering event. To meet the diagnosis of DMDD, the outbursts typically occur in multiple types of environments with a frequency of several times per week.

Gifted students with DMDD may struggle due to low frustration tolerance. High-ability students with DMDD who are placed in gifted programs or classes with challenging coursework may need significant support to succeed. Some gifted students with this disorder may go unidentified because they become frustrated during the screening and testing process as test items get progressively more difficult.

Most mental health and neurodevelopmental disorders do not appear to occur more frequently in gifted individuals than they do in the rest of the population. However, people with above-average cognitive ability *do* have a slightly higher risk of BD diagnosis. Below-average cognitive skills are also associated with a higher risk of BD diagnosis (Gale et al. 2012). BD, which is characterized by a manic episode lasting several days, is rare in young children. By adolescence, some students who've experienced symptoms of depression may experience a manic episode, indicating the presence of BD. Students experiencing a manic episode may be euphoric; speak rapidly; experience rapid, tangential thought processes (called "flight of ideas"); and take unnecessary and unsafe risks. Gifted students with BD cycle through episodes of depression, mania, and normal moods; episodes of each must last several days or weeks to qualify for BD diagnosis.

Either DMDD or BP may qualify a student for an educational diagnosis of emotional disturbance and special education services through an IEP. IEP services can provide support to help these students learn to regulate their emotions and can provide staff to assist when they become dysregulated. Students who are less affected on a daily basis or who have found medication that reduces their symptoms may find that a 504 plan serves their needs sufficiently.

Social and Emotional Considerations for Gifted Students with Mood Disorders

Developing an awareness of the social and emotional needs unique to gifted students with mood disorders can help educators support them beyond their academic needs. It is vital to understand the risk of suicide for gifted learners as well as the impact of existential depression, self-injury, and self-harm and to provide a safe place for students to disclose their emotions. School counselors may work with students who are dealing with mood disorders, but teachers often have stronger relationships with individual students. This is especially true for gifted and special education teachers because of their smaller class sizes. Being prepared with strategies to understand and triage student concerns provides a safety net for students who need it.

Talking to Kids and Teens About Depression

A student dealing with depression needs an adult they can talk to and trust. A teacher is often that person. If you notice symptoms that suggest the student is struggling, it is important to open that conversation with them. As a school counselor, I did my best to keep my finger on the pulse of students' lives, but unless a student talked to a teacher or peer first, they were usually in crisis before I knew they needed help. If you are a student's gifted or special education teacher, it is more likely that you know the child well enough to recognize a problem or that they trust you enough to ask you for help.

One common myth about students dealing with depression or thoughts of suicide is that they won't talk about it. A second myth is that talking about suicide frankly will increase the likelihood of a suicidal thoughts or actions. Many well-meaning people dismiss signs of distress when a student writes fiction about suicide, draws artwork depicting self-injury, or frequently talks up or jokes about dying. These are red flags that should not be dismissed. If a student is sharing with you in these subtle ways, reaching out to them personally is the best thing you can do. An immediate referral to a counselor or administrator the student doesn't know well or doesn't trust can cause them to shut down and internalize their feelings. Opening the conversation, letting them know they aren't alone, and coming up with a plan to get help are the first steps to the support the student. You can ask for their permission to share what they've told you with a parent, guardian, or counselor or make an agreement that they will tell somebody and you will follow up with that person within a specific time frame to be sure they've been helped. Generally, students are relieved to be heard and have help. Some students may ask what you are required to share before disclosing their thoughts. Assure them that you will keep the conversation between the two of you as long as you know they are safe, but that safety is your number one priority. Make sure to follow your state's requirements or school procedures for mandated reporting if you are concerned the child is in danger.

If you are someone a child or teen trusts enough to tell about their struggle, the best thing you can do is provide a judgment-free place for them to share. Be careful not to make statements that are well intentioned but come across as minimizing. See **figure 12-1** for some examples of reframing minimizing statements into supportive ones. Remember that gifted children and teens sometimes struggle with vulnerability. They are the kids who've never needed help and whom the other students have always looked up to. Dealing with depression can make them feel weak, and they may insist everything is fine, even when it's not. When you provide an environment built on unconditional positive regard, you give kids a safe place to ask for help.

Figure 12-1 Reframing Statements

Instead of . . .	Try . . .
"Look at all the good things you have going in your life!"	"I know how hard it is when it looks to the outside world like everything is great but inside you're hurting."
"Why would you want to hurt yourself? That won't help solve your problem."	"People who self-injure have lots of reasons why they feel like it helps. How do you feel like it helps you?"
"Look at the bright side of this situation. It is all going to work out."	"When you are feeling down, it is hard to imagine how it will ever get better. But I'm here to listen until it does."
Calling the student's parents or guardians without their knowledge	"I am always here for you to talk to, but I think we need to talk to someone else who can help. Who is someone we could talk to that you trust? Do you want me to call them for you?"

Existential Depression in Gifted Learners

One of the symptoms of asynchrony in gifted learners is a discrepancy between their level of existential awareness and the life experience needed to resolve their existential questions. At a young age, gifted kids will ask questions about what happens after death, the purpose of their lives, and the feeling of isolation in the universe. Most kids don't truly grasp the permanence and universality of death until adolescence. Without being told, gifted students make these connections at much younger ages. But young gifted students don't have the emotional maturity to find their own sense of meaning in the world. Even older teens struggle, wondering about their place in the world and if they'll ever make sense of it all.

Gifted kids often become aware of famine, war, and other tragedies earlier than their peers do. Students who are insulated from these types of events may realize the inequity between their own lives and the suffering around them; those who are experiencing such events directly can feel helpless and hopeless to make any changes. Many adults find ways to rationalize or set aside this awareness, or they do what they can to rectify the wrongs they see. Children and teens who desperately want to make a change cannot rationalize or set aside their awareness, and they feel helpless when they can't actually do something about the injustice they see.

Multipotentiality is another factor that can contribute to existential depression. Children may become paralyzed with the fear of making the wrong choice when they recognize the number of possible life paths they can take. Multipotentiality can contribute to existential depression—possibly leading to clinical depression—when it's combined with awareness of isolation within the human experience and questioning the meaning of life.

When students feel helpless or believe life is pointless, they lose a sense of purpose and motivation. Whether a 2e student's diagnosis is depression or something else, we need to be prepared to help them process their emotions. Service projects, especially student-driven ones, empower children and help them overcome existential depression. We can help guide them forward to find their place in this world.

TAYLOR'S STORY

Taylor began thinking about existential issues from a young age. She worried about children in countries with no clean food or water and felt intense guilt about living a life of relative comfort. She recognized the injustice of the world and felt helpless to change it. As she got older, she showed symptoms of clinical depression, and her existential worries were a part of this. "I feel bad about taking up the air I breathe," she described, "like I don't really deserve it."

Taylor's great difficulty was her feeling of helplessness. A middle school student, Taylor didn't have money to give to charity or a car to drive back and forth to volunteer. Her ideas about how to help were often grand. When she struggled with the logistics of her ideas, she fell deeper into frustration and guilt.

I worked with Taylor to build the skills necessary to reframe her thoughts and tolerate the waves of emotion caused by her depression using cognitive behavioral therapy and other techniques. While these skills helped some, they did not resolve her stress and worry about the world and her role within it. Finally, during one fall session, Taylor entered the session excited. Halloween had been the previous week, and she and a friend had finally had a success. Overcoming her social anxiety, Taylor had distributed flyers to her neighbors telling them that she'd be coming around to trick-or-treat but would be collecting canned food to donate to the local food pantry instead of candy for Halloween. Several wagonloads later, Taylor felt that she'd accomplished something good, and in her mind, she had evened the score by helping others. She continued to struggle with such worries, but finding ways to be of service empowered her. ∎

Suicide

Information about gifted students and suicide is sparse, although some information can be gleaned from research evidence. For example, one study found that feeling successful at school through academic achievement was a protective factor for students against suicidal ideation (Taliaferro and Muehlenkamp 2013). In another study, expressed poor self-concept related to students' academic abilities was a predictor for future suicidal actions (Martin et al. 2005). When 2e students struggle academically, we put them at risk by not providing the support they need for success in school.

The book *What Made Maddy Run* by Kate Fagan tells the heartbreaking story of an elite college athlete and high-achieving student who died by suicide. Maddy felt pressure to live up to unbending societal expectations, and this made it hard for her to ask for help and advocate for her own needs, which ultimately led to her death. Maddy's story doesn't indicate whether she was cognitively gifted, but the parallels are impossible to miss. She clearly experienced feelings of socially prescribed perfectionism, as do many gifted and 2e students.

Self-Injury

It's scary for a teacher to realize that a student has been cutting or engaging in some other type of self-injury. Sometimes we become aware of self-injury when we notice the marks on the student ourselves. Other times, a student may engage in self-injury in our presence. Some 2e learners who experience severe emotional dysregulation may bite themselves or hit their head on the desk as a form of self-injury.

Self-injury is sometimes called nonsuicidal self-injury (NSSI) in the field of psychology. The difference between NSSI and suicidal gestures is that NSSI is a way to regulate emotions without any intent or desire to attempt or complete suicide. Cutting or other types of self-injury are a maladaptive coping skill for many people. We can help our students find better ways to release or express those uncomfortable emotions.

If self-injury is not directly tied to suicidal ideation, why might 2e students self-injure? Understanding the possible reasons can help us determine ways to prevent it in the future. Here are a few possible reasons for self-injury:

- A student may have feelings of guilt, worthlessness, or inadequacy. Self-injury is sometimes used to punish oneself for not being good enough.

- If a student is emotionally dysregulated, self-injury can serve two purposes. The physical pain of self-injury can distract from the emotional pain the student is experiencing. And if a student is unable to verbalize their emotions, self-injury can be a way to communicate their level of dysregulation.

- Self-injury can be a way to externalize uncomfortable emotions, especially if the student is unable to identify the exact source of their discomfort. If a student doesn't understand why they hurt internally, a visual and tangible exhibit of pain through self-injury helps validate their internal struggle.

- Students who are feeling depressed often describe feeling numb. Self-injury provides a physical sensation instead of numbness.

- Many people will describe self-injury as a "cry for help" or "attention-seeking" behavior. For students who are unable to ask for help, visible self-injury may indeed be a way of asking for somebody to notice their struggle and provide support.

If you become aware of a student engaging in self-injury, consult the appropriate school personnel, who can assess the student's immediate needs. Once the immediate concern has been addressed, understanding what may be causing self-injury can help you modify the support you provide in the classroom for this student.

Key Points

■ Students who have a sudden change in behavior and seem low, sad, or negative may be experiencing a depressive disorder. Lack of motivation and drive are also symptomatic of students dealing with depression.

■ Providing an open and supportive environment where kids can share their thoughts and feelings without fear of being judged or having their feelings minimized is important for kids with mood disorders.

■ Existential depression in gifted kids can develop at an early age. Young students don't have the life experiences to put their thoughts and worries into context.

■ Self-injury is not necessarily caused by a desire to die.

Gifted, 2e, or Mood Disorder?

Gifted Characteristics	Characteristics of Gifted Students with Mood Disorders	Characteristics of Mood Disorders
Feelings of self-efficacy		
Gifted students who are emotionally and mentally healthy typically show self-confidence and willingness to take risks.	Gifted students with mood disorders may experience a drop in feelings of self-efficacy and may avoid taking academic risks. Students with high verbal abilities may frame negative self-talk with sarcasm or humor to mask their feelings.	Negative self-talk related to feelings of not being good enough or feeling overly guilty about minor incidents are common in students with mood disorders.
Levels of motivation		
Motivation is related to interest in the topic and feelings of competence.	Even in areas where a student previously felt successful or exhibited high levels of achievement, students dealing with symptoms of depression often see a decrease in motivation. This may not be evident in their grades if their cognitive ability is masking their struggles.	A decrease in motivation to pursue previously enjoyed activities is a common symptom of depression.
Existential awareness		
Gifted students often experience heightened levels of existential awareness and questioning, but this awareness does not cause them distress.	Gifted students with depression often have existential questions beyond what is common for their age. These concerns contribute to their feelings of hopelessness and helplessness.	Nongifted students with depression may have existential concerns that are commensurate with their age.
Quality of work or grades		
Quality of work is typically consistent for gifted children. Some evidence of perfectionism may be evident.	Gifted students with depression may struggle to complete work on time, or their quality of work may suffer compared to their typical levels of achievement. Perfectionism can drastically increase, with students refusing to attempt tasks. Objective measures of achievement (grades) may not drop if the student is masking their struggles.	Students with depression often see a dramatic drop in the quality of their work and grades.

Accommodations and Modifications for Gifted Students with Mood Disorders

Major Life Activity	Possible Accommodation or Modification
Concentrating	
Low mood inhibits active engagement in lessons and activities. Inability to concentrate makes it hard for student to complete work in a timely manner.	• Instructional: Provide work in chunks to avoid overwhelming student. • Instructional: Give extended time on assignments and homework.
Learning	
Student's feelings of low self-worth lead to learned helplessness and unwillingness to attempt tasks perceived as difficult.	• Behavioral: Set microgoals to build student's feelings of success with positive feedback and encouragement.
Thinking	
Negative thought patterns and low self-esteem impede thinking.	• Instructional: Provide manageable amounts of work that are carefully scaffolded for student's ability.
Communicating	
Low mood appears as resistance or defiance. Low mood leaves student unable to engage in group work effectively.	• Behavioral: Establish a communication strategy to use if a student becomes dysregulated (like a hand signal or cue word) to quickly reassure a student you are there to support them and give permission to take a break. • Environmental: Provide a safe alternative location if student needs a break from the classroom. • Instructional: Provide option for student to work independently or structure collaborative work clearly to provide scaffolding to struggling student.

The Neurodiverse Classroom 13

When I think about the number of students over the years who have been dismissed, unserved, or ignored because their needs were misunderstood or invisible, my heart breaks. But here's the good news: our understanding of neurological and psychological development throughout the human lifespan is continually growing, and as it grows, it broadens our awareness of the varying needs of individuals. We are living in a new world that acknowledges and appreciates neurodiversity.

As an educator, you are in the unique position of helping your neurodivergent students nurture their strengths and develop their ability to become independent and curious adults. Twice-exceptional kids need someone who understands them. They need someone who is willing to learn what it means to be neurodivergent and how to help them with their unique learning profile. They need someone like you.

You are one of the first people with whom your students may develop a significant, influential relationship outside their families. Who was the teacher that stood out for you? How did they make a positive impact on your life? What did they help you believe about yourself? How do you feel when you think about them? You can be that person for your students.

Normalizing Neurodiversity

People with neurological and psychological diagnoses, as well as their families, face a great deal of stigma. This social disapproval creates shame and prevents people from seeking help or talking about their struggles. They fear judgment from others who just don't "get it." The fear of using a label or diagnosis to describe a student's struggles reminds me of how, in the Harry Potter stories, almost everyone calls the archvillain He-Who-Must-Not-Be-Named, You-Know-Who, or the Dark Lord. But Professor Dumbledore tells Harry, "Call him Voldemort, Harry. Always use the proper name for things. Fear of a name increases fear of the thing itself" (Rowling 1997, 298). I think Dumbledore's right. It's easier to fight the monster underneath your bed when you turn on the light.

Of course, neurodiversity is neither a dark wizard nor a monster under our bed. But acting as if neurodiversity doesn't exist or is shameful or can't be discussed makes overcoming the struggles next to impossible.

Feeling isolated in a diagnosis is one of the major obstacles faced by 2e learners' families. Parents and guardians ask themselves, "What does this mean for the future?" Kids want to know if they'll ever fit in. When I'm having these conversations, I like to remind families of this saying: *The only normal people are the ones you don't know very well.*

In episode 51 of *The Neurodiversity Podcast,* guest Colin Seale talked about being diagnosed with ADHD as an adult. He'd been diagnosed only a week before our interview and was still processing what it meant to have gone through school as a gifted student without the diagnosis of ADHD. It meant he was constantly in trouble and that he was called a "hot mess." Colin wondered how his life might have been different if he'd been diagnosed in childhood as a 2e learner.

We talked about how Colin overcame his struggles. We discussed how being gifted with ADHD had actually served him through his life. As we chatted, Colin said something I think is important to remember, especially for adults who work with 2e kids: we need to start looking at individuals who have succeeded *because of* their differences, instead of *despite* them.

Can we help our 2e learners believe that their unique learning profile can be both strength and struggle? That learning to handle the struggle will help them in the future? I'm not saying that we should look at the world through rose-colored glasses. We can't pretend that having ADHD or ASD or dyslexia or a mood disorder isn't a disability. I'm just suggesting we need to move from an either-or mentality to a both-and mindset: "Yes, I have these struggles. And they bring strengths along with them. They both make me who I am."

Teaching Students About Neurodiversity

Students need to learn about neurodiversity—and not just the kids who are neurodivergent. Our schools educate students to understand racial and ethnic diversity. Our counselors teach kids how to use empathy. Antibullying messages are heard in our hallways, assemblies, and cafeterias. Let's teach our student bodies about the needs of neurodiverse learners too.

Teaching students about neurodiversity can have long-term benefits, both individually and systemically. Neurodivergent individuals who know that others have a basic understanding of neurodiversity are better able to self-advocate. People who understand neurodiversity learn to pause when a miscommunication occurs and ask themselves if there's a possible explanation before replying. (Was the person feeling anxious? Did they misunderstand what I said?) A basic awareness and acceptance of neurodiversity creates an environment that helps neurodivergent learners feel safe and accepted in the world.

There are many opportunities for integrating neurodiversity awareness into our schools and classrooms. Schools can invite neurodivergent speakers to share their experiences with students. Teachers can encourage students to research well-known individuals with varied neurological and psychological needs (see sidebar at right). Professional development helps educators create neurodiversity-supporting classrooms. Twice-exceptional kids can form a student task force to make their school a more accommodating environment.

Self-Advocacy for 2e Learners

What do 2e students need? Right now, on day one, they need your help. They need accommodations and modifications. They need strategies to support their areas of struggle. But you aren't going to be there all day, every day. And you probably won't be their teacher next year or when they get to the next level—middle school, high school, or college.

So, what gift can you give 2e students to take with them? What skills and beliefs can you help them internalize that will stay with them through adulthood? You can teach them to advocate for themselves. They need to understand what will help them be successful and how to access those tools in a variety of environments.

Accepting and understanding the nature of their neurodivergence is the first step in this process. Some types of learners discussed in this book may go through episodes during which they struggle, and then balance returns—for example, those who experience depression or anxiety. Other learners, like those with ADHD, autism, or dyslexia, will need to be constantly aware of their environment and what supports they need to succeed. Neurodivergence never goes away, even if it looks from the outside as though it has.

The second step is to help 2e students find their voice. Teach them to speak up and ask for what they need. This skill carries forward to their futures as college students or employees communicating with their bosses when they enter the workforce. Confidence and self-esteem are key to self-advocacy. Twice-exceptional kids need to know their needs are valid and they have the right to access the supports that help them. They need strategies to effectively communicate those needs with the people who can provide help. Deb Douglas has written an excellent guide called *The Power of Self-Advocacy for Gifted Learners*. If you are looking for an in-depth resource on this topic, I recommend checking it out.

NOTABLE NEURODIVERGENT PEOPLE

- Muhammed Ali—boxer—dyslexia
- Simone Biles—Olympic gymnast—ADHD
- Wayne Brady—actor—depression
- Cher—singer—dyslexia
- Carrie Fisher—actor—bipolar disorder
- Lady Gaga—singer, actor—depression, anxiety
- Whoopi Goldberg—actor—dyslexia
- Selena Gomez—singer—depression, anxiety
- Temple Grandin—activist, author—ASD
- John Green—author—anxiety, OCD
- Salma Hayek—actor—dyslexia
- Lisa Ling—journalist—ADHD
- Alicia Keys—singer—depression
- Demi Lovato—singer—bipolar disorder
- Howie Mandel—television host, comedian—OCD
- Marcus Morris—NBA player—depression, anxiety
- Michael Phelps—Olympic swimmer—ADHD
- Daniel Radcliffe—actor—OCD
- John Elder Robison—author—ASD
- Michelle Rodriguez—actor—ADHD
- Kanye West—singer—bipolar
- Henry Winkler—director, actor—dyscalculia and dyslexia

Your Classroom Isn't an Island

I know that people who dedicate themselves to a career in education do so because they believe that classrooms are where our future lies. I believe teachers are idealists who want all children to succeed. I also recognize it isn't realistic to expect every teacher to keep up on every trend in education. So the job of initiating support for your 2e kids is up to you.

Twice-exceptional students need wraparound support. Whether you teach in a gifted, special education, or general education classroom, do you know what is happening to your 2e learners when they go to their other teachers? Accommodations and modifications in your classroom are great, but your 2e students may still need strategies when they go to physical education class or when they're in the cafeteria. If they have a behavior issue, will the staff at your school recognize it within the context of their disability?

Opening a conversation with the other stakeholders in your school or district is key to supporting your 2e students. Figure out your starting point. Whose support do you need right now? Is it a principal, counselor, or psychological examiner? Maybe it is the classroom teacher of a student you've had on your mind while reading this book. Help your colleagues understand the concept of masking skills and struggles. This is the foundation for understanding a student who shows cognitive giftedness in some situations but struggles greatly in others. Continue your conversation so you can collaboratively find areas of flexibility in the school system and meet the needs of your 2e students.

Try. Tweak. Transform.

Dr. Stephen Shore, an autism expert and professor of special education who is autistic himself, says, "If you've met one person with autism, you've met one person with autism" (Lime Connect 2018). This truth can be extrapolated to all the exceptionalities we've discussed in this book. There is no single easy solution for every 2e kid you'll teach.

My goal throughout this book has been to give an inside look at a wide range of 2e students and a variety of ideas to support them. But I can promise you that none of the strategies I've suggested is a quick fix. You will use a lot of trial and error when you are working with your 2e students. It is through this trial and error that the change happens.

Kids' emotions are valid. Their experiences are authentic, and their stress is real. When we, their teachers, let our students know that we are *with* them, we set the stage for collaboration and connection. Together with our students, we can walk through the process of change discussed in this book. We **try** new ideas and let students have a voice in the process. We note how well an idea works and figure out how to **tweak** what we were doing to have greater success. We build momentum as we refine our goals and see gradual progress. And through this process, we see our 2e students **transform**. They transform into independent, creative, intelligent people, ready to find success wherever they choose.

TRY. TWEAK. TRANSFORM.
The three T's lead to exponential growth for 2e kids.

$$3T = 2e^x$$

References and Resources

Academy of Orton-Gillingham Practitioners and Educators. 2018. "What Is the Orton-Gillingham Approach?" ortonacademy.org/resources/what-is-the-orton-gillingham-approach.

American Psychiatric Association. 2000. *Diagnostic and Statistical Manual of Mental Disorders: Fourth Edition: Text Revision.* Washington, DC: American Psychiatric Association.

American Psychiatric Association. 2017. *Diagnostic and Statistical Manual of Mental Disorders: Fifth Edition.* New Delhi: CBS Publishers and Distributors, Pvt. Ltd.

Arnsten, Amy F. T. 2009. "The Emerging Neurobiology of Attention Deficit Hyperactivity Disorder: The Key Role of the Prefrontal Association Cortex." *Journal of Pediatrics* 154 (5): I–S43. doi:10.1016/j.jpeds.2009.01.018.

Assouline, Susan G., Nicholas Colangelo, and Joyce VanTassel-Baska, eds. 2015. *A Nation Empowered: Evidence Trumps the Excuses Holding Back America's Brightest Students.* Iowa City: Belin-Blank Center. accelerationinstitute.org/Nation_Empowered.

Barnard-Brak, Lucy, Susan K. Johnsen, Alyssa Pond Hannig, and Tianlan Wei. 2015. "The Incidence of Potentially Gifted Students Within a Special Education Population." *Roeper Review* 37 (2): 74–83. doi:10.1080/02783193.2015.1008661.

Brown, Brené. 2010. *The Gifts of Imperfection: Let Go of Who You Think You're Supposed to Be and Embrace Who You Are.* Center City, MN: Hazelden.

Cederberg, Charles D., Lianne C. Gann, Megan Foley-Nicpon, and Zachary Sussman. 2018. "ASD Screening Measures for High-Ability Youth with ASD: Examining the ASSQ and SRS." *Gifted Child Quarterly* 62 (2): 220–229.

Center on the Developing Child. 2019. "Executive Function and Self-Regulation." developingchild.harvard.edu/science/key-concepts/executive-function.

Colangelo, Nicholas, Susan G. Assouline, and Miraca U. M. Gross, eds. 2004. *A Nation Deceived: How Schools Hold Back America's Brightest Students.* Iowa City: Belin-Blank Center. accelerationinstitute.org/nation_deceived.

Cooper-Kahn, Joyce, and Laurie Dietzel. 2019. "What Is Executive Functioning?" LD OnLine. ldonline.org/article/29122.

Crogman, Maryam T., Jeffrey W. Gilger, and Fumiko Hoeft. 2018. "Visuo-Spatial Skills in Atypical Readers." In *Twice Exceptional: Supporting and Educating Bright and Creative Students with Learning Difficulties*, 229–265. New York: Oxford University Press.

Cross, Jennifer Riedl, and Tracy L. Cross. 2015. "Clinical and Mental Health Issues in Counseling the Gifted Individual." *Journal of Counseling and Development* 93 (2): 163–172. doi:10.1002/j.1556-6676.2015.00192.x.

Cross, Tracy L., and Jennifer Riedl Cross. 2018. "Suicide Among Students with Gifts and Talents." In *APA Handbook of Giftedness and Talent*, 601–614. Washington, DC: American Psychological Association.

Danielson, Melissa L., Rebecca H. Bitsko, Reem M. Ghandour, Joseph R. Holbrook, Michael D. Kogan, and Stephen J. Blumberg. 2018. "Prevalence of Parent-Reported ADHD Diagnosis and Associated Treatment Among U.S. Children and Adolescents, 2016." *Journal of Clinical Child and Adolescent Psychology* 47 (2): 199–212. doi:10.1080/15374416.2017.1417860.

Davis, Joy Lawson, and Shawn Anthony Robinson. 2018. "Being 3e, a New Look at Culturally Diverse Gifted Learners with Exceptional Conditions: An Examination of the Issues and Solutions for Educators and Families." In *Twice Exceptional: Supporting and Educating Bright and Creative Students with Learning Difficulties*, 278–289. New York: Oxford University Press.

Delisle, James R. 1986. "Death with Honors: Suicide Among Gifted Adolescents." *Journal of Counseling & Development* 64 (9): 558–560. doi:10.1002/j.1556-6676.1986.tb01202.x.

Endrew F. v. Douglas County School Dist. RE-1, 580 U. S. ___ (2017)

Frye, Devon. 2016. "Children with ADHD Avoid Failure and Punishment More Than Others, Study Says." additudemag.com/children-with-adhd-avoid-failure-punishment.

Fugate, C. Matthew. 2018. "Attention Divergent Hyperactive Giftedness." In *Twice Exceptional: Supporting and Educating Bright and Creative Students with Learning Difficulties*, 191–200. New York: Oxford University Press.

Gale, Catherin R., G. David Batty, Andrew Mark Mcintosh, David J. Porteous, Ian J. Deary, and Finn Rasmussen. 2012. "Is Bipolar Disorder More Common in Highly Intelligent People? A Cohort Study of a Million Men." *Molecular Psychiatry* 18 (2): 190–194. doi:10.1038/mp.2012.26.

Ghandour, Reem M., Laura J. Sherman, Catherine J. Vladutiu, Mir M. Ali, Sean E. Lynch, Rebecca H. Bitsko, and Stephen J. Blumberg. 2019. "Prevalence and Treatment of Depression, Anxiety, and Conduct Problems in US Children." *Journal of Pediatrics* 206: 256–267. doi:10.1016/j.jpeds.2018.09.021.

Gnanavel, Sundar, Pawan Sharma, Pulkit Kaushal, and Sharafat Hussain. 2019. "Attention Deficit Hyperactivity Disorder and Comorbidity: A Review of Literature." *World Journal of Clinical Cases* 7 (17): 2420–2426. doi:10.12998/wjcc.v7.i17.2420.

Greene, Ross. 2008. "Kids Do Well if They Can." *Phi Delta Kappan* 90 (3): 160–167.

Heider, Fritz. 1958. *The Psychology of Interpersonal Relations.* New York: John Wiley and Sons.

Hyman, Susan L. 2013. "New DSM-5 Includes Changes to Autism Criteria." American Academy of Pediatrics. aappublications.org/content/early/2013/06/04/aapnews.20130604-1.

Katusic, Maja Z., Robert G. Voigt, Robert C. Colligan, Amy L. Weaver, Kendra J. Homan, and William J. Barbaresi. 2011. "Attention-Deficit Hyperactivity Disorder in Children with High Intelligence Quotient: Results from a Population-Based Study." *Journal of Developmental and Behavioral Pediatrics* 32 (2): 103–109. doi:10.1097/DBP.0b013e318206d700.

Kaufman, Scott Barry, ed. 2018. *Twice Exceptional: Supporting and Educating Bright and Creative Students with Learning Difficulties.* New York: Oxford University Press.

Lerner, Matthew D., and Rebecca M. Girard. 2018. "Appreciating and Promoting Social Creativity in Youth with Asperger's Syndrome." In *Twice Exceptional: Supporting and Educating Bright and Creative Students with Learning Difficulties*, 201–212. New York: Oxford University Press.

Lime Connect. 2018. "Leading Perspectives on Disability: A Q&A with Dr. Stephen Shore." limeconnect.com/opportunities_news/detail/leading-perspectives-on-disability-a-qa-with-dr-stephen-shore.

Little, Lauren M., Evan Dean, Scott Tomchek, and Winnie Dunn. 2017. "Sensory Processing Patterns in Autism, Attention Deficit Hyperactivity Disorder, and Typical Development." *Physical & Occupational Therapy in Pediatrics* 38 (3): 243–254. doi:10.1080/01942638.2017.1390809.

Lovecky, Deirdre V. 2018. "Misconceptions about Giftedness and the Diagnosis of ADHD and Other Mental Health Disorders." In *Twice Exceptional: Supporting and Educating Bright and Creative Students with Learning Difficulties*, 83–103. New York: Oxford University Press.

Macdonald, Kelly, Laura Germine, Alida Anderson, Joanna Christodoulou, and Lauren M. McGrath. 2017. "Dispelling the Myth: Training in Education or Neuroscience Decreases but Does Not Eliminate Beliefs in Neuromyths." *Frontiers in Psychology* 8 (1): 1314. doi:10.3389 /fpsyg.2017.01314.

Maddocks, Danika L. S. 2018. "The Identification of Students Who Are Gifted and Have a Learning Disability: A Comparison of Different Diagnostic Criteria." *Gifted Child Quarterly* 62 (2): 175–192. doi:10.1177/0016986217752096.

Martin, Graham, Angela S. Richardson, Helen A. Bergen, Leigh Roeger, and Stephen Allison. 2005. "Perceived Academic Performance, Self-Esteem and Locus of Control as Indicators of Need for Assessment of Adolescent Suicide Risk: Implications for Teachers." *Journal of Adolescence* 28 (1): 75–87. doi:10.1016/j.adolescence.2004.04.005.

Martin, Laurie T., Rachel M. Burns, and Matthias Schonlau. 2009. "Mental Disorders Among Gifted and Nongifted Youth: A Selected Review of the Epidemiologic Literature." *Gifted Child Quarterly* 54 (1): 31–41. doi:10.1177/0016986209352684.

McCoach, D. Betsy, and Jessica Kay Flake. 2018. "The Role of Motivation." In *APA Handbook of Giftedness and Talent*, edited by Steven I. Pfeiffer, Elizabeth Shaunessy-Dedrick, and Megan Foley-Nicpon, 201–213. Washington, DC: American Psychological Association.

McMahon, Kibby, Deepika Anand, Marissa Morris-Jones, and M. Zachary Rosenthal. 2019. "A Path from Childhood Sensory Processing Disorder to Anxiety Disorders: The Mediating Role of Emotion Dysregulation and Adult Sensory Processing Disorder Symptoms." *Frontiers in Integrative Neuroscience* 13: 22. doi:10.3389/fnint.2019.00022.

Montgomery County Public Schools. 2015. *Twice Exceptional Students: A Staff Guidebook*. Rockville, MD: Office of Curriculum and Instruction and Office of Special Education and Student Services. montgomeryschoolsmd.org/uploadedFiles/curriculum/enriched/programs/gtld/0470.15 _TwiceExceptionalStudents_Handbook_Web.pdf.

Morgado, Pedro, and João J. Cerqueira. 2018. "Editorial: The Impact of Stress on Cognition and Motivation." *Frontiers in Behavioral Neuroscience* 12: 326.

Mueller, Christian E. 2009. "Protective Factors as Barriers to Depression in Gifted and Nongifted Adolescents." *Gifted Child Quarterly* 53 (1): 3–14. doi:10.1177/0016986208326552.

Mullet, Dianna R., and Anne N. Rinn. 2015. "Giftedness and ADHD: Identification, Misdiagnosis, and Dual Diagnosis." *Roeper Review* 37 (4): 195–207. doi:10.1080/02783193.2015.1077910.

Musgrove, Melody (US Department of Education Office of Special Education and Rehabilitative Services). 2013. Letter to Dr. Jim Delisle. December 20. ed.gov/policy/speced/guid/idea /memosdcltrs/13-008520r-sc-delisle-twiceexceptional.pdf.

Musgrove, Melody (US Department of Education Office of Special Education and Rehabilitative Services). 2015. Memorandum to State Directors of Gifted Education. April 17. ed.gov/policy /speced/guid/idea/memosdcltrs/041715osepmemo15-082q2015.pdf.

National Center for Education Statistics. 2017a. "Table 203.70. Percentage Distribution of Enrollment in Public Elementary and Secondary Schools, by Race/Ethnicity and State or Jurisdiction: Fall 2000 and Fall 2015." nces.ed.gov/programs/digest/d17/tables/dt17_203.70.asp?referer=raceindicators.

National Center for Education Statistics. 2017b. "Table 209.10. Number and Percentage Distribution of Teachers in Public and Private Elementary and Secondary Schools, by Selected Teacher Characteristics: Selected Years, 1987–88 through 2015–16." nces.ed.gov/programs/digest/d17/tables/dt17_209.10.asp.

Nicpon, Megan Foley, Allison Allmon, Barbara Sieck, and Rebecca D. Stinson. 2011. "Empirical Investigation of Twice-Exceptionality: Where Have We Been and Where Are We Going?" *Gifted Child Quarterly* 55 (1): 3–17. doi:10.1177/0016986210382575.

Peters, Scott J., Karen Rambo-Hernandez, Matthew C. Makel, Michael S. Matthews, and Jonathan A. Plucker. 2017. "Should Millions of Students Take a Gap Year? Large Numbers of Students Start the School Year Above Grade Level." *Gifted Child Quarterly* 61 (3): 229–238. doi:10.1177/0016986217701834.

Posny, Alexa. (US Department of Education Office of Special Education Programs). 2010. Letter to Anonymous. January 13. ed.gov/policy/speced/guid/idea/letters/2010-1/redacteda011310eval1q2010.pdf.

Reis, Sally M., Karen L. Westberg, Jonna Kulikowich, Florence Caillard, Thomas Hébert, Jonathan Plucker, Jeanne H. Purcell, John B. Rogers, and Julianne M. Smist. 1993. *Why Not Let High Ability Students Start School in January?: The Curriculum Compacting Study* (Research Monograph 93106). Storrs: University of Connecticut, National Research Center on the Gifted and Talented.

Renzulli, Joseph S. 2005. "The Three-Ring Conception of Giftedness: A Developmental Model for Promoting Creative Productivity." In *Conceptions of Giftedness*, edited by Robert J. Sternberg and Janet E. Davidson, 246–279. New York: Cambridge University Press.

Rinn, Anne N. 2018. "Social and Emotional Considerations for Gifted Students." In *APA Handbook of Giftedness and Talent*, 453–464. Washington, DC: American Psychological Association.

Ritchotte, Jennifer A., Chin-Wen Lee, and Amy K. Graefe. 2019. *Start Seeing and Serving Underserved Gifted Students: 50 Strategies for Equity and Excellence*. Minneapolis, MN: Free Spirit Publishing.

Robinson, Shawn Anthony. 2017. "Phoenix Rising: An Autoethnographic Account of a Gifted Black Male with Dyslexia." *Journal for the Education of the Gifted* 40 (2): 135–151. doi:10.1177/0162353217701021.

Rowling, J. K. 1997. *Harry Potter and the Sorcerer's Stone*. New York: Scholastic.

Ruggeri, Amanda. 2017. "The Dangerous Downsides of Perfectionism." BBC Future. bbc.com/future/article/20180219-toxic-perfectionism-is-on-the-rise.

Ryan, Richard M., and Edward L. Deci. 2018. *Self Determination Theory: Basic Psychological Needs in Motivation, Development, and Wellness*. New York: Guilford Press.

Sak, Ugur. 2004. "A Synthesis of Research on Psychological Types of Gifted Adolescents." *Journal of Secondary Gifted Education* 15 (2): 70–79. doi:10.4219/jsge-2004-449.

Shaw, Philip, Deanna Greenstein, Jason Lerch, Liv Clasen, Rhoshel Lenroot, Nitin Gogtay, Alan Evans, Judith L. Rapoport, and Jay Giedd. 2006. "Intellectual Ability and Cortical Development in Children and Adolescents." *Nature* 440 (7084): 676–679. doi:10.1038/nature04513.

Silverman, Linda K., Gilman, Barbara J., Lovecky, Dierdre V., and Maxwell, Elizabeth. 2019. Adapted from Silverman, L., and Maxwell, B. 2010. *Teacher Checklist for Recognizing Twice-Exceptional Children.* Denver: Gifted Development Center.

Sisk, Victoria F., Alexander P. Burgoyne, Jingze Sun, Jennifer L. Butler, and Brooke N. Macnamara. 2018. "To What Extent and Under Which Circumstances Are Growth Mind-Sets Important to Academic Achievement? Two Meta-Analyses." *Psychological Science* 29 (4): 549–571. doi:10.1177/0956797617739704.

Sousa, Nuno. 2016. "The Dynamics of the Stress Neuromatrix." *Molecular Psychiatry* 21 (3): 302–312. doi:10.1038/mp.2015.196.

Taliaferro, Lindsay A., and Jennifer J. Muehlenkamp. 2013. "Risk and Protective Factors That Distinguish Adolescents Who Attempt Suicide from Those Who Only Consider Suicide in the Past Year." *Suicide and Life-Threatening Behavior* 44 (1): 6–22. doi:10.1111/sltb.12046.

US Department of Education. 2017. "Individuals with Disabilities Education Act: Sec. 300.8 (c) (1) (i)." sites.ed.gov/idea/regs/b/a/300.8/c/1/i.

US Department of Education Office for Civil Rights. 2016. "Parent and Educator Resource Guide to Section 504 in Public Elementary and Secondary Schools." ed.gov/about/offices/list/ocr/docs/504-resource-guide-201612.pdf.

US Department of Education Office for Civil Rights. 2018. "Protecting Students with Disabilities." ed.gov/about/offices/list/ocr/504faq.html.

van Stralen, Judy. 2016. "Emotional Dysregulation in Children with Attention-Deficit/Hyperactivity Disorder." *ADHD Attention Deficit and Hyperactivity Disorders* 8 (4): 175–187. doi:10.1007/s12402-016-0199-0.

Webb, James T., Janet L. Gore, Edward R. Amend, and Arlene R. DeVries. 2007. *A Parent's Guide to Gifted Children.* Scottsdale, AZ: Great Potential Press.

WebMD. 2019. "Executive Function and Executive Function Disorder." webmd.com/add-adhd/guide/executive-function#1.

Wegmann, Kate M., and Brittanni Smith. 2019. "Examining Racial/Ethnic Disparities in School Discipline in the Context of Student-Reported Behavior Infractions." *Children and Youth Services Review* 103: 18–27. doi:10.1016/j.childyouth.2019.05.027.

Wiebe, Chris. 2019. "Episode 25: Thinking Twice About Ways to Help Twice Exceptional Students." Interview. *The Neurodiversity Podcast* (audio blog), February 6. neurodiversitypodcast.com/home/2019/2/6/episode-25-thinking-twice-about-ways-to-help-twice-exceptional-students.

Yudin, Michael K. (US Department of Education Office of Special Education and Rehabilitative Services). 2015. Letter to Dear Colleague. October 23. ed.gov/policy/speced/guid/idea/memosdcltrs/guidance-on-dyslexia-10-2015.pdf.

Zentall, Sydney S., Sidney M. Moon, Arlene M. Hall, and Janice A. Grskovic. 2001. "Learning and Motivational Characteristics of Boys with AD/HD and/or Giftedness." *Exceptional Children* 67 (4): 499–519. doi:10.1177/001440290106700405.

Index

E

F

G

Goals and goal-setting. *See also* Microgoals
    building executive function skills with, 117–118
    executive function, 116
    hierarchy of, 102
    motivation and, 99–100
    rewards for reaching, 109–110
    self-advocacy integrated into, 110
    SMART goals, 101
    student autonomy for, 109
    student story on, 99, 101
Goal vaulting, 99
Grade skipping, 36
Grants, 9
Graphic organizers, 40, 42, 143, 170
Greene, Ross, 167
Grouping, cluster, 34
Group learning/projects, 195, 196, 197
Growth mindset, 76, 77

H

Handwriting difficulties, 141, 142
Harm obsessions, 200
Hearing, sensory processing disorder related to, 187
High-functioning individuals with autism, 163
Hoarding, 200
Holistic perspective, 3, 34
Holistic thinking, 38, 39–41, 49, 113
Homework, 61, 139, 155
Hyperactive-impulsive ADHD, 148
Hyperactivity, 148, 164, 165
Hypersensitivity, 186
Hyposensitivity, 187

I

Identification
    academic self-concept and, 54
    of ASD in gifted learners, 160–166
    based on cognitive ability *versus* academic achievement, 9
    creativity inventory for, 45
    of generalized anxiety disorder (GAD), 193
    of gifted and learning disabled (GLD) students, 128–135
    normative *versus* intraindividual scores used for, 130–133
    Response to Intervention (RTI) and, 19
    for special education, 18–19
    of specific learning disabilities in English language learners (ELLs), 129–130
    of students with ADHD, 148–150
    3e learners, 13–15
    training staff in characteristics of 2e learners, 11
    2e learners with physical disabilities, 15–16
Identified regulation, 79, 92, 97
Identity-first language, 4
IEPs (individualized education programs), 2–3, 16
    about, 17
    anxiety diagnosis and, 192
    diagnosis type and, 16, 17
    educators advocating for, 19
    for emotional and behavioral disorders, 191
    establishing, 18–21
    504 plans compared with, 17
    IDEA's educational diagnosis of ASD and, 165
    for mood disorders, 211
    parents advocating for, 18–19, 21–22
    sample learning profiles for SLD, 131–133
    setting goals for, 100–101
    for students with ASD, 161
    for students with specific learning disabilities, 135–136
    supporting families through process of, 25
Improvisation, 172, 179
Impulsivity, 13, 148, 151, 164–165

Inattention, 13, 149–150, 164
Inattentive ADHD, 1, 147, 148, 149. *See also* ADHD
Individuals with Disabilities Education Act (IDEA), 7, 9, 16, 18, 19, 20
    dyslexia and, 138
    educational diagnosis of ASD under, 165–166
    emotional and behavioral diagnoses under, 191
    on mood disorders, 208
    on specific learning disabilities, 128, 138
Infographics, 42
Inquiry-based instruction, 45
Instruction. *See also* Strength-based approach
    differentiation, 36–37
    multisensory, 139–140
    social skills, 55
    technology used for, 46
    of 2e students with math specific learning disabilities, 144
    of 2e students with reading specific learning disabilities, 139–141
    of 2e students with writing specific learning disabilities, 142–143
Instructional accommodations, 33, 120, 146, 159, 177, 190, 206, 218
Integrated regulation, 79, 92, 97
Interdisciplinary approach, 2–3. *See also* Teams and team approach
Internal attribution, 78
Internalization of ADHD symptoms, 152–153
International Classification of Diseases: Tenth Edition (ICD-10), 16
Interoceptive system, 186, 188
Interventions. *See also* Accommodations; Instruction
    for autistic gifted learners, 171–172
    enrichment, acceleration, and placement options, 34–36
    for reading difficulties, 136
Intraindividual scores, 130–133, 134
Intrinsic motivation, 79, 80–81, 82, 86, 92, 97, 100, 108
Introjected regulation, 79, 80, 92, 97
Introversion, 195
Intrusive thoughts, 199, 200
Iowa Acceleration Scale (IAS), 36
IQ tests/scores, 14, 137
Irritability, 193, 209, 210

J

Javits grants program, 9

K

Kindergarten, early entrance to, 36

L

Labels, diagnostic, 25
Language arts, differentiation in, 37
Language barriers, 59
Learned helplessness, 56, 64–65, 66–67, 77
Learning disabilities, 8. *See also* Gifted and learning disabled (GLD); Specific learning disabilities
    talking to children about, 57–59
    working memory and, 141
Legislation, 8–9
Lesson planning, strength-based, 49–50, 52
Logical thinking, 38, 43–44, 49, 57
Lovecky, Deirdre, 10

M

Major depressive disorder (MDD), 191, 207, 208–211
Manic episodes, in bipolar disorder, 211
Masking difficulties
    with anxiety, 194
    ASD and, 160, 163
    with depression, 209–210
    by gifted learners with ADHD, 152–153
    with OCD, 199
    Paired Student Data Observation and, 20
    processing disorders, 183
    of 2e learners, 10, 22
    for writing, 142

DIGITAL VERSIONS OF ALL REPRODUCIBLE FORMS CAN BE DOWNLOADED AT
freespirit.com/**2e-forms**. Use password **2succeed**

About the Author

Emily Kircher-Morris, M.A., M.Ed., LPC, inspired by her own experiences as a twice-exceptional (2e) learner, is dedicated to supporting 2e children—including her own—in a way she wasn't during her academic years. She has taught in gifted classrooms, has been a school counselor, and is now in private practice as a licensed professional counselor, where she specializes in helping gifted and twice-exceptional kids.

Emily is the president and founder of the Gifted Support Network and speaks at statewide and national conferences. She also hosts *The Neurodiversity Podcast*, which explores parenting, counseling techniques, and best practices for enriching the lives of high-ability people. Emily lives near St. Louis, Missouri.

Other Great Resources from Free Spirit

Start Seeing and Serving Underserved Gifted Students
50 Strategies for Equity and Excellence
by Jennifer Ritchotte, Ph.D., Chin-Wen Lee, Ph.D., and Amy Graefe, Ph.D.

For educators and administrators of grades K–8.
192 pp.; PB; 8½" x 11"; includes digital content.

Free PLC/Book Study Guide
freespirit.com/PLC

The SEL Solution
Integrate Social-Emotional Learning into Your Curriculum and Build a Caring Climate for All
by Jonathan C. Erwin, M.A.

For K–12 administrators and teachers.
200 pp.; PB; 8½" x 11"; includes digital content.

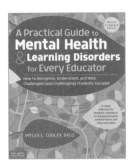

A Practical Guide to Mental Health & Learning Disorders for Every Educator
How to Recognize, Understand, and Help Challenged (and Challenging) Students Succeed (Revised & Updated Edition)
by Myles L. Cooley, Ph.D.

For educators and counselors, grades K–12.
256 pp.; PB; 8½" x 11"; includes digital content.

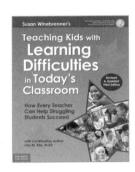

Teaching Kids with Learning Difficulties in Today's Classroom
How Every Teacher Can Help Struggling Students Succeed (Revised & Updated 3rd Edition)
by Susan Winebrenner, M.S., with Lisa M. Kiss, M.Ed.

For K–12 teachers, administrators, higher education faculty.
288 pp.; PB; 8½" x 11"; includes digital content.

Free PLC/Book Study Guide
freespirit.com/PLC

Teaching Gifted Kids in Today's Classroom
Strategies and Techniques Every Teacher Can Use (Updated 4th Edition)
by Susan Winebrenner, M.S., with Dina Brulles, Ph.D.

For teachers and administrators, grades K–12.
256 pp.; PB; 8½" x 11"; includes digital content.

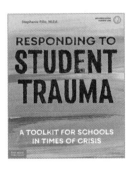

Responding to Student Trauma
A Toolkit for Schools in Times of Crisis
by Stephanie Filio, M.Ed.

For educators and counselors, grades K–8.
80 pp.; PB; 8½" x 11"; includes digital content.

Free PLC/Book Study Guide
freespirit.com/PLC

Teach for Attention!
A Tool Belt of Strategies for Engaging Students with Attention Challenges
by Ezra Werb, M.Ed.

For educators, grades K–8.
208 pp.; PB; 6" x 7½".

Interested in purchasing multiple quantities and receiving volume discounts?
Contact edsales@freespirit.com or call 1.800.735.7323 and ask for Education Sales.

Many Free Spirit authors are available for speaking engagements, workshops, and keynotes.
Contact speakers@freespirit.com or call 1.800.735.7323.

For pricing information, to place an order, or to request a free catalog, contact:

Free Spirit Publishing • 6325 Sandburg Road, Suite 100 • Minneapolis, MN 55427-3674
toll-free 800.735.7323 • local 612.338.2068 • fax 612.337.5050
help4kids@freespirit.com • freespirit.com